PENTAGON PRESS

COMMITTED TO SERVE THE ARMED FORCES

Towards Social Justice

Towards Social Justice

Edited by

C. Joshua Thomas

and

Padmakshi Kakoti

ICSSR-NERC

PENTAGON PRESS

Towards Social Justice
Editors: C. Joshua Thomas & Padmakshi Kakoti

First Published in 2018

ISBN 978-93-86618-44-3

Disclaimer: The views expressed in this book are those of the authors and do not necessarily reflect those of the editors.

Published by
PENTAGON PRESS
206, Peacock Lane, Shahpur Jat
New Delhi-110049
Phones: 011-64706243, 26491568
Telefax: 011-26490600
email: rajan@pentagonpress.in
website: www.pentagonpress.in

Printed at Avantika Printers Private Limited.

CONTENTS

SECTION III
STATUS OF DALITS: EXPERIENCE OF STATES

SECTION IV
EMPOWERING THE DALITS IN NORTH-EAST INDIA

भारतीय सामाजिक विज्ञान अनुसंधान परिषद
पूर्वोत्तर क्षेत्रीय केन्द्र
ICSSR-NERC
INDIAN COUNCIL OF SOCIAL SCIENCE RESEARCH
NORTH EASTERN REGIONAL CENTRE
NEHU Campus, Shillong - 793022

Phone : 0364 - 2550436 (O)
0364 - 2538333 (R)
Fax : 0364 - 2550428
e-mail : icssr_nerc@hotmail.com
website : www.icssrnerc.org

Professor L.S. Gassah
Honorary Director

2nd December 2017

FOREWORD

The North Eastern Regional Centre of the ICSSR, Shillong, as a part of its academic and research activities has initiated a series of state level seminars on the impact of positive discrimination on marginalised communities with special reference to Scheduled Caste groups in North-East India by inviting scholars from within and outside the region to discuss issues related to the status of the marginalised communities. Some of those seminar proceedings were published in book forms in the past years by the organisers themselves.

Now, we are pleased to present selected articles presented in the national seminar organised by the regional centre on *Towards Social Justice: Impact of Positive Discrimination on Marginalised Communities with Special Reference to Scheduled Caste Groups in India* during the 21st and 22nd September 2017 at the NERC Complex, NEHU Campus, Shillong.

As Professor Gopal Guru mentioned in his paper, "concepts like social justice are classical as they are of timeless essence and universal relevance." The papers put together in this volume with great care by Joshua Thomas & Padmakshi Kakoti are relevant for the governments both at the Centre and at the State level while making policies in order to alleviate the problems of people belonging to the marginalised groups.

(L.S. Gassah)

CONTRIBUTORS

C. Joshua Thomas, Deputy Director, ICSSR-NERC, Shillong. cjoshuathomas@gmail.com

Chintamani Rout, Associate Professor, Department of Law, North Eastern Hill University, Shillong. drchintamanirout@gmail.com

Debasish Chowdhury, Controller of Examinations, Sikkim University, Gangtok. coe@cus.ac.in

G. C. Pal, Associate Professor & ICSSR Senior Fellow, Indian Institute of Dalit Studies, New Delhi. gcpal24@gmail.com

Gopal Guru, Centre for Political Studies, Jawaharlal Nehru University, New Delhi. gopalguru2001@yahoo.com

H. Srikanth, Professor, Department of Political Science, North Eastern Hill University, Shillong. hskant@gmail.com

Jenny Rowena P, Assistant Professor, Department of English, Miranda House College, University of Delhi. jenny.chithra@gmail.com

K.V. Reddy, Professor and Head, Department of Political Science, Mizoram University, Aizawl. kvidyasagarr@gmail.com

Korvi Vinayakala, Research Scholar, Department of English, University of Delhi, Delhi. korvikala@gmail.com

M. Lilee Devi, Assistant Professor (S2), Department of Sociology, Manipur University, Imphal. lilee.mayanglambam@gmail.com

Padmakshi Kakoti, Research Associate, ICSSR-NERC, Shillong. padmakshi.kakoti1@gmail.com

Pallavi Devi, Assistant Professor, Assam Rajiv Gandhi University of Co-Operative Management, Sivasagar, Assam. pen2pallavi@gmail.com

Paul Pudussery, Director, Holy Cross College, Agartala, Tripura. pudusseryp@gmail.com

Sangita Yadav, Research Scholar, CSDE/SSS, Jawaharlal Nehru University, New Delhi. sangita.csde@gmail.com

Sarmistha Das, Assistant Professor, Department of Sociology, Tezpur University, Tezpur. sharmishtha.k@gmail.com

Surojit Sen Gupta, Assistant Professor, Maharaja Bir Bikram College, Agartala, Tripura. meghaboy@yahoo.com

V. Bijukumar, Associate Professor, Centre for Political Studies, School of Social Sciences, Jawaharlal Nehru University, New Delhi. vbijuk@yahoo.co.in

Vijaylakshmi Brara, Associate Professor, Centre for Manipur Studies, Manipur University, Manipur. vbrara11@gmail.com

Visakhonü Hibo, Principal, Japfü Christian College, Nagaland. visakhonu99viraho@gmail.com

Visi Yhokha, Assistant Professor, Department of Economics, Japfü Christian College, Kigwema, Kohima, Nagaland.

INTRODUCTION

The terms, 'social justice', 'positive discrimination', 'affirmative action' have become popular both in developed and underdeveloped countries. In countries like Canada, Finland, Brazil and the USA, the term is used to refer to different discriminatory policies that governments have introduced for the benefit of marginalized communities—the indigenous people, the Blacks or the ethnic minorities. The policy of positive discrimination in India has its roots in anti-caste movements during the Freedom Movement, when the national leaders highlighted the history of oppression and social discrimination experienced by the marginalized communities and began pressurizing the colonial government for legal reforms to ensure social justice. After independence, in line with the spirit of the Constitution of India, the Indian government made provision for reservations for the socio-economic development of the Scheduled Castes (SC), Scheduled Tribes (ST) and other socially and educationally backward communities now recognized as Other Backward Classes (OBC). Although the policy was initially conceived for only ten years, the quota-based reservations in the fields of education, employment and politics has now become a permanent feature of the Indian political system. Apart from the policy of reservations, the Government of India has established various institutions, introduced many laws and implemented diverse schemes for the development of the marginalized communities to ensure social justice. The theory and practice of positive discrimination has evoked passionate debate and movements in India. While the advocates of positive discrimination support the government policies as indispensable for the development of the marginalized communities, the critics have raised the issues of equality, merit, justice and national progress.

The policies of positive discrimination are aimed at targeting the unequal and undemocratic nature of the caste system and empower the marginalized communities in India. Six decades of democratic politics, planned development and the policies and programs of positive discrimination have indeed brought about some changes in the nature of the caste system and in the status of the dalits. What exactly are the changes that have taken place in India following the pursuit of the policy of positive discrimination? How far has the practice of reservation been successful in ensuring social, economic and political development of the marginalized communities? What do the empirical studies say about the status of the dalit and tribal communities in India today? Have these policies and programmes meant for the development of the Scheduled Castes (SC) been implemented effectively in all regions and in all SC communities? Have the atrocities and discrimination against the SCs reduced over the decades? Has the policy weakened the caste system and helped in empowering the dalits? How committed and responsible are leaders and parties in addressing the issues of social discrimination and economic inequalities in society? Does the philosophy of social justice or the policy of positive discrimination continue to be relevant or adequate in the contemporary phase of liberalization and globalization, where the market plays the determining role? Should the policy of positive discrimination be reviewed in the light of new developments taking place in the country? What more needs to be done to ensure justice to the marginalized communities?

These are some of the questions that need to be discussed dispassionately in the light of the experience of the last six decades. In pursuit of the answers for these questions, ICSSR-NERC, organized a two-day National Seminar on *Towards Social Justice: Impact of Positive Discrimination on Marginalized Communities with Special Reference to Scheduled Caste Groups in India* at the ICSSR North Eastern Regional Centre, NEHU Campus, Shillong, on 21 and 22 September 2017 and brought together policy makers, academicians and activists to discuss various aspects related to the social justice and empowerment of dalits in India. This volume contains some of the selected articles presented in the seminar and has been arranged under four sections: interrogating the idea of social justice; strategies for empowering dalits: problems and perspectives; status of dalits: experiences from states; and empowering the dalits in North-East India.

Section I entitled **Interrogating the Idea of Social Justice** comprises five papers. Gopal Guru, in his paper on 'The Classical and the Radical in the Concept of Social Justice' emphasizes on a fourfold argument on the concept of social justice. He examines first, the concept of social justice to be classical and considers it to be a needed principle for radical formation. Social justice is one such concept that has acquired timeless relevance in societies that are divided across the globe. The relevance of this concept has a universal dimension in the sense that it has been universally relevant for almost all societies including those in India. Second, he argues that injustice is the result of natural and historical conditions. Injustice can be termed as natural to the extent that it resulted from the natural placement of population. The twin conditions of uneven habitation of population or social groups on geographical territory and the hierarchical social arrangement of society give rise to the need for social justice. It is a fact that the concept of social justice derives its purpose and essence from nature-generated injustice and man-induced injustice. Thirdly, he feels that the route to rectify the social and material imbalance is not through the market but through the state and that the concept of social justice has to be mobilized, particularly in favour of the marginalized communities, through the intervention of the state. But, ironically, the state has been shifting its responsibility to the corporate through Corporate Social Responsibility (CSR). And, lastly, he opines that a more sensitive approach to social justice would demand on our part the moral responsibility to adopt fair consideration even for institutions. The need is to emphasise on the symbiotic relationship between individual interest and institutional well being. That is to say, individuals and institutions need to grow together and not at the cost of each other's interest.

Guru further puts forth the question as who should be concerned about the state and institutions as the major source of delivering social justice. The target, he says, is always the dalits and the tribals. He also opines that dalits are not to be found using justice as the ground on which they can attempt a critique of the state. Instead, some of them consider the market as the ground for equality and attempt to condemn the state as an obstacle in the progress of the dalit.

In his paper, 'Access to Social Justice: Intersection of Caste, Class and

Identity', G. C. Pal examines the legitimacy of the Reservation Policy (RP) and Prevention of Atrocities (PoA) Act with special reference to marginalized communities keeping in view the discriminatory and exclusionary practices against them at structural and behavioural levels. His paper sheds light on the need to replace caste with economic criteria and, likewise, recent campaigns against POA in the form of allegedly misuse of the law by SCs and STs have been stated. Drawing evidence from multiple sources, the paper uncovers the weakness of the arguments against the two protective measures. He mentions how the state and the law implementation mechanisms that are mandated to ensure 'rights to equality' have not been successful in providing 'social protection' and 'social justice' to SCs in contemporary society.

V. Bijukumar in his paper, 'Social Justice in Contemporary India: Receptivity of Recognition and Redistribution', tries to examine the possibility of synthesizing the Ambedkarite notion of recognition and the Marxist conception of redistribution in the challenges posed by the unleashing of market forces and Hindu nationalist politics. The recent Dalit upsurge in Una in Gujarat and the Dalit Asmita Yatra (Dignity March) demand for livelihood and land reforms is a clear manifestation that contemporary Ambedkarites go beyond the sheer politics of recognition to the politics of redistribution and the strong participation of the Marxists in the movement convey the clear message that delinking the struggle for recognition from redistribution is the death-knell for the emancipatory project of social justice in India. He mentions the demand for recognition, representation and redistribution and the role of organisations in the movement.

The last paper in this section is on 'Social Justice and Positive Discrimination'. In this, Chintamani Rout speaks about the policies of positive discrimination that aim at mitigating the unequal and undemocratic nature of the caste system and empowers the marginalized communities in India. He further tries to examine whether these policies and programmes meant for the development of the marginalized groups have been implemented effectively and have achieved their objectives.

In the second section on **Strategies for Empowering Dalits: Problems and Perspectives**, there are three papers. The first is by K. V. Reddy on

'Dalit Empowerment in India: Problems and Prospects' and views B.R. Ambedkar and his Constitutional efforts and the 'reservation' mechanism that has certainly raised the standard of living of about 60-70 lakh dalits in the country. As part of governmental efforts, many a program, including 'reservations' towards improving the living conditions of the dalits, have been initiated. He identifies the main problems that affected the process of dalit empowerment in India and offers some ways to overcome them so that the state and society direct their efforts in that direction. The paper recognizes the process of dalit disempowerment as the starting point that explains why this community is being given primacy today. The paper further argues that the success of dalit empowerment lies in the political empowerment of marginalized communities like the SCs, STs, OBCs and religious minorities *en masse*.

Korvi Vinayakala and Jenny Rowena, in their joint paper 'The New Media and Empowering the Marginal Communities 'reflect upon the media as the fourth pillar of democracy and how it plays the role of the voice of the people ensuring that every section of society is represented without any bias. But despite such concepts on the role of the media, in India it has failed to represent 'caste' and the dalit cause of exploitation and oppression. Their paper highlights the construction of dalit images in different historical accounts and how the oppressed themselves have begun to deconstruct and reconstruct real images of dalits in the newer public sphere. Through surveys, they identify and critique the mainstream media perspectives and at the same time theorize the perspectives of dalits in the mass media.

Pallavi Devi, the author of the last paper in this section, 'Caste or Reservation: Who is Damaging Society? An Analytical Study of Caste-Based Reservation in India in Society,' argues that reservations should not be mixed with the welfare activities of the state; reservations are not meant for conferring benefits to the poor and thus caste is primarily damaging society not reservation.

The third section on **Status of Dalits: Experience of States** has two contributors. H. Srikanth's paper, 'Dalit Movement in Telugu Region: Limits of Identity Movements for Social Justice' focuses on the trajectory of dalit movement in the Telugu region and shows how autonomous dalit movements that arose to address the caste question and ignored by mainstream political parties tend to become prey to philistinism and exclusionary politics and finally get absorbed in mainstream politics, making the state and ruling class final arbitrators or dispensers of social justice. He emphasizes on caste, reservation and positive discrimination rather than structural reforms and highlights the fact that the state comes as a mediator when the need for revolution is ignored; it seeks the help of the state in the name of social justice. He mentions that the Indian state sees no threat in the existence of reservation policies to legitimize its power and should go ahead with its policy of liberalization and privatization, affecting the interest of poor dalits.

The last paper in this section 'Social Justice and Women Empowerment through Reservation in PRIs: SCs in Uttar Pradesh' by Sangita Yadav questions the idea of social justice and women empowerment, especially in the context of SC women. She cautions that unless reservations are accompanied by independent voting rights, literacy and change in the status in the family and society, women will continue to act as mere namesake representatives of their male counter parts in the household and will not be given justice in decision making. According to her, in order to keep the transformation process sustainable, a fresh look should be given by which embedment will be removed to make the mission of women empowerment genuine, effective and result-oriented at all levels of the panchayat system.

The fourth section deals with **Empowering the Dalits in North-East India** and consists of eight papers. The first, 'Issues and Challenges of Scheduled Castes Population in Nagaland: Select Case Studies from Kohima' presented by Dr. Visakhonu Hibo and Ms.Visi Yhokha examines the presence of the Scheduled Caste population in Nagaland after the creation of the State in 1963. While elaborating on the issues of migrant SC workers on the basis of certain case studies, they point out the issues and challenges faced by them in present day Naga society which are indicative of a deteriorating Naga society that requires major structural and functional changes. The elevation of Scheduled Castes migrant workers to higher occupations is in sharp contrast to their assigned castes and, therefore, is a clear indication of occupational mobility. They observe that the Scheduled Caste migrant workers are often reluctant to reveal their true caste in the

Hindu status ladder but would claim higher than their actual status even when they respond to queries.

Elaborating on the issues of caste and reservation policies in Manipur, Vijaylakshmi Brara in her paper, 'Caste, Tribe and Reservation in Manipur: A Critique' focuses on four important points. Firstly, she speaks on the power equations based on the proximity to the ruler but not to hierarchy as every clan is an exogamous unit with no exclusions on the basis of the ascribed status. Secondly, she discusses the historical antecedents of the conversion of the Meitei into the Vaishnav Hindu fold. Thirdly, she analyses the creation of an SC category to fulfil the policy of reservation, ascribing the SCs in Manipur to be not even part of the Hindu religion. Fourthly, she draws attention to the fact whether the reservation policies have really benefitted all the people in the selected list or there is a new elite emerging within the marginalised. These aspects need to be enquired into to define the reservation policies ensuring social justice.

In 'Constitutional Justice to *Lois* of Manipur: Comparative Village Profiles', M. Lilee Devi explores a detailed comparative profile of the Scheduled Caste and Non-Scheduled Caste *Loi* locales in Manipur and presents a sociological insight into the similarities and differences between SC and non-SC *Loi* locales of Manipur. She examines how the '*Loi*' inhabitants of *Loi* locales have suffered from constitutional injustice by their inclusion in the list of SCs being delayed or by denying their identity as Scheduled Caste to a few. Such constitutional injustice to some sections of *Lois* is despite the fact that all *Loi* locales shared similar historicity and experiences.

Sarmistha Das, in her paper, 'Locating the 'Dalit' in a Multi caste Assamese Village' tries to understand the meaning of caste in mundane and everyday life experiences of people. While the tentacles of social discrimination seem to wane from Indian society, its challenges continue to persist. The paper aims to raise certain elementary questions like: what is caste? How do people in their everyday practices negotiate caste? She focuses on an important site of social interaction in the village, i.e., the *satra* (neo-Vaishnavite monasteries), and aims at understanding the meanings that people give and derive from it. How the polity, economy and social rhythm of the *satra* vis-à-vis the village gives meaning to the idea of being who they are in the village. She refers to caste as attaining a benchmark position in the individual production process and in the lives of the SCs in the village who are divided into two groups; *kaibarta* in fishing and *hira* in pottery.

Paul Pudussery's paper on 'Social Justice: Fusion of Polarities, A Peep into the Approach to the SCs of Tripura' mentions social justice as the exerciser of altering, disrupting and subverting arrangements that promote marginalization and exclusionary processes. He says social justice is a social reconstruction by a process of deconstruction with a certain determined impetus to have an inclusive society by fusing certain polarities that exist in any given society. This conscientious effort has to be a positive discrimination so as to set the stage for the fusion of polarities of various types. Taking the SC community of Tripura into consideration, he mentions how the state of Tripura has engendered this fusion with thirty-four communities as Scheduled Castes. Development works taken up are in the area of education, health, housing, drinking water, link roads, power, irrigation and income-generating schemes. This study will appraise the construction of a society by the positive discrimination. In his final note, he calls the road ahead as 'the collaboration and cooperation in three major SC communities', because all the three communities, in a way, are equally strong and require concerted effort to bring a better fusion, better integration and better living lifestyle in Tripura.

The paper, 'Dr. B. R. Ambedkar and Scheduled Caste: A Brief Scenario of Scheduled Castes in Tripura' presented by Surojit Sen Gupta talks about Dr. Ambedkar' s vision for the upliftment of the down-trodden classes and who stood for a social system based on right relations between man and man in all spheres. He talks about the two philosophical aspects of Ambedkar that were both negative and positive; in the negative he wanted to destroy the unjust social whereas in the positive aspect it was a concern for justice against untouchability. He mentions how Ambedkar believed that the root of untouchability lay in the caste system which, in the hands of the orthodox, has been a powerful weapon for persecuting the reformers. Citing examples from the state of Tripura, Sen Gupta adds that the SC villages have been recognised and the interrelation with the SC with other communities in

Tripura appeared to be a harmonious one in the social context. He claims that the SCs in Tripura in modern politics, education, economic and other processes have undergone significant changes in their lifestyle and that the system of caste has been undermined. He states that various organizations have created mobility among the SCs in Tripura; their lifestyle and modern ideology had also played an important part among the SCs and concludes by saying that the spread of equality, ideology, government welfare programmes and social mobilization reveals that a fundamental change has taken place among SCs in Tripura.

Debasish Chowdhury in his paper, 'Social Justice and the Scheduled Castes: A Sikkim Narrative' presents a brief profile of Sikkim which is the 22nd state to become a part of the Indian Republic in 1975. He mentions that social justice may be understood as the task of ensuring that the collective essentials of a society, its wealth, opportunities, authorities and privileges are fairly shared without prejudice. According to him, positive discrimination has never maintained a uniform standard; it has its supporters as well as opposition dating back to the 1950s when this was challenged. But he says that there are large numbers of supporters who feel that compensation is necessary and should be accepted because the kind of society we live in cannot do away with such a privilege. Giving a basic profile of the Scheduled Caste population in Sikkim, he states that the state has been able to meet the demands for social justice for the deprived and that it has been carrying out the responsibilities in a sensible fashion. But despite having Central and government institutions, they are unable to achieve a 100 percent literacy rate. Even though reservations have helped in situations like this, they should not only serve as a fundamental object. He finally adds that it may seem like utopia to serve for an individual's right and fight for justice but in course of time this utopia shall drive the progress of society with undiminished zeal.

The last paper, 'Impact of Social Justice in North-East India: A Study from the States of Assam, Manipur and Tripura' presented by C. Joshua Thomas and Padmakshi Kakoti puts forward a glimpse of the Scheduled Caste population in the three states of Assam, Manipur and Tripura. Based on a field survey, this paper attempts to primarily examine the education status and level of achievement among the scheduled caste communities in these three numerically strong SC-populated states of North-East India. It also tries to ascertain the quality of higher education in these States vis-a-vis the employment status. This is an effort to be acquainted with the measures undertaken by the Government of India for the SCs, namely, the reservation policy and its impact on the socio-economic and political conditions of the people in these states. They conclude with an understanding that the policies in favour of social justice and positive discrimination have, no doubt, been able to touch the lives of a smaller section from the community, but the majority, who are rural dwellers and under the shadow of extreme poverty and illiteracy, remain still deprived. This can be effective only when policies related to job reservations in the private as well as public sectors are implemented. And this would be possible only when there is ample opportunity and access to quality-based education in the schools and higher educational institutions not necessarily meant for the elite classes. The shattering effects of caste segregation in educational vis-a-vis the employment sector in these States have remained submissive and in a helpless position.

We take this opportunity to express our appreciation for all the help which the Indian Council of Social Science Research (ICSSR) extended toward this research project and the seminar. We are grateful to Professor S. K. Srivastava, Vice-Chancellor, NEHU & Chairman, ICSSR-NERC, for his encouragement for the seminar. We appreciate the valuable support and advice of Professor L. S. Gassah, Honorary Director of the NERC, not only in the research project but throughout the seminar. We are grateful to all the contributors and we put on record the valuable assistance extended by the young staff in the Centre, particularly, Mrs. Kalari I. Lyngdoh for her meticulous copy editing. Lastly, we appreciate Mr. Rajan Arya of Pentagon Press for having agreed to undertake this publication. We only wish that our volume finds a wide readership and helps the governments, both at the Centre and in the States, while making policies towards the marginalized groups and empower them!

C. Joshua Thomas

Padmakshi Kakoti

SECTION I

Interrogating the Idea of Social Justice

1

THE CLASSICAL AND THE RADICAL IN THE CONCEPT OF SOCIAL JUSTICE

Gopal Guru

In this particular keynote address I am making four-fold arguments. First, certain concepts like social justice are classical as they have timeless essence and universal relevance. Social justice has been one such concept that has acquired timeless relevance in societies that are divided across the globe. Hence, the relevance of this concept has a universal dimension in the sense that it has been universally relevant for almost all societies including that in India. But the concept of social justice does not have a bright theoretical past as it is yet to receive a proper, adequate treatment. We have to still wait for the arrival of an Indian John Rawls who could assign a proper theoretical treatment. However, the principle of social justice which was arguably developed in the West can be locally applied covering the forms of injustice which may not have a universal character. For example, in the USA it is race that forms the basis of justice whereas in India it is caste that provides the ground for the articulation of the principle of justice. The concept of social justice has acquired seminal importance without which no morally sensitive country can manage its social relationships. Social justice also performs another discursive function, that is, to minimise the tension between liberty and equality. The concept of social justice has been devised to moderate the tension between liberty and equality. Here, it is individual liberty that, in its ambition to achieve utmost satisfaction for itself, tends to undermine the expansive capacity of the concept of equality. Possessive Individualism is in constant contradiction with egalitarian equality. The concept of liberal justice imposes certain limits over possessive Individualism, thus making equality accessible to the underprivileged. Thus equality does not remain an elitist value or a sectoral reality. In neo-liberalism, it is only sectoral equality that is thought to be desirable. Through the intervention of justice, equality acquires a democratic character. To argue, equality reaches to dalits and adivasis/tribals via social justice.

Second, I am going to argue that injustice is the result of natural and historical conditions. Injustice could be termed as natural to the extent that it results from the natural placement of population. The uneven habitation of population or social groups on geographical territory and the hierarchical social arrangement of society give rise to the need for social justice. Hence, social justice is a necessary principle. Certain sections of the population came to be residing in particular geographical regions that did not create a sense of discrimination, backwardness and deprivation. But it is the force of modernity that created this sense of injustice. Thus, the imbalance that resulted in skewed development between the rural, mountainous areas and the plains, and between one sub-region and another within the same region created the experience of injustice among the people. A similar social division of society on the basis of caste, religion, region and gender and language also created a deep sense of injustice. Social justice has come into being from the very day human beings sought its separation from nature. In fact, the concept of social justice derives its purpose and essence from nature-generated injustice and man-induced injustice. What is missing in the available literature on the functioning of social justice is the natural and ecologically unfair division of productive resources (for example, in the Himalayas the eastern side of the mountains has thick vegetation while the western side is plain). One might argue in favour of nature which had the nature principle of justice in such division of the mountain. One could hence argue that the side with thick jungle is for the judicious use of human beings and the side which grows only grass can be used as fodder for cattle. Thus one could argue that since there is a win-win situation, nature is without a sense of injustice. It is then the unequal appropriation and occupation of natural resources that generates a deep sense of injustice among members of society. In our country, those who came to occupy privileged positions used caste and gender as the potent resource to maintain their privileged positions across time and space. For example, the tribals and the dalits have been forced to settle in places that are far from water sources. For example, certain regions have been endowed with rich bountiful resources; it is human intervention that has to rectify the social and material imbalance.

Third, I am going to argue that the route to rectify this imbalance is not through the market but through the state. I am further arguing that the concept of social justice has to be mobilised particularly in favour of marginalised communities through the intervention of the state. But ironically, the state has been shifting its responsibility to the corporate through the Corporate Social Responsibility (CSR). Social justice at the theoretical level ceases to be the energy that is necessary for the exercise of rights. The concept of social justice which has the potential to acquire a radical edge seems to be losing it through the language of philanthropy.

Fourthly, until today we thought of social justice in terms of individual interest and we made institutions subordinate to such interest. In the Rawlsian sense, institutions have been thought in terms of giving concrete expression to an abstract principle of social justice. But the more sensitive approach to social justice would demand on our part the moral responsibility to adopt fair consideration even for institutions. We need to emphasise the symbiotic relationship between individual interest and institutional well being. This means that individuals and institutions need to grow, not at the cost of each other. Today, political parties in power and outside the formal political power seem to have adopted the attitude that seems to be quite unfair to the interest of welfare-oriented institutions. In a modernist sense, institutions need to survive on the basis of merit and not narrow ideology. Once conservative ideologies replace modernity, public institutions are bound to suffer. The lead question that one has to ask is who should be concerned about the state and institutions as the major source of delivering social justice? Obviously, it is the tribals and the dalits who should care about these institutions more. Put differently, those who are without any ancestral assets and who cannot rely on the market for obvious reasons have to put their entire faith in the basket of the state. The question that is pertinent for us to ask is: are the dalits and tribals paying any attention to this basic question? The answer is unfortunately in the negative. We do not find dalits using justice as the ground on which they can attempt a critique of the state. Instead, some of them consider the market as the ground for equality and attempt to condemn the state as an obstacle in the progress of the dalits.

2

ACCESS TO SOCIAL JUSTICE: INTERSECTION OF CASTE, CLASS AND IDENTITY

G. C. Pal

ABSTRACT

With the recognition of specific problems of the Scheduled Castes (SCs) and Scheduled Tribes (STs), the Constitution of India provides legal safeguards for their empowerment. The state therefore has the obligation to promote their socio-economic interests and ensure access to social justice through specific legislations and policies. In recent times, unlike many other legal measures for SCs and STs, the Reservation Policy and the Prevention of Atrocities (PoA) Act; which have a common goal of promoting social equality, face perpetual resistance in one form or another. The focal argument against these two is that they have achieved limited success. While the argument against the reservation policy revolves mainly around setting a time limit for its application and replacing caste by economic criteria; the campaign against the PoA Act has been allegedly misuse of the law by the SCs and STs. Against this backdrop, this paper examines the legitimacy of reservation and the PoA Act with special reference to SCs in view of the discriminatory and exclusionary behaviours that this social group face in mainstream society. Drawing evidence from multiple sources, the paper argues that the reservation policy has a definite positive impact despite limitations in terms of low coverage. Further, the positive impact of the policy is very often misconstrued. The PoA Act which aims to protect SCs and STs against human rights violations is not misused by the beneficiaries of the Act; rather a large majority of the victims are denied justice because of unresponsiveness of law enforcement officials and several implementation gaps. The State mechanisms have not been successful to ensure 'rights to equality' and 'social justice' in contemporary society.

Key Words: Caste, specific legislations and policies, resistance, denial of social justice

Introduction

The Constitution of India recognizes the Scheduled Castes (SCs) and Scheduled tribes (STs) as two of the most marginalized social groups, hence, they should be provided with special social protection. A number of constitutional safeguards have been declared to address all forms of discrimination against them and protect them from social injustice. Article 46 of the Constitution states that "The State shall promote with special care the educational and economic interests of the weaker sections of the people and, in particular, of the SCs and STs, and shall protect them from social injustice and all forms of exploitations." The government's approach towards these social groups therefore has been shaped by various provisions of the Constitution. There have been two-fold strategies for the promotion of the social, educational, economic and political interests of the SCs and STs; and for providing them social protection. These include provisions of positive policies and specific legislative measures against discrimination, exploitation and violence.

Although there are several specific laws and policies for the empowerment of SCs and STs, unlike many others, in recent years, the reservation policy, 1950 and the anti-discrimination and atrocity legislation in the form of the Prevention of Atrocities (PoA) Act 1989, later on amended as the PoA Amendment Act, 2015; have been matters of serious contestation and debate and discussion. The reservation policy aims to ensure a fair share for SCs and STs in the spheres of education, employment and the legislature. It has a larger goal, that is, improvement in the relative position of the lower castes and restructuring of the institutionalized social relationships on democratic lines through creation of openings in the hegemonic hold of certain sections of society over public resources and services (Thorat and Senapati, 2006). Similarly, the PoA Act aims to provide protection against discrimination and atrocities and ensure equal citizenship rights. Despite the implementation of the reservation policy and the PoA Act since long, they face perpetual resistance in one form or another. The arguments against the policy have been manifold. It is argued that the policy has achieved limited success in helping the poor among the SCs and STs; that the economically better off have benefited more; and that it derecognizes merit and encourages inefficiency. Accordingly, there has been a demand either to discontinue the reservation policy or replace caste with economic criteria. Similarly, there has been a lot of resistance against the PoA Act 1989. After the amendments were made in 2015 to strengthen the existing provisions in the Act, there has been a strong argument that the Act is being misused by the SCs and STs and hence, there is need to scrap it.

This paper deals with a few pertinent questions such as: Are there any substantial bases of arguments against the reservation policy and the PoA Act?; Why do the SCs and STs continue to suffer from lower access to higher education and employment, and suffer from discrimination and atrocities of various forms despite the implementation of a positive discrimination policy and anti-discrimination and anti-atrocities laws respectively? What implications do these campaigns against reservation and the PoA Act have on SCs and STs in a democratic society? This paper basically aims to offer some explanations as to how SCs and STs, despite legal safeguards, are denied access to social justice and how structural barriers and interplay of caste, class and identity matter in the discourse of accessing social justice. Evidence is drawn from multiple sources, which constitute diverse official data sets, empirical research findings and other relevant literature on the issues of focus. Aligned with the focus of this paper, the analysis is broadly structured into two major sections. Firstly, there has been a focus on reservations in the spheres of education and employment keeping in view the recent debate on reservation and the overall structural changes that have taken place in these two spheres. Secondly, the legitimacy and efficiency of the PoA Act is examined to understand the underlying processes in regard to human right violations affecting access to social justice.

Reservation in Education and Employment: Misconstructions

In recent times, the issue of reservation in education and employment, for SCs and STs in particular, has drawn wide attention. Some sections of society argue that the reservation policy has achieved limited success in solving their problems in these two spheres. There has also been a demand for reservation by certain other sections of the population. There is no doubt that the SCs and STs continue to suffer from relatively lower socio-economic status despite the benefits of the reservation policy for a long time. But this cannot be attributed entirely to the fact that reservation has not helped these groups. Studies have clearly demonstrated that, overall, the reservation policy has been reasonably successful in providing more education and job opportunities to SCs and STs; thereby it has brought positive changes in their social and economic life (Borooah *et al.*, 2007; Dubey, 2016; Haq, 2012; Jogdand, 2007; Pais, 2007). While commenting on 'shortcomings in reservation', one also needs to see the 'limitations in reservation policy' that affect the changes in social and economic status (Thorat, Tagde and Naik, 2016). It is a fact that in political spheres, the impact of reservation is more explicit as reflected through political representations of various social groups at different levels of the political system. But, this has not been so in the case of education and employment. Thus, there is a need to understand the limitations in reservation in education and employment while arguing against its impact.

Understandably, there are shortcomings in implementation of the reservation policy. As claimed, the system of reservation has succeeded in the creation of creamy layers within the marginalized social groups to the extent that the percolation of benefits has been marginal and differentially accessed. There have been reported cases where SCs and STs are discriminated and denied their rights through the non-implementation of the reservation policy. There have not been legal provision of 'checks' against those who wilfully avoid the implementation of the policy. As a result, the policy was not implemented in a true spirit over many years. Only in mid-2000, did the government provided an impetus to implement the reservation policy by incorporating several provisions for action against those who wilfully derailed its implementation. Thus, though rules regarding reservation are in place, the problem lies in its implementation. It may be noted that in recognition of implementation-related problems, the Ministry of Personnel, Public Grievances and Pensions has developed procedural safeguards to overcome them. Moreover, reservation being relevant in the public sector, given the increasing trend of privatization, the scope of the policy has been restricted to a large extent. An attempt is made in the following sections to examine the effectiveness of reservation in education and employment and also limitations in the reservation policy.

Access to Education: Disparities across Social Groups

There is a plethora of writings to show how the exclusionary nature of institutional structure and other social relations impede equal access of certain groups to their entitlements. There is also striking evidence to suggest that education development has a clear caste dimension. Educational programmes are often fraught with unequal educational opportunities. This in fact creates conditions for poor educational development of marginalized sections such as SCs and STs. This section examines the access to education across social groups with a specific focus on higher education. Analysis is structured along the dimensions of inequality across social groups in access to various levels of education, types of educational institutions, and growth in access to higher education in particular.

It is a fact that there has been an impressive educational expansion leading to considerable increase in the educational attainment of all social groups. But the question is, 'have all social groups benefitted equally from this educational growth?' In the recent past, there has been a phenomenal growth of private educational institutions catering to the needs of specific groups. Many students from excluded communities like SCs and STs are deprived of this market-oriented education owing to the costs involved in it. Moreover, other constraints associated with household characteristics deter their access to such an education system. Before getting into a detailed discussion on this issue, an attempt is made here to provide a glimpse of the educational inequalities in access to education across social groups (Table 1). According to Census 2011, of the total SC and ST population, about 70 per cent SC and 75 per cent ST population had an education below secondary level whereas it was about 58 per cent for the non-SC/ST population. As compared to 10 per cent non-SC/ST population, only 3.4 per cent ST and 4.9 per cent SC population had access to higher education. According to NSSO data 2014, there were no significant differences among social groups up to the elementary level. But the proportion of high castes (HCs) with secondary and higher education was significantly higher than the proportion of SCs, STs and OBCs. The share of the SCs, STs and OBCs at the higher education level was found to be considerably low.

Table 1: Access to Various Levels of Education across Social Groups in India

Education Level	*Census, 2011*				*NSSO, 2014*				
	SCs	*STs*	*Non-SCs/STs*	*Total*	*SCs*	*STs*	*OBCs*	*HCs*	*Total*
Below Primary	22.9	29.0	17.7	19.3	17.9	19.1	17.9	15.4	17.3
Primary	27.8	28.1	23.1	24.1	14.5	14.6	14.4	13.7	14.2
Middle	19.4	17.8	17.2	17.6	13.6	12.8	13.6	13.8	13.6
Secondary	11.7	9.1	14.7	13.9	7.8	6.7	9.9	13.0	10.1
Higher Secondary	7.9	6.3	11.0	10.2	4.9	3.8	6.4	9.1	6.6
Diploma	0.8	0.5	1.2	1.1	0.7	0.6	1.1	1.7	1.1
Graduate and >	4.9	3.4	10.2	8.9	2.9	2.6	4.8	11.9	6.2

Sources: (i) Census 2011, Office of Registrar-General and Census Commissioner, Govt. of India. (ii) NSSO data, 71st Round, Participation in Education Survey, Govt. of India

Educational inequalities across social groups in terms of gross attendance ratio (GAR), defined as the number of persons at different levels of education to the number of persons in the corresponding official age groups indicated that at the primary and middle levels, the GAR across social groups was remarkably high (Table 2). The overall GAR at the secondary and higher secondary levels was 78 per cent, with noticeable differences among social groups. But the GAR at the higher education level was very low and the group inequalities were more prominent.

Table 2: Gross Attendance Ratio (GAR) at Different Levels of Education Across Social Groups, 2014

Social Group	*Primary & Middle*	*Secondary & Higher Secondary*	*Graduate & Above*
ST	96.1	67.8	15.2
SC	95.8	73.1	20.1
OBC	96.9	76.2	26.5
HC	99.5	88.5	36.7
Total	97.2	77.9	26.9

Source: Based on NSSO data, 71st Round, Participation in Education Survey, Govt. of India

Besides the issue of inequalities in access to different level of education, the rapid growth of private-unaided institutes places challenges in attaining the goals of equity and cultural diversity. There have been huge disparities in access to different types of educational institutions across social groups.

The NSS data indicated that SCs and STs had considerably lower access to private institutions across all levels of education. The distribution of students in different types of higher educational institutions revealed that a considerably higher proportion of SCs and STs was in public (government and private-aided) institutions. Besides lower access to private educational institutions, normally believed to be imparting 'quality' education, the access of SC and ST students to different types of courses also reflected their exclusion from courses having a greater significance on employment opportunities. The NSS data also showed that the representation of students from SC and ST communities as compared to other social groups was found significantly lower in various professional courses. Thus, the private education system and professional courses excluded many SC and ST students, having greater implications on their human development. In the context of reservation, access of SCs to higher education in particular, as compared to 'Others' (excluding STs) are discussed in detail in the following section.

Access of Scheduled Castes to Higher Education: Relevance of Reservation

Despite the expansion of higher education, the challenge of achieving equity in access to higher education still persists. Another concern is the public-private divide in higher education, which further intensifies the deprivation among SCs and STs. In this context, the role of reservation appears significant to ensure equity in higher education, as caste is seen as conferring privilege on some sections. This section examines the growth rate in GER at the higher education level between SCs and 'Others' to reflect the potential role of reservation in the growth of GER among SCs in particular. The NSS data over two time points (the 52nd round, 1995 and 71st round 2014) clearly indicated that the overall GER in higher education increased significantly from about 7 per cent in 1995 to about 27 per cent in 2014. However, the growth rate in GER varied significantly across institutional types. The share of government institutions decreased from about 57 per cent to 41 per cent during the corresponding period with the per annum growth rate of (minus) 1.7 per cent whereas in the share of private-aided institutions, it decreased from about 36 to 25 per cent with the per annum growth rate of (minus) 1.9. On the contrary, the share of private-unaided institutions increased from about 7 per cent to about 33 per cent with the per annum growth rate of about 9 per cent.

However, despite the decrease in the overall percentage share of government institutions, as per the NSS data, 2014, the highest percentage of students still attended these institutions followed by private-unaided institutions and private-aided institutions. If we look at the gap in the growth rate of GER in higher education between SCs and 'Others' over the period from 1995 to 2014, the per annum growth rate had been about 9 per cent for SCs and about 7 per cent for 'Others' which itself suggests that reservation has helped in the access of SCs to higher education. Further, the gap in the growth rate between SCs and 'Others' was found higher in urban areas (1.9) than rural areas (0.5), obviously due to higher growth of private institutions in urban areas besides other socio-economic constraints of SCs to get enrolled in public higher educational institutions.

The relevance of reservation could further be examined from the access of SCs to different types of higher educational institutions. The fact is that reservation is provided only in the government and private-aided institutions; hence, beneficiaries of reservation are those who are enrolled in these institutions. The percentage share of enrolment in higher education by institution type showed that about half of the SC students were in government institutions whereas another 22 per cent were in private-aided institutions, leaving about 29 per cent SC students who attended private institutions (Graph 1); hence, they were not benefitted by the reservation

Graph 1: Share of Enrolment by Institution Type and Social Groups, 2014

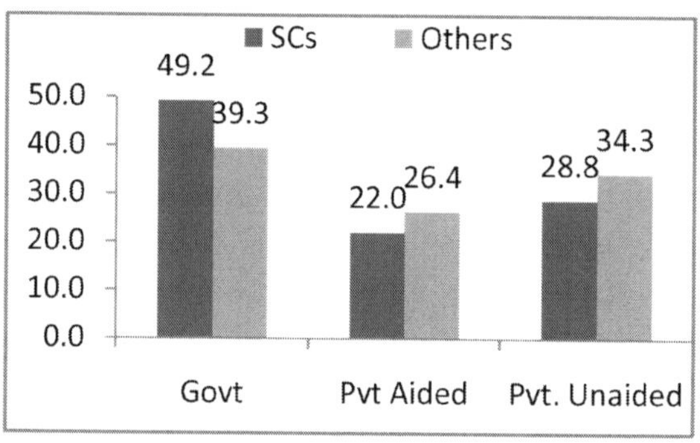

policy. It should also be noted that of the 71 per cent SC students in public institutions, all may not be beneficiaries of reservation, as a certain section of students gets enrolled based on past performance or merit.

Although enrolment of SCs and 'Others' increased in all types of institutions during 1995-2014, the growth rate was found significantly higher in private-unaided institutions than government and private-aided institutions (Graph 2). Another important question is 'did students from higher income groups take advantage of reservations only?' A recent study (Khan, 2017) revealed that GER of SCs and 'Others' belonging to different income groups increased but the increase was relatively higher for higher-income groups. Interestingly, the growth rate in GER was found relatively higher among lower-income groups for both caste groups. Further, there was a significant difference in the GER growth of SCs and 'Others' belonging to the low-income group (income ranging from 0 to 40) as well as middle-income group (income ranging from 41 to 80). Among higher income groups, GER growth for SCs was higher than 'Others'. An analysis of the share of enrolment among SCs and 'Others' across institution types and the three broad income groups indicated that the share of government and private-aided institutions went down for every income group during 1995 to 2014 (ibid). The decrease in the share of enrolment in these two types of institutions was distinctively higher for the higher income groups. On the contrary, there was considerable increase in the enrolment share of SCs and 'Others' in private-unaided institutions. The changes in the

Graph 2: Growth in Enrolment by Institution Type and Social Groups, 1995-2014

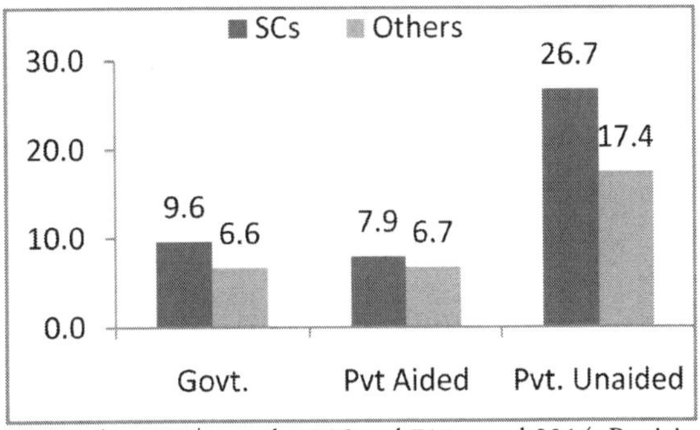

Source: Based on NSSO data, 52nd round, 1995 and 71st round 2014, Participation in Education Survey, Govt. of India

percentage share of both SCs and 'Others' in private-unaided institutions were also found to be positively related to the income range.

To sum up, the overall access to higher education across social groups has been very low. But SCs and STs are in the most disadvantaged position. The share of private-unaided higher educational institutions has increased disproportionately. The share of SCs and STs in these institutions has been significantly low. The growth patterns in enrolment across income groups, particularly for SCs, suggest that it is the lower-income groups that attend government institutions; hence, they are the main beneficiaries of the reservation policy. In such a scenario, the argument that reservation benefits to SC students from better-off families only, does not appear to have strong ground.

Reservation in Employment: How much does it Matter?

Broadly, the objective of providing reservations for SCs and STs in employment is not only to increase their representation in public sector jobs but also to improve their relative status in critical human development indicators. An understanding of the impact of reservation therefore calls for ascertaining the percentage share in public sector employment among SCs and STs; and changes in their employment position. With considerable growth in access to higher education among these two groups, there is also need to examine their employment status in various levels of employment. The key questions that are addressed in this section are: 'what have been inter-social group positions in the realm of public sector employment?'; 'how many have benefitted from reservation?'; and 'is there a need to extend the reservation policy?'

To ascertain the employment status of SCs, STs and non-SC/STs in public sector employment, this paper deals with Central Government services only, although reservation is applicable in other sector jobs such as public sector undertakings (PSU), nationalized banks (NB) and nationalized insurance companies (NIC). This is done keeping in view the jobs directly under the Central Government and lack of viability within the scope of this paper to deal with various aspects of employment using diverse sources of data. For the purpose of analysis, the employment status of social groups is examined in terms of the percentage share of employment, both horizontally (percentage share of a respective social group out of total Central Government jobs), and vertically (percentage share of a respective social groups in different categories of jobs). In addition, the employment status of social groups in higher educational institutes under the Central Government is discussed to shed light on the linkage between higher education and employment in the context of reservation. For the purpose of analysis, the paper uses official data from various sources which include the Ministry of Personnel, Public Grievances and Pensions; All India Survey on Higher Education (AISHE) by the Ministry of Human Resource and Development (MHRD) and NSS data on Employment Survey. The questions that are considered for analysis are: 'Are there any variations across social groups in Central Government employment?'; 'Have there been significant changes in the representation of SCs and STs in Central Government employment over the years?'; and 'What is the proportion of SCs and STs who receive benefits from the reservation policy?'

The data on the number of SCs, STs and non-SCs/STs in Central Government employment in India by social groups over five decades (1960-2010) revealed that the total number of SC employees in Central Government jobs increased from about 2.3 lakh in 1960 to 4.9 lakh in 2010 (Graph 3). The corresponding figures for STs were about 38 and 215 thousand. Similarly, the number of non-SCs/STs increased from about 16 lakh in 1960 to nearly 23 lakh in 2010. The data on the net change in the number of SCs and STs in Central Government employment over five decades revealed a growth of about 115 per cent for SCs, 472 per cent for STs and 43 per cent for non-SCs/STs. The data also showed that after 2000, there was a marginal decline in the number of SC and ST Central Government employees. The decline in the number of non-SCs/STs employees was found to be higher than SC and ST employees.

The decadal percentage share in Central Government employment showed a consistent increase for STs, but for SCs it varied slightly over decadal points. However, the data for non-SCs/STs showed a decreasing trend. No remarkable changes were noticed in the percentage share of SCs

Graph 3: Trend in Central Government Employment by Social Groups, 1960-2010 (Figures in '000)

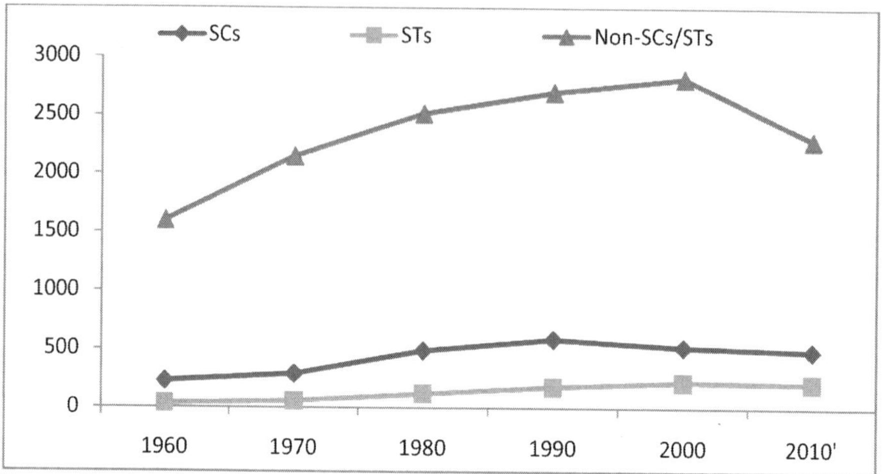

Source: Based on data, Ministry of Personnel, Public Grievances and Pensions, Government of India, New Delhi

and non-SCs/STs in Central Government employment after 1990. An analysis of the decadal average in this employment revealed that the decadal average for SCs increased till the 1990s, but slightly decreased in the 2000s. The decadal average for STs showed a consistent increase. Like SCs, the figures for non-SCs/STs showed a steady increase till the 1990s and decreased in the 2000s. Further, an analysis of the decadal annual growth rate revealed that for SCs, it increased marginally from 5.18 per cent in the 1960s to 5.40 per cent in the 1970s. But the growth rate in the subsequent decades declined sharply. The change was found negligible in the 1990s, and there was about two per cent negative growth in the 2000s. A similar trend was noticed for STs till 1990, but there was no negative growth in the 2000s. The growth rate for non-SCs/STs was found quite low over the decades, and like the SCs, there was a negative growth in the 2000s.

The trend in the percentage share of social groups in government employment over five decades thus suggested that reservation helped SCs and STs to increase their representation in it. Government employment is however not a homogenous category; rather it is divided into different categories. Group A and B jobs are generally considered as high category. The data revealed variations in the share of social groups in different categories of Central Government employment (Table 3). An analysis of data, particularly from 1990 onwards, the time around which the economic growth in India looked up, revealed that the share of SCs in Group A jobs was far behind the proportion of their population, though it showed an increase from 8.64 per cent in 1990 to 11.60 per cent in 2010. A similar situation was found for STs, though the growth was higher than SCs. Thus, till 2010, the share of SCs and STs in Group A jobs was found lower than their assigned quota.

Table 3: Percentage Share of Social Groups in Different Categories of Jobs, 1990-2010

Year	*Group A*		*Group B*		*Group C*		*Group D*	
	SCs	*STs*	*SCs*	*STs*	*SCs*	*STs*	*SCs*	*STs*
1990	8.64	2.58	11.29	2.39	15.19	4.83	21.48	6.73
1995	10.15	2.89	12.67	2.68	16.15	5.69	20.53	6.48
2000	10.97	3.48	12.54	3.09	15.88	6.33	17.38	6.66
2005	11.90	4.27	13.71	4.45	16.39	6.47	18.31	6.91
2010	11.60	4.50	15.27	5.72	15.95	7.43	18.59	7.17

Note: Group D jobs exclude 'sweepers'. Under each category of job, the remaining percentage share is for non-SCs/STs

Source: Based on data, Ministry of Personnel, Public Grievances and Pensions, Government of India, New Delhi

The share of SCs and STs in Group B jobs went up from 11.29 per cent and 2.39 per cent respectively in 1990 to 15.27 per cent and 5.72 per cent in 2010. Thus, SCs had a representation in Group B jobs as per their reserved quota whereas the representation of STs was lower than the quota. However, the percentage share of STs in Group B jobs increased more than double between 1990 and 2010, and the increase was significantly higher than the increase in the percentage share of SCs. The share of SCs and STs in low-paying Group C jobs was found little higher than their population share. In Group D jobs, the share of SCs was remarkably higher than their population share. The share of SCs in Group D jobs was recorded as high as 21.48 per cent in 1990 and it came down to 18.59 per cent in 2010. It is believed that Group D jobs being in the lower category accounted for a higher percentage share of SCs. But the same was not found true for STs. An analysis of the percentage share of employees from different social groups in each category of jobs suggested job mobility among SCs and STs as their share in group A and group B jobs increased over the years. This also suggests the impact of reservation on the employment status of SCs and STs, though they still have a higher representation in the lower category of jobs.

Given that SCs and STs have been marginalized in the access to higher education over the years and the reservation policy along with other special measures have been implemented to facilitate their access to higher education, an attempt was made to examine their representation in teaching jobs in higher educational institutions under the Central Government. It was revealed that the percentage share of teaching staff belonging to SCs and STs in institutes of higher education was not as per the reservation quota although reservation helped them to get employment. According to the data provided by All India Survey on Higher Education (AISHE), in 2010-11, the share of SC and ST teaching faculty in institutions of higher education was still lower than the share of their population. In 2011-2012, the share of SCs increased marginally whereas the share of STs decreased slightly (Graph 4)

Graph 4: Percentage Share of Teaching Staff in Institutes of Higher Education

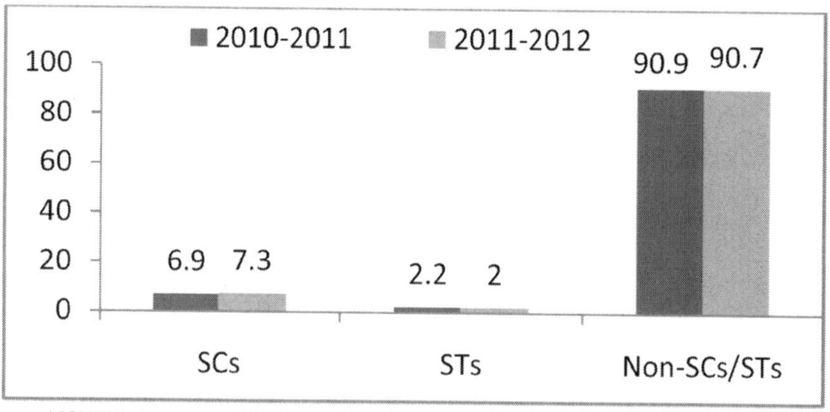

Source: AISHE 2010-11 and 2011-12, MHRD, Govt. of India

The data also revealed that the representation of the teaching faculty belonging to SCs and STs in Central Government institutions of higher education varied by types of institution. The AISHE data showed that the share of SCs and STs in some premier central government educational institutions like Central Universities (CUs), management institutes like IIMs and other scientific and technical institutions like IITs and IIITs, was considerably lower than their population proportion. This is believed to have been caused by several factors. The reservation in faculty positions in scientific and technical institutions is, as a rule, implemented at the entry level. Moreover, there has been a considerably lower participation of SCs and STs in professional and technical courses. Because of the remarkable growth of these courses in private institutions and the high cost involved, these groups have less access to them. As a result, a limited number of degree holders are available among SCs and STs to take up teaching jobs in these premier institutions.

To sum up, the analysis indicates that there has been an improvement in the representation of SCs and STs in different categories of Central Government services, suggesting the significance of the reservation policy. The representation of SCs in some categories of Central Government jobs was found slightly higher than the stipulated quota. The representation of STs in Central Government jobs, though showing improvement, is still keeping them in a disadvantageous position as compared to SCs. However, the representation of SCs and STs in the highest-ranked government and teaching jobs in scientific and technological institutions in particular is less than the stipulated quotas.

One of the arguments against reservation in employment is that it dilutes merit and deprives 'other' social groups of their entitlements. But, the limitation of reservation in terms of its narrow coverage is hardly recognized (Thorat, Tagade and Naik, 2016). The total share of SCs in permanent public employment signifies a positive impact of the reservation policy on employment. But the policy has narrow coverage due to two reasons—firstly, the exclusion of private sector jobs, and secondly, the exclusion of temporary government jobs from reservation (ibid). This results in the confinement of reservation in employment to a minuscule segment of permanent government employees only. As per the NSS data, 2011-12, of the total regular salaried employees in the non-farm sector, about 70 per cent were employed in the private sector; hence, the remaining 30 per cent were employed in the public sector. Of these public sector employees, about 40 per cent were temporary; hence they were not covered by the reservation policy. Eventually, about 60 per cent of public sector employees who were permanently employed were covered under reservation. This in fact constitutes less than one-fifth of the total non-farm regular salaried employees; hence, a large majority of SCs were outside the purview of reservation. Thus, the coverage of government jobs under reservation is very small and it is likely to have a limited impact on the overall economic 'well-being' of SC communities.

Another argument against the reservation policy is that those who are economically better off among the SCs have benefited more from reservation. As discussed earlier, SC employees have relatively higher representation in Grade C and D jobs, indicating a significant use of reservation by the weaker sections among SCs through recruitment in C and D category jobs. Further, the NSS employment data provided the number of SC government employees under reservation by their education level. As reported (Thorat, Tagade and Naik, 2016), about two thirds of permanent SC employees were educated below secondary and higher secondary levels or were diploma holders. These people also generally belonged to the economically weaker sections; hence, a larger proportion of SCs from weaker backgrounds have benefited from reservation. Further, based on analysis of the NSS data on land holding by households with different education levels, they also argue that poor SCs (with low land holding) from all educational levels have been benefited from reservation in government employment. When a large proportion of SC employees with higher levels of education possessed small acres of land, this itself highlights their relatively weak financial status. It justifies that the educated poor have also been benefited from reservation in employment. Thus, when there is a question mark on the continuity of the reservation policy, it should be recognized that the purpose of the policy to protect SCs and

STs from inequality has not been fulfilled. The gaps between SCs/STs and 'Others' on the economic and educational status persist. The SCs/STs also continue to face discrimination in access to civil, cultural, social and economic rights. There are a number of studies to show that discrimination is deeply embedded in social relations and persists in a significant measure in all spheres of life, having significant consequences on the socio-economic life of the SCs, in particular. Moreover, the victims of caste-based discrimination and atrocities have limited access to social justice despite the protective laws. In the following section, the effectiveness of the PoA Act which aims to protect SCs and STs from civil rights violations and atrocities is dealt with to shed light on challenges in access to social justice.

Caste-based Discrimination and Atrocities: Denial of Social Justice

The National Crime Records Bureau (NCRB) data reveals that there has been a consistent increase in registered cases of atrocities against SCs and STs. Although, the official figures on caste-based discrimination and atrocities have limitations in terms of poor reflection on the magnitude of such human rights violations; still it provides insights into the patterns of human rights violations against SCs and STs. The analysis of fact-finding reports, case studies and experiential accounts of victims and human rights activists shows that a majority of the victims of discrimination and atrocities are denied justice for various reasons (Pal, 2015, 2014, 2012; Pal and Lal, 2010). Delivery of justice to victims of atrocities is affected by dilution of scope, applicability and meaning of the provisions under the laws. Failure on the part of the judicial system to provide justice in a large majority of cases multiplies the suffering of the victims. The aftermath of the atrocities has larger consequences on the overall 'well-being' of SC victims and other members of their communities (Pal, 2015). The challenging task therefore is not only to prevent atrocities against SCs and STs, but to also deliver justice to the victims and ensure social security for them.

This section examines the magnitude of atrocities against SCs in particular and the responses of the state machinery under the criminal justice system to them to provide a glimpse of the effectiveness of specific legislation and access to justice. However, keeping in view the specific focus on 'social justice' and scope of the paper, the analysis primarily deals with access to social justice following human rights violations in the form of atrocities though an attempt is made to highlight the patterns of atrocities against SCs based on the official data. An analysis of registered cases of atrocities provided by the NCRB clearly showed a rise in the number of atrocities against SCs. According to the NCRB data, during 2001-2015, on an average, about 33.5 thousand crimes against SCs were registered annually. The registered cases increased distinctively from 2014 (Graph 5). The data on the crimes registered under the PoA Act, considered as 'atrocities', revealed that on an average, around 14.5 thousand cases of atrocities were registered against SCs annually. This is despite the fact that many cases of atrocities remain unreported due to various reasons; hence, figures are always underestimations of the actual magnitude. Moreover, several cases of crimes committed by high-castes member against SCs are very often not registered under the PoA Act wilfully as it invites more punishment. The data thus suggests that the PoA Act has not been a deterrent to curb atrocities.

Graph 5: Trends of Total Crimes and PoA Crimes, 2001-15

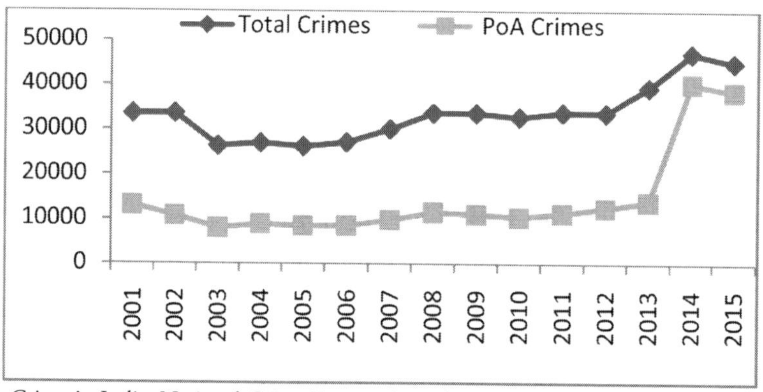

Source: Crime in India, National Crime Bureau Record, MHA, Govt. of India, New Delhi

However, the major concern has been the outcome of the registered atrocity cases. How many victims of atrocities are provided with justice through conviction of the accused? The PoA Act Rules 1995 makes specific provisions for the speedy disposal of crimes at the administrative level so that charge-sheets are submitted in court within a specific time period. Recently, the PoA Amendment Act Rules 2016 prescribes time limits for court trials for the quick delivery of justice. The timely disposal of cases thus would indicate the efficiency of the state machinery in dealing with atrocity cases. According to the NCRB data, on an average, more than 90 percent of the total valid cases were charge-sheeted at the end of each year during 2001-15. (Graph 6). However, the disposal of cases by courts has been far from satisfactory. The disposal assessed in terms of pendency and conviction rates revealed that, on an average, 80 per cent of cases remained pending at the end of each year during the corresponding period. The average pendency percentage for PoA crimes (atrocities) in courts was considerably higher than the overall crimes against SCs. But the issue that draws serious attention is the low conviction rate. Of the tried cases on overall crimes, the accused were convicted in only one third of them. The conviction rate for PoA crimes was dismal. The data clearly suggests that despite protective provisions under the PoA Act, delivery of social justice to the victims of atrocities has been depressing.

Graph 6: Trend of Charge-sheet Rate (CSR), Pendency Percentage (PP) and Conviction Rate (CR) for Total Crimes, 2001-15

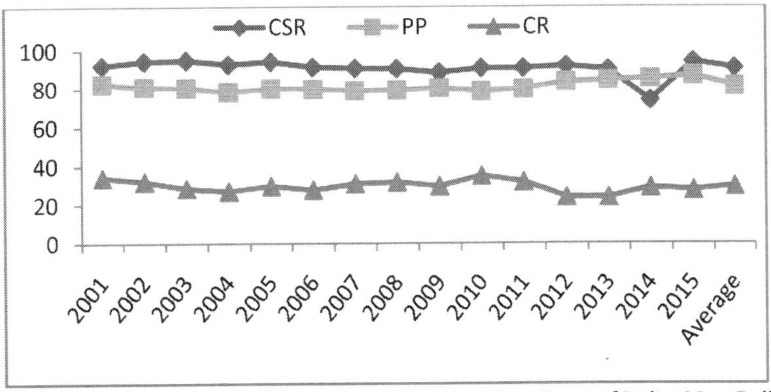

Source: Crime in India, National Crime Bureau Record, MHA, Govt. of India, New Delhi

The reasons for the low conviction rate have been multifarious. The analysis of fact-finding report and case studies (Pal, 2015, 2014; 2012) reveals that reasons for low conviction range from delay in framing charge sheets to dilution of evidence against the accused, non-availability of eyewitnesses, delay in court trials, forced compromises and so on. Another concern is that the delay in disposal of cases and the rate of high acquittal very often become potential causes of atrocities as legitimate response to resentment, retaliation and revenge remain prominent to protect social identity (Pal, 2015, 2012). Other mechanisms such as atrocities against SC women and influential persons from the SC community, and constant threatening of victims (dropping subtle hints of dire consequences) and social boycotts or ostracisms against entire SC communities are also used as means of retaliation (Pal, 2015, 2014; Pal & Lal, 2010).

The fact is that the state machinery has an obligation to ensure social security and social justice to the victims of atrocities. Increase in atrocities despite the powerful legislation of the PoA Act and further low conviction rate clearly point to the failure of the state machinery in implementation of the law in the proper spirit. An examination of the gaps in the enforcement of the PoA Act based on fact-findings reports, case studies, and experiential accounts of human rights activists working on atrocities at the grassroots level revealed that SCs face several obstacles while seeking justice through the criminal justice system (Pal, 2015, 2014, 2012; Pal and Lal, 2011). Some provisions under the law are predisposed to misinterpretations which often lead to denial of justice to victims. A growing number of instances show misuse of laws by implementing officers, even in cases of heinous atrocities. Several PoA cases are often registered under wrong legal provisions to shield the accused from arrest and prosecution. An analysis of court cases revealed that in a majority of cases, the acquittal of the accused takes place on procedural grounds, but the victims are denied social justice (Pal and Thorat, 2017). Implementation of the PoA Act to provide justice to the victims of discrimination and atrocities requires performance of duties by not merely going by the law but also having a commitment to deliver social justice. Subramanian (2009) views that "implementation of legislation like the PoA Act call for qualities of head and heart, in addition to professionalism." The acts of omission and commission by law enforcement agencies shake the people's faith in the rule of law (NHRC, 2004). The high rate of pending cases in courts manifests not only delay in judgment but also denial of justice. Delay causes disposal of many cases outside the 'law of the state' rather than court verdicts, which is nothing but denial of social justice, as these outcomes deprive victims of their entitlement to several compensatory and rehabilitation provisions. Thus, the critical issue is that the implementation of law normally overlooks the challenges that victims of atrocities normally face after the incident, and their further vulnerability to the vicious cycle of caste atrocities.

Conclusion

This paper basically offers an alternative view to the arguments against the two protective measures of the reservation policy and the PoA Act. There are many misconceptions about the reservation policy, leading to constant debate. The paper argues that despite many shortcomings in the reservation policy, it has a definite positive impact. It has helped SCs and STs to achieve socio-economic mobility. The benefits of reservation reach a small proportion of SCs and STs. As a result, social inequalities on socio-economic indicators continue. It should be recognised that SCs and STs were given reservation because they are vulnerable to discrimination, exploitation and oppression. There can be no disagreement with the fact that one of the most shameful realities of life in India today is caste-based discrimination and atrocities. The problem of discrimination is deep rooted and the public system has failed to provide social security and justice to marginalized groups like SCs and STs. The problem is not something that arises only at the level of employment or higher education; rather it exists in different spheres of life. As evident from the data on access to higher education, they were deprived of 'quality' education because of the rapid privatization of higher education. Though overall access to higher education across social groups has been low, SCs and STs are in a most disadvantageous position because of the disproportionate increase of private unaided higher educational institutions. This further deprives them of opportunities for 'high' ranked jobs. As is evident, the representation of SCs and STs in highest-ranked government jobs and teaching jobs in management and scientific and technological institutes is still below the stipulated quota. It is reservation that has helped them to move a few steps forward. But they have a long way to go, particularly in the context of the privatization of the educational and employment sectors as a large majority of them remain outside the purview of the reservation policy. The argument that reservation benefits SC and ST students from better-off families only does not have strong ground. There has been an improvement in the representation of SCs and STs from different income groups in different categories of Central Government services, suggesting the significance of the reservation policy.

There is no doubt that SCs, STs and other socially weaker sections remain largely affected so far education and employment opportunities are concerned. The practice of discrimination against them further serves as an instrument to marginalize them. Like the positive discrimination policy in the form of reservation, the anti-discrimination and anti-oppression law in the form of the PoA Act which aims to protect SCs and STs against human rights violations is also fraught with several gaps in implementation. As a result, violations of rights of SCs and STs continue, which sometimes act as a deterrent to socio-economic equality. The economic privilege, high social status and other vested interests of socio-economically dominant social groups continue to motivate them to discriminate in multiple spheres. Very often, it is not simply the factor of 'caste' that makes SCs and STs vulnerable to subjugation, exploitation and unequal development; rather it interacts with the social class and identity associated with it. As is evident, any act of assertion by SCs and STs against caste-based discrimination and violence triggers retaliation or/and social ostracism by members of dominant social groups as a matter of disrespect to their group position. Sometimes, the unresponsive behaviour of the state machinery towards human rights violations against SCs and STs are guided by 'significant' social actors and 'power relations'. This again accentuates conditions for increased vulnerabilities to further discrimination and violence. Similarly, the privatization of education and employment creates a sense of 'different class' and 'distinct identity' among certain sections of the population that have access to it. As a result, SCs and STs often face the vicious cycle of discrimination, violence and poor socio-economic development, enforcing their subordinate position in society. In such a social environment, the reservation policy and the PoA Act remain highly significant. However, human development cannot be ensured with the presence of laws and policies only. The state mechanism, which is mandated to ensure 'rights to equality' and 'social justice' for SCs and STs, needs to see that these legal tools are effectively used to bring changes in the life of marginalized groups of society and ensure delivery of social justice.

REFERENCES

Borooah, V. K., et *al.,* 2007, "The effectiveness of jobs reservation: Caste, religion and economic status in India," *Development and Change,* Vol. 38, No. 3, pp. 423-445.

Dubey, A. 2016. *Effectiveness of Job Reservation in India*, Project Report, Indian Institute of Dalit Studies, New Delhi.

Haq, R. 2012, "The managing diversity mindset in public versus private organizations in India," *The International Journal of Human Resource Management*, Vol. 23, No. 5, pp. 892–914.

Jogdand, P. G., 2007, "Reservation policy and empowerment of Dalits," In S. M. Michael (ed.) *Dalits in Modern India: Vision and Values,* New Delhi: Sage Publications, pp. 315-335.

Khan, K. 2017, *Access of Scheduled Castes and Scheduled Tribes to School and Higher Education: A Gap Analysis.* Research Report, Indian Institute of Dalit Studies, New Delhi.

National Crime Record Bureau (NCRB) (Various years). *Crimes in India,* Ministry of Home Affairs, Government of India, New Delhi.

National Human Rights Commission (2004). *Report on Prevention of Atrocities against Scheduled Castes.* National Human Rights Commission, Government of India, New Delhi.

Pais, R. 2007, "Scheduled caste, employment and social mobility," In S. M. Michael (ed.) *Dalits in Modern India: Vision and Values*, New Delhi: Sage Publications.

Pal, G. C., 2012, "Mapping Caste-based Atrocities in Uttar Pradesh," Project Report No. 49, Indian Institute of Dalit Studies, New Delhi.

Pal, G. C., 2014, "Access to justice: Social ostracism obstructs efforts by Dalits for equal rights," *Journal of Social Inclusion Studies*, Vol. 1, No. 1, pp.122-134.

Pal, G. C., 2015, "Social exclusion and mental health: The unexplored aftermath of caste-based discrimination and violence," *Psychology & Developing Societies*, Vol. 27, No. 2, pp. 189-213.

Pal, G. C. and Lal, L. D., 2011, *Mapping Caste-Based Atrocities in India with a Special Focus on Dalit Women: Annual Report 2010-11,* Project Report No. 41, Indian Institute of Dalit Studies, New Delhi.

Pal, G. C. and Lal, L. D., 2010, *Mapping Caste-based Atrocities in India: Status Report,* Project Report No. 39, Indian Institute of Dalit Studies, New Delhi.

Pal, G. C. and Thorat, S., 2017, Violation of Civil Rights and Atrocities in Maharashtra, *Working Paper*, Indian Institute of Dalit Studies, New Delhi.

Subramanian, K. S., 2009, *Political violence and the police in India,* New Delhi: Sage Publications.

Thorat, S. and Senapati, C., 2006, Reservation Policy in India—Dimensions and Issues, *Working Paper Series*, Vol. 1, No. 2, Indian Institute of Dalit Studies, New Delhi.

Thorat, S., Tagade, N. and Naik, A. K., 2016, Prejudices against reservation policies: How and why? *Economic& Political Weekly*, Vol. 51, No. 8, pp. 61-69.

3

SOCIAL JUSTICE IN CONTEMPORARY INDIA: RECEPTIVITY OF RECOGNITION AND REDISTRIBUTION

V. Bijukumar

ABSTRACT

In India, Marxists and Ambedkarites are counterpoising each other on the issue of social justice. For a long time, Marxism as an emancipatory ideology and its emancipatory potentiality is often questioned by the Ambedkarites and the later overemphasis on identity-based recognition was interrogated by the Marxists as it erodes class mobilisation. However, contemporary India is witnessing a united slogan of 'Jai Bhim' and 'Lal Salaam' combining the emancipatory projects of both Marxism and Ambedkarism. The article tries to examine the possibility of synthesizing the Ambedkarite notion of recognition and the Marxist conception of redistribution in the challenges posed by the unleashing of market forces and Hindu nationalist politics. The recent dalit upsurge in Una in Gujarat and the Dalit Asmita Yatra (Dignity March) demand for livelihood and land reforms is a clear manifestation that contemporary Ambedkarites go beyond the sheer politics of recognition to the politics of redistribution and the strong participation of Marxists in the movement convey the clear message that delinking the struggle for recognition from redistribution and vice versa is the death knell for the emancipatory project of social justice in India.

Key Words: social justice, redistributive, Marxists, Ambedkarites, caste system, Una dalit protest, chaturvarna

Introduction

In contemporary India, the discourse on social justice has assumed a new dimension as it came out of the straightjacket formulation of the politics of recognition and redistribution. In contrast to the politics of redistribution, it is commonly equated with class politics, while the politics of recognition is associated with identity politics related to assertions by gender, sexuality, nationality, ethnicity, race and caste. The two main protagonists of social justice such as the Marxists and Ambedkarites have realized that the insulation of recognition from redistribution and vice versa would jeopardize the achievement of the grand idea of social justice and the realization of the project of social emancipation for the marginalized.

Marxism as a meta-narrative for liberation based on economic egalitarianism in which redistribution of material resources is the paramount goal. Though Marxism does not explicitly propound any theory of justice, the Marxian conception of justice can be traced in the Marxist analysis of the inhuman conditions attached to capitalism. As such, the Marxist conception of justice depends on its totality of the capitalist system for it breeds inequality. Marx's critique of capitalism is based on the inherent problems of alienation and exploitation and domination. Marx was even critical of the trickledown effect in the capitalist system which would not bring justice to the working class. Unlike liberalism, the Marxist conception of justice is not related to liberty and rights. In its critique of capitalism, it argues that property rights perpetuate inequality and exploitation.

The redistributive model of social justice does not confine only the Marxist conception. Even the liberals emphasized some form of redistributive form of social justice. This model found its expression in the writings of Rawls, Sen and Dworkin. Rawls describes justice as fairness and distribution of primary good. Sen is creating capabilities among the people. Dworkin emphasizes on 'equality of resources'. Resource allocation is a way to achieve a redistributive society. Keynesianism emphasizes on state intervention in monetary and fiscal policies by enhancing government spending on social sector investment.

Fraser's Social Justice

The idea of recognition and redistribution in the literature on social justice was emphasized by Nancy Fraser in the mid-1990s when she warned feminists of the risk of neglecting redistribution in favour of recognition, a key feature of post-socialist condition. (Fraser, 1997 & 2003). For Fraser, redistribution and recognition must be regarded as two mutually irreducible elements of an account of social justice. In her view, cultural recognition and economic redistribution must go hand in hand. According to Fraser, the politics of redistribution and politics of recognition would synergize towards achieving the goals of social justice. In other words, Fraser emphasizes on a combined socialist politics of redistribution and deconstructive politics of recognition. Recognition ultimately related to achieving distributive justice which is possible through the emphasis on redistribution. It is often seen that economic issues are sidelined in the age of identity politics and there is a need to address economic marginalization, economic disempowerment, unemployment, etc. She was sceptical of the more emphasis on the more identity-based social justice project. With the rise of identity politics, the politics of egalitarian redistribution was undermined. The setback of socialist regimes, advent of free market ideology and the rise of identity politics overshadowed the demand for redistributive politics. The recognition argument is based on the assumption that social inequality emanates from cultural differences and brings injustice to certain communities. On the other hand, the redistribution argument based on the assumption that inequality emerged out of unequal material possession—unequal access to income and asset, private ownership—leading to injustice. In other words, redistribution is addressing the material inequality rooted in the political-economic structure of society, economic marginalization and deprivation. Fraser identified three constitutive features of the 'post socialist' condition—firstly absence of any credible progressive vision of an alternative to the present order after the collapse of the socialist order; secondly, shift in the grammar of political claims, making claims for the recognition of group difference and thirdly, the resurgence of economic liberalism (Fraser, 1997: 1-3). The reification of recognition and the displacement of redistribution are often seen as a crisis of class politics in the post socialist era. It is claimed that the assertion of identities and identity-based politics is the result of the negation of class politics.

Indian Marxism and the Question of Social Justice

The Indian Marxist approach to social justice is based on an understanding of the nature of capitalist development in India. The capitalist development in India did not destroy the caste system; on the other hand, it cemented it for its expansion leading to creating more hurdles for the communist movement to penetrate into the Indian society. The distinctiveness of Indian capitalism is its hobnobbing with caste loyalties and relationships that perpetuate the caste-based agrarian relationship. As much as for capitalism taking a grip in India, caste loyalties and consciousness also develop leading to the weakening of class politics. The bourgeoisie landlord system has failed to put an end to caste oppression. The communists argue that the caste system contains both social oppression and class exploitation. Since there is an intertwining relationship of caste and class in India, social justice can be achieved through intertwining the struggles against class and caste oppression. It believed that the guarantee of education, employment and health facilities to the socially marginalized through redistributive policies is the way to address social deprivation.

Marxism in India, while emphasizing the need for redistribution, is aware of the social injustices due to the caste system. In fact, Marx himself correctly argued that the caste system of India was based on the hereditary division of labour, which was inseparably linked with the unchanging technological base and the subsistence economy of the Indian village community. However, initially, the Marxists did not pay much attention to the politics of recognition as it denigrates the idea of redistribution and reifies identity politics though they believed that the bourgeois-landlord system has also failed to put an end to caste oppression which resulted in the scheduled castes being the worst sufferers. Indian Marxism once believed that the dalit movement was merely a 'politics of recognition' as it was not having revolutionary potentialities.

It is not true that the early Indian Marxists did not take up the issue of the caste question in the larger agenda of emancipation and establishing egalitarian society. The early communist leaders like EMS Namboodiripad and B.T. Ranadive address the caste questions on the class line. Ranadive even admitted at some point of time that "there has been a certain neglect in the ideological struggle against caste and communalism," and that "the common consciousness generated through the economic struggle cannot be pushed forward without such struggle and direct intervention of the movement on caste oppression" (Ranadive, 2002:145). In some pockets of India, the Marxists tried to integrate the caste oppression with class oppression, but that could not be extended to the all-India level and their commitment to synthesise the issues of caste with class was confined only to some geographical segments. Patnaik states that "the communist movement in India is not a homogenous thing. Bengal communism is quite different from Kerala communism. Kerala is one state in which the communist movement and the social emancipation movement went hand in hand, which is why communists are very powerful among the Ezhavas. In Bengal, that is not the case. There, it was much more a trade union thing, which of course made inroads into the peasantry later when it became powerful. The communist movement in Bengal never had a history of fighting for social emancipation." (Patnaik, 2017). In Kerala, the Marxists were able to combine the social and political struggles and thereby combined the struggle for recognition and redistribution. According to Guru, "In the Indian context, the Left has not been averse to the dalit demand for inclusion.... But, the Left has to pay the political price of postponing the project of forging solidarity based on unified class consciousness" (Guru, 2016: 23).

Ambedkarite Conception of Social Justice

The conception of the Ambekarites of social justice is premised on the critical of the caste system legitimized by the Hindu Social Order (HSO). Accordingly, the social division of labour based on an inscriptive identity breeds social injustice for the underprivileged sections in Indian society. The HSO, which is based on graded inequality, breeds social injustice. The *varna* ideology based on untouchability strengthening *varnashrama dharma* leads to the denigration of social justice. In the HSO, caste as a traditional social institution, fails to bring justice in society. The HSO seldom discussed the ideas of social equality and social justice though it is pronouncing on universal equality and brotherhood, harping on *Vaskdhaiv Kutumbkam*. In HSO, human relationships are based on the principle of purity and pollution which creates unequal citizens based on unequal rights. Ambedkar believed that since the HSO is based on hierarchy, it lacks rationality. In the HSO, both *chaturvarna* and *karma* propose inequality and suffering. Ambedkar understands that a society based on domination and subordination seldom has scope for distributive justice. Ambedkar believed that the HSO survives only because of the inequality sanctioned by the Hindu religion. The Great Indian Tradition is not based on justice because in the HSO, Brahmanism interfaced with tradition faced breeds inequality. The HSO is not only based on segregation and exclusiveness, but also on institutionalized inequality and injustice through traditional institutions. Ambedkar believed that liberating people from tradition is the ultimate objective of his emancipatory project. The HSO is a stratified social order based on the social division of labour and founded on the values of *Varnashrama Dharma* that is a negation of social justice. The early Ambedkarite movement showed much commitment to representation, access to public offices, employment and education rather than on economic empowerment through redistribution of material resources. In the 1980s, the Dalit parties such as the Bahujan Samaj Party (BSP) raised the slogan, *vote hamara, raj tumhara nahin chalega, nahin chalega* (our vote, your regime, no more, no more) reasserting the politics of representation.

Ambedkarites' Critique of Indian Marxism

Though caste-based injustice was recognized as a social reality by both the Ambedkarites and the Marxists, there is no consensus on joining a common platform in addressing this issue. On the other hand, these two groups question the strategies and commitment of each other in addressing this problem. The Ambedkarites were critical of the nature and the social base of the communist leadership and their policy priorities for dalit emancipation. They often accused Indian Marxism of Brahmanical

Marxism as most of the Indian Marxists are Brahmins and their dominance still exists in the party organizational structure. The Ambedkarites often use Ambedkar's criticism of the nature of the Communist leadership in India. According to him, a revolutionary movement for the emancipation of the poor and the workers had been rendered impotent because its leadership was in the wrong hands. As Ambedkar said:

> "The Communist Party was originally in the hands of some Brahmin boys—Dange and others. They have been trying to win over the Maratha community and the Scheduled Caste. But they have made no headway in Maharashtra. Why? Because they are mostly a bunch of Brahmin boys. The Russians made a great mistake to entrust the communist movement in India to them. Either the Russians did not want Communism in India—they wanted only drummer boys—or they did not understand." (Government of India, 2014:425)

The Ambedkarite criticism is based on the nature of the communist leadership as the early communists primarily came from the upper caste, particularly from West Bengal. The Marxist conception of modernity could not emancipate the socially marginalized due to the upper-caste base of Indian Marxism. The Left has not given much representation, even formal, to the socially marginalized in party structures, especially in the highest decision-making body. The emancipatory potentiality of Marxism is often challenged by the Ambedkarites by arguing that Indian Marxists failed to address the issue of caste in the true sense of the cause. The Ambedkarites often accused Marxism of giving primacy to class over caste. In the ideological realm, Marxism was often demeaned as a derivative ideology and based on Euro centrism. As a meta-narrative based on universalism cannot be applied to the Indian context the Marxist conception of justice is more 'political' than 'social' and delinking the political with the social may not create a just society in India. It is argued that the 'class dogmatism' of the Marxists leads to hostility between these two. In India, the Marxist conception of modernity is linked with the upper strata of society. The Ambedkarites' are often sceptical of the sincerity of the Indian Marxists in addressing the issue of social justice and emancipation. The Left was accused of undermining caste oppression and of looking down suspiciously on identity politics. The communists always looked in the prism of class and class struggle and failed to understand the caste structure within the class system. The Marxist preoccupation with economic structure makes it difficult to recognize social justice. According to Guru, "...the Indian Left seems to have followed a symbolic approach to deal with the caste question. Unfortunately the Left leaders paid only rhetorical attention to the caste question." (Guru, 2016: 24)

Invoking Ambedkar's critique on the nature of the communist leadership by the Ambedkarites, however, does not have any kind of theoretical understanding but is based on its praxis. In contrast to the prevalent notion of the Ambedkarites that Ambedkar was against Marxism, the reality is that Ambedkar never doubted the emancipatory potential of Marxism as a meta-narrative. As a pragmatic socialist, he had some differences with the praxis of Marxism in India, especially related to addressing the caste question and social background of Indian Marxists. Ambedkar was primarily an economist who had deep knowledge in neoclassical economics and a clear understanding of India's rural society. Ambedkar himself identified two enemies of dalits in India—capitalism and the caste system and called for the annihilation of both. W.N. Kuber puts it thus:

> "In 1937, (Ambedkar) founded the Independent Labour Party, for sometime joined hands with the communists in the labour field but did not take consistent attitude and fight class battles. Though his community was downtrodden and landless and mostly wage-earners, still he could not make them class-conscious, because of the weakness in his inherent thinking. After the Poona Pact he tried to lead the working class, but failed and left the field for ever, and chose to become the leader of his community." (Kuber, 1973: 304)

Contemporary Marxist Receptivity

In the light of the recent assertion of the Ambedkarites for recognition and redistribution, the Marxists are also in the process of reinventing themselves from their earlier stand on dalit politics. The Marxists in contemporary India show much interest in equal emphasis on the demand for recognition and redistribution as class organizations taking up the issues of caste. In the recent past, the Marxists recognize the importance of recognition along with redistribution as an integrative strategy towards emancipation politics. The great realization is that addressing the caste question is the precondition to ensure social justice in India. It is believed that the struggles for recognition occur in a world of exacerbated material inequality—in income and property ownership, education, healthcare. The renewed assertion is that capitalism is still developing in India and the process of the development of society divided into modern capitalist classes is taking place constantly within the existing caste stratification. According to the Marxists, the question, therefore, is not one of class versus caste. It is this that not only needs to be recognized but also the integration of the struggle against class exploitation with the struggle against social oppression. Perhaps, this realization emerged out of the Marxist praxis of concrete analysis of the concrete situation rather than its theoretical commitment to the realization of a universal goal through the implementation of a grand ideology. For instance, V. I. Lenin in 1919 had said,

> "In this respect you are confronted with a task which has not previously confronted the Communists of the world: relying upon the general theory and practice of communism, you must adapt yourselves to specific conditions such as do not exist in the European countries; you must be able to apply that theory and practice to conditions in which the bulk of the population are peasants, and in which the task is to wage a struggle against medieval survivals and not against capitalism."[1]

The Communist Party of India (Marxist) (CPI-M), the largest parliamentary communist party, is more realistic in its approach to addressing the caste question in India, especially in the context of the rise of identity politics and assertions among the lower castes of society. The CPI-M Programme updated in 2000 succinctly summarizes the caste question that "The bourgeoisie-landlord system has also failed to put an end to caste oppression. The worst sufferers are the Scheduled Castes. The dalits are subject to untouchability and other forms of discrimination despite these being declared unlawful. The growing consciousness among the dalits for emancipation is sought to be met with brutal oppression and atrocities. The assertion by the dalits has a democratic content reflecting the aspirations of the most oppressed sections of the society. The backward castes have also asserted their rights in a caste-ridden society." The Political Resolution of the 18th Congress of the CPI-M held in 2005, a section devoted to 'Caste Oppression and Dalits' says that "the caste system contain both social oppression and class exploitation. The dalits suffer from both types of exploitation in the worst form." A resolution adopted at the All India Convention on Problems of Dalits by the CPI-M in 22 February 2006 emphasized "the need to link the fight against caste oppression with the struggle against class exploitation. At the same time, the class struggle must include the struggle for the abolition of the caste system and all forms of social oppression. This is an important part of the democratic revolution." The CPI (M) Kolkata Plenum held on 27-30 December 2015 identified two problems faced by the people—economic exploitation and social oppression.

However, while taking a proactive stand on the issue of democratic revolution of the dalits, the party is also cautioning against the use of identity politics for consolidating vote banks and thereby detaching them from the larger democratic revolution. Such mobilization "ignores the basic issues of land, wages and fight against landlordism, which is the basis for overthrowing the older order." As Patnaik argues while completely supporting the demands of the identity politics of the oppressed for reservation for affirmative action, etc., he cautions that identity dalit politics is not the annihilation of caste. Caste is not going to disappear through dalit identity politics. And identity politics is something which is perfectly compatible with capitalism. (Patnaik, 2017)

Emerging Sensibilities in India

The emerging grammar of social justice in India is a synthesis of emancipatory projects of both Ambedkarism and Marxism. Such a platform would help in creating mobilization for social justice in the contemporary situation. The emerging solidarity between the left and the dalits can be seen as a movement towards achieving social justice. Such sensibilities emerge out of various factors. Firstly, the growing realization is that the two stumbling blocks in achieving social justice in contemporary India lie in the resurfacing of the unholy alliance between Hayek and Manu. Hayek, in his neo-liberal order, is critical of social justice and the intervention of the state. The neo-liberal order perpetuated by the market, which is considered as a natural order, is antithetical to the conception of social justice. Hayek argues that the term, 'social justice' is 'a hollow incarnation,' is 'empty and meaningless.' (Hayek, 1976: xv-xvi). According to him the idea of equality is incompatible with progress. Since social justice means the distribution of wealth, Hayek was not ready to accept it. Hayek was not in favour of state intervention as essential to ensure social justice and the market order is a reasonable order where justice prevails. In the neo-liberal regime, the rhetoric of growth occupied centre stage over social justice and when economic growth is the prime goal, it undermines the values of social justice. If growth is not inclusive, it has its repercussions on the issue of social justice.

Like the Hayekian natural order of the market, Manu believed in a Hindu social order with caste as a natural order for the stability of Indian society. While the laws of Manu govern the HSO, the ideas of Hayek run the market order; both negate the possibility of creating a just socioeconomic order. The denial of access to social groups was justified, invoking the stability of the institution. Based on the principles of naturalism and optimism of the order, both contribute to the exclusion of certain sections in society. In fact, these two ideological trends negate the idea of social justice and welfare state. It creates inequality as both the conceptions are riddled with the notion of the efficiency syndrome and institutional well-being. For Hayek, the market is a natural order and for Manu, caste is also a natural order. The emerging urge for social justice depends on the demolition of the two natural orders created by Manu and Hayek under the categories of caste and market.

Second is the insulation of higher educational institutions from the democratic commitment to social justice. In India, institutions are supposed to promote social justice. However, the emerging trend is that public institutions such as the educational ones engage in subverting the social justice agenda. The entry of dalits into educational institutions faces multiple forms of humiliation and discrimination. The tragic end of Rohit Vemula, a dalit research scholar in Hyderabad Central University in January

2016, is a glaring failure of public institutions to implement the agenda of social justice. Moreover, such denial of social justice assumes significance when key institutions are insulated from the democratic pressures of social justice. The protagonists of institutional well-being often contend that when public institutions succumb to democratic pressure from society, it would be a disaster for the institutional wellbeing (Beteille, 1991). The growing violation of institutional injustice is the manifestation of insulating democracy from public institutions and to protect institutional well-being. Universities and other public-funded higher educational institutions show insensitivity to the cause of social justice, precisely because they want to insulate these institutions from social demands for justice.

Una Dalit Protest—New Grammar of Social Justice

The Una dalit protest in August 2016 was a clear indication of the changing ethos of the direction towards social justice. Abandoning the traditional caste-based mobilization, the contemporary Ambedkarite movements demand redistribution along with self-respect and dignity. Unlike past movements, land reforms assumed centre stage and a greater realization that such reforms would boost agrarian economy by way of increasing purchasing power. The Una movement began after a shocking video of seven dalit men being brutally beaten up by *gaurakshaks* (cow protectors) went viral. Subsequently, in protest against the brutal attack, dalits refused to remove the carcasses of the dead animals which is the traditional work assigned to them by the caste hierarchy. Led by Jignesh Mevani, the convener of the Una Dalit Atyachar Ladi Samiti (UDALS), the slogan that resounded in the *Asimita Yatra* (dignity march) was *gay ki punch tum rakho, hume hamari zameen do* (You keep the cow's tail, give us our land). Though, the immediate reason for the movement was the brutal attack and the denial of self-dignity to the dalits, the roots of the simmering discontent is related to the economic condition of the dalits. Shah traces the context of the Una movement by arguing that "the informal neoliberal political economy of Gujarat has seemingly given a new lease of life to primordial identity politics by promoting social capital for social security." (Shah, 2017: 62)

The Una movement gave a message that it is not the segmented struggles but the united struggles with a conglomeration of dalits, women, workers and Muslims that would lead to ushering in an era of social justice. Mevani claims that the Una movement is an inclusive movement of all the oppressed sections of society including farmers, labourers, Muslims and tribal groups. The movement, while reaching out to all the marginalized sections of society beyond ideological and caste limitations, asserted that the demand for recognition alone would not deliver justice to the socially marginalized sections. On the other hand, an integrative approach of the struggles for recognition and redistribution is considered essential for emancipation. In other words, recognition-oriented social justice may not be able to fully achieve its. Even the constitutional recognition and guarantee of affirmative action could not lead to the transformative agenda for emancipation due to the absence of a follow-up policy of distribution. According to Gopal Guru, "social justice demands a fair distribution of primary goods such as self-respect and material resources. The articulation of this language could be found in the peasant and Dalit struggles for the redistribution of surplus land and a different identity name respectively." (Guru, 2010: 364)

The Una movement declares that dalit politics should not be focused on only the avenues of recognition such as reservation, other political benefits, symbolism and power politics, but on a positive agenda of redistribution. It is argued that "dalit politics cannot move forward unless it is willing to articulate the material aspirations of the dispossessed. Similarly, Left politics has no future unless it recognizes that annihilation of caste is vital for any progressive politics." (Sampath, 2016).The new demands include land ownership and employment which are essential for the material existence of dalits when the state is abdicating its duties in the age of market expansion.

The new form of social justice is a manifestation of 'Neel Salam' and 'Lal Salaam'. In an interview, Mevani categorically stated that the dalit movement cannot move forward by ignoring class issues. According to him, if one wants to annihilate caste, one needs to address the issue of not just caste but of class also. In his opinion, in the last two decades after India started pursuing liberalization and globalization policies, the condition of the working class has deteriorated. In fact, dalits are the most affected by the policies of globalization. So ignoring class is detrimental to the cause of dalit emancipation. He asserts that the limitation of the identity politics lies here as it is ignoring this aspect altogether. Stressing too much on identity, in his view, would not help to annihilate caste; rather it would strengthen that identity. At the same time, there are cultural issues that also need to be addressed comprehensively in the fight against the caste system. Both the fights should be carried out together (Mevani, 2016).

According to Mevani, there is now scope for greater cooperation with the dalit movement and the Indian Left. The dalit movement will have to engage with Marxism sooner or later as, for the emancipation of dalits, they would have to develop a kind of Marxian approach. Reminding Ambedkar's identification of two enemies of dalits—capitalism and Brahmanism—Mevani asserts that if the dalit movements are genuine then you would have to understand how classes came into being and how they survived over time. For this, one needs a Marxist framework (Mevani, 2016). Echoing the same argument, Sampath argues that "The dalits need the Left because there is no other political formation that programmatically raises working class issues such as a living wage, job security, pensions and abolition of contract labour. As for the Left, sheer survival requires it to raise dalit issues. Given that the overwhelming majority of dalits are working class, there is a natural affinity of political interests." (Sampath, 2016). In the wider connotations, Vivek Chibber underscores that the movement of the oppressed can be sustained and strengthened by issues of economic justice because majority of the dalits are wage labourers and most of them are in the informal sector (Chibber, 2016).

Conclusion

The emerging sensibilities of social justice in India go beyond the water-tight compartmentalization of the ideas of recognition and redistribution. Such a pragmatic approach emerges out of the manifestation of the concrete analysis of the concrete situations emerging out of contemporary Indian reality. The emerging sensibilities of social justice in contemporary India is based on the realization that when Manu strikes a deal with Hayek, Ambedkar and Marx can join hands to counter them to ensure social justice to the marginalized. Any attempt either on the part of the Marxists or the Ambedkarites to create a binary between the ideas of recognition and redistribution would disrupt the realization of the larger agenda of social justice. The Una protest, dalit refusal to perform traditional work and the demand for land reforms not only scripted a new history in achieving social justice in India but also gave a positive signal for a possible alliance between the Left and the Ambedkarites to meet the challenges emerging out of neo-liberalism and Hindu nationalism.

NOTE

1. https://www.marxists.org/archive/lenin/works/1919/nov/22.htm

REFERENCES

Beteille, Andre. 1991, "Distributive Justice and Institutional Well Being," *Economic and Political Weekly*, Annual Number, March, pp. 591-600.

Chibber, Vivek. 2016, "Dalit movement has to see itself as part of a class-wide movement," in interview with Meera Srinivasan, *The Hindu*, March 3.

Fraser, Nancy. 1997, *Justice Interrupts: Critical Reflections on the "Post socialist" condition*, New York: Routledge.

——. 2003, "Social Justice in the Age of Identity Politics: Redistribution, Recognition, and Participation," in Nancy Fraser and Axel Hornet (eds.), *Redistribution or Recognition? A Political-Philosophical Exchange,* London and New York: Verso, pp. 7-109.

Government of India. 2014, *Dr. Babasaheb Ambedkar: Writings and Speeches*, Vol. 17, Part-1, New Delhi: Ministry of Social Justice & Empowerment.

Guru, Gopal. 2016, "Shifting Categories in the Discourse on Caste and Class," *Economic and Political Weekly*, Vol. LI, No. 47, November 19, pp. 21-25.

——. 2010, "Social Justice," in Niraja Gopal Jayal and Pratap Bhanu Mehta (eds.), *The Oxford Companion to Politics in India,* Delhi: Oxford University Press, pp. 361-377.

Hayek, F. A., 1976, *Law, Legislation and Liberty*, Vol. II: The Mirage of Social Justice, London: Routledge and Kegan Paul.

Kuber, W. N., 1973, *Ambedkar: A Critical Study*, New Delhi: People's Publishing House.

Mevani, Jignesh. 2016, "Dalit movement can't move forward ignoring class issues," Accessed from http://en.southlive.in/politics/2016/10/20/jignesh-mevani-says-for-dalit-emancipation-addressing-class-issue-is-vital. Accessed on 12 September, 2017.

Patnaik, Prabhat. 2017, Interview*: Prabhat Patnaik on Contemporary Capitalism and the Shape It Takes in India,* Accessed from https://thewire.in/159148/prabhat-patnaik-interview-capitalism/ . Accessed on 26 July, 2017.

Ranadive, B. T., 2002, "Caste, Class and Property Relations," in Ghanshyam Shah (ed.), *Caste and Democratic Politics in India,* Delhi: Permanent Black, pp. 134-161.

Sampath, G., 2016, "When Jai Bhim meets Lal Salaam," *The Hindu*, 14 October.

Shah, Ghanshyam. 2017, "Neoliberal Political Economy and Social Tensions: Simmering Dalit Unrest and Competing Castes in Gujarat," *Economic and Political Weekly*, Vol. LII, No. 35, September 2, pp. 62-70.

4

SOCIAL JUSTICE AND POSITIVE DISCRIMINATION

Chintamani Rout

ABSTRACT

The policy of positive discrimination in India goes back to its origin during the freedom movement, when the national leaders stressed the history of oppression and social discrimination experienced by the marginal communities and pressurized the British Government for legal reforms to ensure social justice. After Independence, as per the provisions of the Constitution of India, the Government of India made provision for socio-economic development of the Scheduled Castes (SCs), Scheduled Tribes (STs) and other socially and educationally backward communities or Other Backward Classes (OBCs). The policy of reservation was conceived in the fields of education, employment and election to Parliament and State Legislative Assemblies. The policies of positive discrimination are aimed at mitigating the unequal and undemocratic nature of the caste system and empower the marginalized communities in India. Positive discrimination is a contentious issue both politically and socially. The reasoned debate about it has questioned whether the practice of reservation has brought success in ensuring the social, economic and political development of the marginalized communities. This paper will discuss what distinguished positive discrimination is from other practices with which it has been confused. The paper will further examine arguments that attempt to justify in terms of justice itself and to identify the circumstances in which its use might be justified in India. Have these policies and programmes meant for the development of the SC/ST/OBC been implemented effectively and have they achieved their objective?

Key Words: Constitution, scheduled castes, reservation, employment, religion, untouchability

Introduction

The system of reservation in India comprises a series of affirmative action measures, also known as 'positive discrimination' in the UK, such as reserving access to seats in various legislatures, to government jobs and to enrolment in higher educational institutions. It is intended to favour historically disadvantaged castes and tribes listed as Scheduled Castes and Scheduled Tribes by the Government of India. The reservation is undertaken to address the historic oppression, inequality and discrimination faced by members of those communities. It is intended to realize the promise of equality enshrined in the Constitution. The Constitution prohibits untouchability under Article 17 and obligates the state to make special provision for the betterment of the scheduled castes and scheduled tribes, also spelling out that such special provisions would not be considered discriminatory as it would address existing inequality.

Over the years, the categories for affirmative action have been expanded beyond the lists of Scheduled Castes and Scheduled Tribes to include a special category of Other Backward Classes (OBCs). Consideration has also been given to economically backward people in providing reservations. Reservation is governed by constitutional laws, statutory laws and local rules and regulations. The Scheduled Castes (SCs), Scheduled Tribes (STs) and Other Backward Classes (OBCs) and, in some states, backward classes among Muslims under a category called BC(M), are the primary beneficiaries of the reservation policies under the Constitution—with the objective of ensuring a level of equality among all. The primary objective of the present-day Indian reservation system is to enhance the social and educational status of underprivileged communities and thus improve their lives.

The Origin and History of the Positive Thought of Social Justice

A reservation system favouring certain castes and other communities existed before Independence in several areas of British India. Demands for various forms of positive discrimination had been made; for example, in 1882 and 1891, Sahuji, the maharaja of the princely state of Kolhapur, introduced reservation in favour of non-Brahmin and backward classes, much of which came into force in 1902. He provided free education to everyone and opened several hostels to make it easier for them to receive it. He also tried to ensure that people thus educated should be employed, and he appealed both for a class-free India and abolition of untouchability.

The British administration also introduced elements of reservation in the Government of India Act of 1919 and there were many other measures put in place prior to independence. A significant one emerged from the Round Table Conference of June 1932, when the prime minister of Britain, Ramsay Macdonald, proposed the Communal Award, according to which separate representation was to be provided for Muslims, Sikhs, Indian Christians, Anglo-Indians and Europeans. The depressed classes were assigned a number of seats to be filled by election from constituencies in which only they could vote, although they could also vote in other seats. The proposal was controversial: Mahatma Gandhi fasted in protest against it but many among the depressed classes, including their leader, B.R. Ambedkar, favoured it, and after negotiations Gandhi reached an agreement with Ambedkar to have a single Hindu electorate with dalits having seats reserved within it. Electorates for other religions such as Islam and Sikhism remained separate.

After the independence of India in 1947, there were some major changes in favour of the Scheduled Tribes (STs), Scheduled Castes (SCs) and Other Backward Classes (OBCs). A common form of caste discrimination in India has been the practice of untouchability. Scheduled Castes were the primary targets of this practice which was outlawed by the new Constitution of India.

In 1954, the Ministry of Education suggested that 20 per cent of seats should be reserved for SCs and STs in educational institutions with a provision to relax minimum qualifying marks for admission by 5 per cent, wherever required. In 1982, it was specified that 15 percent and 7.5 percent of vacancies in public sector and government-aided educational institutes should be reserved for SC and ST candidates, respectively.

A significant change began in 1978 when the Mandal Commission was established to assess the situation of the socially- and educationally-backward classes. The commission did not have exact population figures for the OBCs and so used data from the 1931 census, thus estimating the group's population at 52 per cent. In 1980, the commission's report recommended that a reserved quota for OBCs of 27 per cent should apply in respect of services and public sector bodies operated by the Union Government. It called for a similar change in admissions to institutes of higher education, except where states already had more generous requirements. It was not until the 1990s that the recommendations were implemented in Union Government jobs.

The Constitution of India in Part III under fundamental rights, in Article 16(4) says: "Nothing in [article 16] or in clause (2) of article 29 shall prevent the State from making any special provision for the advancement of any socially and educationally backward classes of citizens or for the Scheduled Castes and the Scheduled Tribes." Article 46 of the Constitution states that "The State shall promote with special care the educational and economic interests of the weaker sections of the people and, in particular, of the Scheduled Castes and the Scheduled Tribes, and shall protect them from social injustice and all forms of exploitation."

The Supreme Court of India ruled in 1992 that reservations could not exceed 50 percent; anything above it would be judged as violating equal access as guaranteed by the Constitution. It thus put a cap on reservations. However, there are state laws that exceed this 50 per cent limit and they are under litigation in the Supreme Court. For example, in the State of Tamil Nadu, caste-based reservation stands at 59 per cent and applies to about 87 per cent of the population. In Parliament, caste- and tribe-based reservations are provided to make it more representative.

Today, out of 543 seats in India's Parliament, 84 (15.47%) are reserved for SC dalits and 47 (8.66%) for ST/Tribes. Allocation of seats for Scheduled Castes and Tribes in the Lok Sabha are made on the basis of the proportion of Scheduled Castes and Tribes in the State concerned to that of the total population.

A similar percentage of exclusive seats has been provided for members of scheduled castes and tribes in each state legislature. Local self-governments have a caste, tribe and gender-based reservation system in place.

Reservation in Employment

A fixed percentage of India's government and public sector jobs are made exclusive for categories of people largely based on their caste or tribe.

The 1992 Supreme Court ruling in the Indra Sawhney case said that "reservations in job promotions are 'unconstitutional'" but allowed its continuation for five years. In 1995, the 77th amendment to the Constitution was made to amend Article 16 before the five-year period expired to continue with reservations for SC/ST in promotions. It was further modified through the 85th Amendment to give the benefit of consequential seniority to SC/ST candidates promoted by reservation.

The 81st Amendment was made to the Constitution to permit the government to treat the backlog of reserved vacancies as a separate and distinct group to which the ceiling of 50 per cent did not apply. The 82nd Amendment inserted a provision in Article 335 to enable states to give concessions to SC/ST candidates in promotion.

The validity of all the above four amendments was challenged in the Supreme Court through various petitions clubbed together in *M. Nagaraj & Others vs. Union of India & Others,* mainly on the ground that these type of policies may affect the basic structure of the Constitution. In 2006, the Supreme Court upheld the amendments but stipulated that the concerned state will have to show, in each case, the existence of 'compelling reasons'—which include 'backwardness', 'inadequacy of representation' and overall 'administrative efficiency' before making provisions for reservation. The court further held that these provisions are merely enabling provisions. If a State government wishes to make provisions for reservation to SC/STs in promotion, it has to collect quantifiable data showing backwardness of the class and inadequacy of its representation.

In 2007, the Government of Uttar Pradesh introduced reservation in job promotions. However, citing the Supreme Court decision, the policy was ruled to be unconstitutional by the Allahabad High Court in 2011.

The decision was challenged in the Supreme Court, which upheld it in 2012 by rejecting the government's argument because it failed to furnish sufficient valid data to justify the move to promote employees only on the basis of caste.

Reservations in Education

In India, most of the scholarships or student aid is available only to SCs, STs, BCs, OBCs, women, Muslims and other minorities. Only about 0.7 per cent of scholarships or student aid in India is based on merit.

The University Grants Commission (UGC) provides financial assistance to universities for the establishment of special cells for SC/STs. The cells help universities implement the reservation policy in student admission and staff recruitment processes for teaching and non-teaching jobs. Seats are reserved for people under the following criteria:

Caste

In Central Government-funded higher education institutions, 22.5 per cent of available seats are reserved for Scheduled Caste (SC) and Scheduled Tribe (ST) students (7.5% for STs, 15% for SCs). This reservation percentage has been raised to 49.5 per cent by including an additional 27 per cent reservation for OBCs. This ratio is followed even in Parliament and all elections where a few constituencies are earmarked for those from certain communities (which will next rotate in 2026 as per the provisions of the Delimitation Commission). The exact percentages vary from state to state.

In Tamil Nadu, the reservation is 18 per cent for SCs and 1 per cent for STs, based on local demographics.

In Northeast India, especially in Arunachal Pradesh, Meghalaya, Nagaland and Mizoram, reservation for ST in State government jobs is of a higher percentage.

In Andhra Pradesh, 25 per cent of educational institutes and government jobs are reserved for OBCs, 15 per cent for SCs, 6 per cent for STs and 4 per cent for Muslims.

In West Bengal, 35 per cent of educational institution seats and government jobs are reserved for SC, ST, and OBC (22% SC, 6% ST, 7% for OBC A&B). In West Bengal there is no reservation on religious basis but some economically and educationally backward Muslim castes (basis is surnames pertaining to different professions, e.g., cobbler, weaver, etc.) have been included along with their Hindu counterparts in the OBC list, namely, OBC A and OBC B; in both lists castes from both communities are included. But in higher educational institutions, till now there is no reservation for the OBC community but there is reservation in regard to admission in primary, secondary and higher secondary studies.

In Gujarat, 33 per cent of posts are reserved for females in all government departments and services, such as police, health, education and general administration.

Reservation for Women in Parliament and Legislative Assemblies in the States

The Women's Reservation Bill was passed by the Rajya Sabha on 9 March 2010 by a majority vote of 186 members in favour and 1 against. As of now, the Lok Sabha has not voted on the bill. Critics say gender cannot be held as a basis for reservation alone; other factors should also be considered, e.g., economic and social conditions of women candidates especially when applying reservation for educated women. There is also a growing demand for women's reservation in pre-existing reservations like OBC, SC/ST, physically handicapped, etc., and also that reservation for women should be at least 50 per cent as they comprise 50 per cent of the population.

Religion

There is no reservation granted on the basis of religion in the Central educational institutions at the national level, although reservation has been extended to religious minorities in some states. The Tamil Nadu government has allotted 3.5 per cent seats each to Muslims and Christians, thereby altering the OBC reservation to 23 per cent from 30 per cent (since it excludes persons belonging to Other Backward Castes who are either Muslims or Christians).

The Government of Andhra Pradesh introduced a law enabling 4 per cent reservations for Muslims in 2004. This law was upheld by the Supreme Court in an interim order in 2010 but it constituted a Constitution bench to further look into the issue. The referral was to examine the constitutional validity of quotas based on religion. The Kerala Public Service Commission has a quota of 12 per cent for Muslims. Religious minority (Muslim or Christian) educational institutions also have 50 per cent reservation for Muslim or Christian candidates. The Central Government has listed a number of Muslim communities as backward Muslims, making them eligible for reservation. The Union Government on 22 December 2011 announced the establishment of a sub-quota of 4.5 per cent for religious minorities within the existing 27 per cent reservation for Other Backward Classes. The reasoning given was that Muslim communities that have been granted OBC status are unable to compete with Hindu OBC communities. It was alleged that the decision was announced as the Election Commission announced Assembly elections in five states on 24 December 2011. The government would not have been able to announce this due to the model code of conduct. On 12 January 2012, the Election Commission stayed implementation of this decision for violation of the model code of conduct. Later, Justice Sachar, head of the Sachar Committee that was commissioned to prepare a report on the latest social, economic and educational condition of the Muslim community of India, criticized the government decision, saying, "Such promises will not help the backward section of minorities. It is like befooling them. These people are making tall claims just to win elections." He suggested that instead of promising to give reservations, the government should focus on basic issues of improving administration and governance. On 28 May 2012, the Andhra Pradesh High Court quashed the sub-quota. The court said that the sub-quota had been carved out only on religious lines and not on any other intelligible basis. The court criticized the decision: "In fact, we must express our anguish at the rather casual manner in which the entire issue has been taken up by the central government."

Conclusion and Suggestions

"The term, 'positive discrimination' has become popular both in developed and under-developed countries. In countries like Canada, Finland, Brazil and the USA, the term is used to refer to different discriminatory policies that governments have introduced for the benefit of marginalized communities—indigenous peoples, Blacks or ethnic minorities. The policy of positive discrimination in India has its roots in anti-caste movements during the freedom movement, when the national leaders highlighted the history of oppression and social discrimination experienced by the marginalized communities and started pressurizing the colonial government for legal reforms to ensure social justice. After independence, keeping in line with the spirit of the Constitution of India, the Government of India made provision for reservations for the socio-economic development of the Scheduled Castes (SCs), Scheduled Tribes (STs) and other socially and educationally backward communities, now recognized as Other Backward Classes (OBCs). Although the policy was initially conceived for only 10 years, the quota-based reservations in the fields of education, employment and politics has now become a permanent feature of the Indian political system. Apart from the policy of reservations, the Government of India has established different institutions, introduced different laws and implemented different schemes for the development of marginalized communities to ensure social justice. The theory and practice of positive discrimination has evoked passionate debates and movements in India. While the advocates of positive discrimination support the government policies as indispensable for the development of marginalized communities, the critics have raised the issues of equality, merit, justice and national progress." [the Concept note of the national seminar on "Towards Social Justice: Impact of Positive Discrimination on Marginalised Groups with Special Reference on Scheduled Casts and Schedule Tribes Groups in India"]

After 70 years of independence, planned development and the policies and programs of positive discrimination have indeed brought about some changes in the nature of the caste system and in the status of backward communities in every field of social life. It is suggested that the Government of India should constitute a committee headed by a retired judge of the

Supreme Court to assess the percentage of people benefited by the reservation system and those belonging to Scheduled Caste and Scheduled Tribe families. The benefits given under the reservation system should be extended to other families and the reservation system should be stopped within a stipulated time frame. It should also cover persons belonging to below the poverty line irrespective of caste and religion.

REFERENCES

Adish C. Aggarwala, Constitution of India, 4th revised edition: December 2014.
Constituent Assembly Debates, dated 2-12-1948 at p. 780.
Jain, M. P., *Indian Constitutional Law*, Lexis Nexis Butterworth, Nagpur: Wadhwa Publication.
Kailash Rai, *The Constitutional Law of India*, Allahabad: Central Law Publication.
Shukla, V. N., *Constitution of India*, Lucknow: Eastern Book Co.
The Constitution of India.

SECTION II

Strategies for Empowering Dalits: Problems and Perspectives

5

Dalit Empowerment in India: Problems and Prospects

K. V. Reddy

ABSTRACT

Thanks to Dr. B. R. Ambedkar and his constitutional efforts, the 'reservation' mechanism has certainly raised the standard of living of about 60-70 lakh dalits in the country. As part of governmental efforts, many a program including 'reservations' towards improving the living conditions of the dalits were initiated. Starting with the welfare paradigm, the governments at the Centre and in the states had moved on to various developmental schemes for the benefit of this community. Although a section of dalits had derived a few economic benefits in terms of education and employment, besides political, a vast majority of them is still left out. Meanwhile, the very scheme of reservations is being diluted in numerous ways. Obviously, dalits as such, are yet to be empowered in any way. The less said the better about their social status. Thus they continue to be humiliated and harassed on a regular basis, notwithstanding the number of anti-atrocity acts put in place.

Viewed against this backdrop, this paper is aimed at identifying the main problems that affected the process of dalit empowerment in India and offer some ways of overcoming them so that the state and society would direct their efforts in that direction. The paper recognizes the process of dalit disempowerment as the starting point that explains why this community is being given primacy today. This paper is largely based on a few academic works that focused on the political empowerment of marginalized communities like the Scheduled Castes, otherwise known as the dalits in the recent past. The paper argues that the success of dalit empowerment lies in the political empowerment of marginalized communities like the SCs, STs, OBCs and religious minorities en masse.

Key Words: reservation, empowerment, social inclusion, casteist social hierarchy

Introduction

In India, the Scheduled Castes (SCs), Scheduled Tribes (STs), Other Backward Classes (OBCs) and Religious Minorities (RM) constitute about 80 per cent of the marginalized population. Of them the SCs, also known as dalits,[1] alone are referred to as 'castes.' This paper aims at discerning the main problems that affect the dalits and their socio-economic advancement at the macro level in the country. Although it's a comprehensive study of dalit empowerment in India, the paper identifies the role of various actors that were responsible for their present predicament. Besides, the paper tries to explore various strategies that were attempted to address the problem of dalit disempowerment for over several decades. Based on some empirical findings[2] that stem from a few micro-level studies that were authored by academics as well as social activists belonging to about half-a-dozen states in the country, the paper exposes their conjectural appreciative of the dalit problem.

Moreover, this paper argues that the strategies adopted by state and non-state actors who were actually liable for the genesis and evolution of the dalit problem seem to be superficial and hardly beneficial. Despite the tactic of reservations that offered certain economic opportunities to a fraction of the dalits, political empowerment has not been achieved. In consequence, these communities remained reliant on the *manuwadi*[3] regime for over decades. This paper has also focused on caste[4] and its multiple implications on dalit disempowerment, besides the politics of reservations in the country in the context of globalization. The paper eventually argues that the Ambedkarite position[5] had become reasonably supportive towards achieving the objective of dalit empowerment to an extent.

Indian Social Hierarchy

Caste system: Indian society is largely a plural one due to the existence of the caste system that was formalized into the four-fold social hierarchy (*chaturvarna* system) that was justified by the 'Manusmriti.'[6] At the top were the upper castes, viz., Brahmins, Kshatriyas and Vaishyas and at the bottom were the fourth category, the Sudras. An additional category of 'untouchables', also known as dalits, was not at all considered part and parcel of the Hindu social order! All these terms referred to the graded groups of various artisans and occupational peoples, sometimes called low castes and sub castes[7] in India. Resembling the coloured 'race' in America and Western Europe, colourless 'caste' played havoc in India as both these social categories were compared to 'slavery' in the writings of Dr. B. R. Ambedkar.[8]

The caste system can be described as an elaborately stratified social hierarchy, distinguishing its social structure from other nations. The history of the caste system is multifaceted and complex. Caste is a social evil and untouchability is the product of the caste-based social system. Many struggles were launched against its practice. Under the gifted leadership of Dr. B. R. Ambedkar, the evil effect of untouchability was widely exposed to the Western world. Thus, *manuwadi* society was compelled to social pressure and thereby untouchability was abolished legally. Since 1950, as per our Constitution, the Indian government has enacted numerous laws to benefit their social life. Yet, the government, central and state, were silent when these laws were barely implemented as the root cause of dalit exclusion stems from the casteist social system. Obviously, more than the others, SCs remained disempowered over the centuries.

Due to casteist social hierarchy, the dalit community has been placed at the lowest rung of the social ladder that was based on the birth of an individual. Once born in the compartmentalized social system, the dalits were to continue as such and thereby degraded as the 'lowest caste'. Since degraded in the uneven social spectrum, the community was deprived of all human rights, civil or otherwise. The community was kept at a distance individually and community-wise even in remote areas of habitation. Evidently, any sort of natural resources, viz., land, housing, assets and water that were basic to one's livelihood was invariably denied to them. Besides, the community was barred from getting educated due to the predominance of the *manuwadi* code of social conduct. Those dalits who tried to infringe this unsocial code were dealt with severely and boycotted socially and exploited economically. Failing to secure any advance in status, the community could not improve its livelihood. In other words, the community that suffered the most social and economic exclusion was in no position to stand on its feet, leave alone getting empowered.

Dalit Predicament

Thanks to the scheme of reservations, a section of dalits had become educated as well as employed. Despite their rise in the economic and education levels, caste discrimination acquired a new form that continued to persist. An overview of different forms of untouchability that denied the SCs access to basic public services as was observed by a study[9] vindicates the point. Besides, certain routine media reports of non-dalit children refusing to eat midday meals cooked by dalits in states like Uttar Pradesh and Andhra Pradesh expose the gravity of the problem of casteist discrimination. Even today, news of casteist violence[10] and discriminatory practices stare one in the face despite the inclusion of Article 17 in the Fundamental Rights and numerous other enactments 'within' and 'without' the Indian Constitution. For instance, even after the passage of the SC/ST (Prevention of Atrocities) Act in 1989, the safety and protection of dalits is left to their fate as there is a rise in crime rate against them.

Besides, the National Human Rights Commission (NHRC) noted in its 2002 report, "Under-reporting (atrocities) is a common phenomenon and the police resort to various machinations to discourage SC/ST (persons) from registering their cases, to dilute the seriousness of the violence and to shield the accused persons from arrests and prosecution." This report reflects the ineffectuality of the Act that was elevated beyond all proportions! Even the judiciary can be held accountable for the police lapses as most of the accused under the IPC Act have been acquitted under the SC/ST Act. According to the National Bureau of Crime Report (2006), 27,070 crimes were committed against dalits though many more go unreported. Evidently, data on civil rights cases show that of the total cases registered in 1991, only 1.56 per cent was convicted.[11] Irrespective of one's abilities and skills, the dalits have been subjected to suffer from untouchability as usual.

Empowerment Issues

The general notion of 'empowerment' has been assumed as 'strengthening capacities' which can be achieved through 'full participation' of the people. Of course, strengthening of capacities is crucial to the emancipation of any oppressed group. But one has to see if it is possible to achieve it without removing the structural social restrictions on their capacities. Such a definition does not imply liberation from the burdens that have traditionally and caste-wise constrained fuller realization of human potential in the case of the dalits. Such pressures do operate at various levels including socio-economic structures and the political process which the multidimensional concept of 'empowerment' does not capture. Thus, the term 'empowerment' implies formal rather than substantive power and it involves an external agency to grant power rather than people below seizing it in the course of struggle.

Besides, the concept of empowerment is heavily loaded and its multiple dimensions need to be kept in view. Empowerment is about making one powerful, based on one's inherent individual abilities. It's about creating an environment wherein one can empower oneself. In other words, once an educational environment is created then one can achieve an educational qualification. With educational achievement, one can become empowered educationally. It is not to be understood as 'giving something' externally to those like the dalits for being empowered socially or otherwise. Since the community was deprived of its right to demonstrate its capability and prove its mettle due to external agencies like the upper castes, it was disempowered over the years. Yet, it was the case of Dr. Ambedkar and many others who, having had high-profile education against all odds could still emerge as top-ranking Indians at home and abroad.

Process of Social Inclusion

Notwithstanding the reluctance of civil society, the state and its governmental agencies had inaugurated a new era of affirmative action in independent India. Despite many a limitation, the scheme of reservation aimed at reverse discrimination has certainly helped lakhs of dalits to be educated and thousands of them to be employed in the public sector. Of course, many of them had become a significant part of our political leadership at the Centre and in several states. Overall, a small fraction of the community had become economically uplifted slowly and gradually. Yet, their social empowerment was incomplete. Unless social empowerment is achieved, their inclusive empowerment will be a distant dream. For empowerment is a potential concept that could uplift any community from their prevailing predicament.

Because of social crusaders like Mahatma Jyotiba Phule, Sant Ravidas and Dr. B. R. Ambedkar, the evil of untouchability was questioned over a period of time. Dr. Ambedkar was more forthright in his struggle against casteism at home and abroad. Owing to his serious efforts of educating and organizing the untouchable communities, the process of social liberation was initiated long before India attained Independence. In consequence, he was instrumental in getting certain safeguards assured for the disadvantaged sections from the British government. Be it settlement of land or a separate electorate it was approved in the Round Table Conferences held at London. At home, certain attempts were made to bring the discriminated communities into the mainstream.[12] Thus, the alien rulers had also enacted a few social policies whereby the untouchables and others were liberated from the age-old clutches of caste discrimination.

Besides, thanks to Dr. Ambedkar again, political equality was achieved ever since there surfaced a political situation of 'one man-one vote, and one vote-one value' in the country. Since the dalits have got their proportional strength, politically if not otherwise, the political parties had to cultivate their electorate on a regular basis. Thus, the rise of 'vote bank' politics had been witnessed for over a few decades after independence. However, due to their rising political awareness, the dalit votes could not be taken for granted any more, as was the case for long. In fact, one could witness the rise of social movements that were organized by the dalits and also under their leadership in various states.

Incidentally, various political parties and pressure groups have accordingly endorsed the will of the state that is reflected in the Preamble to the Constitution. Numerous Constitutional provisions exist clearly safeguarding the interests of this community. Suffice it to cite the case of such provisions like the Fundamental Rights (FRs) as well as the Directive Principles of State Policy (DPSP). Besides, several Acts and enactments were formulated at various points of time in several states. Theoretically speaking, the community is the most protected one in the country. However, contrary to that, is the experience of the dalits under various regimes.

Besides, it is the state and Centre that launched a few programmes of socio-economic nature. Yet, the state and Government cannot initiate any radical programme that would undermine the interests of dominant stakeholders like the upper castes in Indian society. Even if there was one it could not be implemented to its logical end. Thus, one observes a formulation of frequent Acts and enactments that were aimed at manipulating the dalits. A series of schemes and programmes were notified and introduced. Yet, none of them were fulfilled to any extent so that the dalits could be benefitted. This is what one could observe from the cases of dalit-oriented socio-economic programmes incorporated in plans and sub-plans. As a consequence, the dalits had always been at the mercy of those political regimes that acted contrary to their interests.

Politics of Reservations

Thanks to B.R. Ambedkar's instrumental role in Constitution-making, the reservation policy has been devised to undo the prevailing/age-old reservations to the upper castes from time immemorial. The policy was conceived as a short-term measure to promote social justice on the basis of the principle of distributive justice and compensation for the disadvantages of the past. In a way, it was described as a measure of 'reverse reservation'. And the governments were bound to implement the policy of reservations only in the public sector areas like education and employment which employed not more than 10 per cent of the workforce in the country[13]. Even such a little gesture or tokenism as a reservation policy was implemented half-heartedly in the public sector. For the public sector was shrinking over a period of time due to the deliberate policies that various governments had been pursuing.

In the context of the remaining 90 per cent of the job market, it was always controlled by the private sector. Several studies[14] on the labour market reveal that an insignificant percentage of these communities was employed while excluding a large majority by way of discrimination. The near and dear or kith and kin (Thanks to *bhai-bhatijavad* type of nepotism) of those in private managements were given jobs beyond their population percentage! In any case, the vast majority of private institutions were rarely queried on providing jobs to dalit communities. Understandably, the private sector was under no obligation to fulfil the constitutional requirements.

These reservations were extended to the political field as well, of course in proportion to their population size. Due to the notorious 'Poona pact,'[15] political reservations have scarcely been gainful to dalits and adivasis. The upper castes have devised different methods of sabotaging even these political reservations. For instance, spineless and selfish representatives of the lower castes will be selected to get them elected as 'reserved' legislators! In other words, the existent territorial constituencies cannot represent/ safeguard the dalits or their community interests at all as the bulk of the voters are invariably non-dalits. Kanshiram[16] termed those 'reserved' legislators who danced to the tunes of their non-dalit (upper caste) masters as stooges.

More than the private sector, the casteist and elitist bureaucracy was reluctant to implement the same. Thus, the concept received a setback as governments retreated on the issue. Meanwhile, as part of the continuity of the privatisation process, the state has pursued the policies of more privatisation since the 1990s. In the wake of the two-decade-long globalisation (1990-2010), the Indian state practised the policies of liberalisation, privatisation and globalisation (LPG), whereby the public sector became under the weather. Still, the private sector was persuaded to take over and own so-called sick units in the public sector at throwaway prices! Thus, the winds of change in the name of 'economic reforms' has slowly shaken the very foundation of the dalits and adivasis. As a consequence, more than anyone else, it is they who were the first to be affected adversely as there was 'no reservation in the private sector'.

Globalisation and After

At a time when the number of the educated among the unprivileged classes was increasing in geometrical progression, their share of jobs in the public sector was dwindling. This was more so during the last two decades, all in the name of the so-called free market and the phenomenon of globalisation. Obviously, these economic reforms envisaged the withdrawal of the state from its social obligations once and for all. In a way, the state has clearly abdicated its constitutional obligation. The trend went on and on over the years. According to a Report of the Working Group[17] on Empowering of SCs, following the LPG policies in 1992-97, 113, 450 SCs lost their jobs in the Central Government (Public Sector) alone. While the private sector enjoys the support of the state in establishing and managing the business ventures, it demonstrates its unwillingness to follow the constitutional regulations on providing employment to marginalised communities.

Meanwhile, some voices were raised against the phenomena of globalisation and its aftermath. At the national level too, there were some attempts to raise the issue of reservations in the private sector at the Bhopal convention in Madhya Pradesh in 2001. The Bhopal declaration aimed at offering better facilities for the underprivileged classes at all levels, including the private sector. Some other states and political parties were also compelled to concede to the demand of private reservations. For instance, the Maharashtra Government under S.K. Shinde tried to implement it but failed following protest and pressure from businesses in 2005. The Mayawati regime had also attempted to move in that direction during her last tenure (2007-12) in Uttar Pradesh, but could not succeed.

While the upper strata of society was in some position to survive the pressures of globalisation because it grabbed some job opportunities in the private sector, marginalised communities that were dependent on state support were left jobless. The globalisation phenomenon elevated those who could afford access to quality education in corporate institutions while the marginalised students ended up studying in government-aided schools and colleges where there were hardly any good facilities. While some economic benefits were accessible to a fraction of the dalit community, their empowerment is yet not achievable to any extent. Overall, the reservation mechanism has been used more for vote-bank politics rather than for benefitting the dalits in any substantial way. Thus, there prevailed an insecure feeling among the dalits as there surfaced different movements that were aimed at diluting their reservations overtly or covertly. Lastly, more than anybody else, it is the dalits and adivasis who were entrapped in the vicious circle of globalisation.

Political Power

While some of the inclusive strategies were initiated by the state and governmental agencies, some others were introduced by civil society organizations t associated with dalits and other marginalized communities in some states. Consequently, the remedial measures that were offered by the state and governmental agencies have hardly uplifted them economically, leave alone socially. Rather, the dalits have been subjected to multiple ways of embarrassment in several states. Even the politics of reservations that helped a small section of marginalized communities to secure some living opportunities in terms of education and employment in the public sector hardly upgraded their socio-cultural identity in the context of globalization. Similarly, the strategies and methods that got underway by some non-state actors like Ambedkarite groups, dalit organizations and dalit-based political parties were helpful to some extent but did not lead to dalit empowerment!

Incidentally, Dr. Ambedkar had stressed that if the SCs were to enjoy the benefits of their constitutional and legal rights, they were to merge all the marginalized groups on the basis of unity and fraternity, bring them on a strong political platform and capture the 'master key' of political power. To cite a few lines from what he had said: "Understand our ultimate goal. Our ultimate goal is to become the rulers of this country. Write this goal on the walls of your houses so that you will never forget. Our struggle is not for the few jobs and concessions but we have a larger goal to achieve. That goal is to become the rulers of the land."

Further, as part of his continuing struggle against casteist exclusion, Dr. Ambedkar appealed to his fellow communities: "Politics should be the life-blood of the Scheduled Castes." Since the politics of the Congress Party, the mouthpiece of the dominant castes, was considered detrimental to the interests of the marginalized, Dr. Ambedkar tried to form a broad-based movement of all the victims of the *manuwadi* social system which came to be described as the Bahujan Samaj. This was taken up later on by Kanshiram. Taking a cue from Ambedkar and his appeal of capturing political power, various dalit groups and parties that subscribed to Ambedkarism began organizing pressure groups along political lines. Thus,

Ambedkar declared the political goal of his struggle that laid the foundation of the Bahujan Samaj movement in the country.

Meanwhile, the emergence of dalit-oriented parties has been noticed. Some dalit leadership-based parties surfaced on the political horizon of the country. Through the efforts of Kanshiram, one witnessed the rise of a dalit missionary movement that came to be known as the *Bahujan Samaj Party* (BSP) in 1984. Kanshiram's socio-political movement of the *Bahujan Samaj* is a case in point. As a movement and party, it has raised the confidence levels of the dalits and other marginalized communities towards empowerment. Within a short span of three decades, the socio-political gathering had become the third largest national party in the country. Owing to its innovative ideas and distinctive strategies, the party became a ruling party in the largest state of India, Uttar Pradesh, several times. Perhaps, this seems to be an important way forward that could help achieve dalit empowerment in the country.

To conclude, due to the divisive role of caste in the Indian social hierarchy, castes and sub-castes have played critical roles in diverse ways. For, on the basis of one's birth in a particular social category alone, one's lifelong achievements would be assessed. Even after one's death, one's place in history would be situated accordingly, indeed! Incidentally, it is one's caste in the social ladder that undermines or elevates an individual. Instead of one's words and deeds that should be counted as a key factor in assessing one's contribution in the casteist society, it is one's birth that decides the person's fate and his status in society.

Owing to Dr. Ambedkar's leading role in Constitution-making, reservations were included and governments are bound to implement them on the basis of the principle of positive discrimination and reimbursement for past disadvantages. The Indian reservation system relies entirely on quotas for scheduled castes and scheduled tribes as per their population figures only, and not beyond! But the policy was restricted only to the public sector that was aided by the state and central government. Despite many an initiative, constitutionally and otherwise, this community had hardly benefitted socially. Leave alone developing on account of various schemes and programmes, the dalit community remained stagnant economically.

Viewed against this backdrop, it is the political empowerment of dalits that would become pivotal to their achievement of socio-economic empowerment in the long run. In other words, political empowerment of the marginalized alone could clinch the issue in their favour. This could be the basic tactic for the formation of *Bahujan* political systems at the Centre and in the states. Perhaps, only such regimes and governments could enforce the constitutional and legal rights in favour of the marginalized and provide the needed opportunities for them to moving forward in all spheres of life and also enable them to lead a life of self-respect and dignity.

NOTES

1. 'Dalit' is a term that was first coined by Dr. B. R. Ambedkar, one of the architects of the Indian Constitution of 1950 and revered leader of the dalit movement. It was taken up in the 1970s by the Dalit Panther Movement, which organised to claim rights for "dalits," and is now commonly used by rights activists
2. Thorat, Sukhdeo, 2013, 'Caste, Social Exclusion and Poverty' (*Critical Quest*, New Delhi)
3. Those who believe in a birth-based caste system are the ones who justify Manu's code of conduct and thereby justify the vertical division of Hindu society.
4. An eminent sociologist G. S. Ghurye observed: "Caste in India is a Brahminic child of the Indo-Aryan culture cradled in the land of the Ganga and Yamuna and hence transferred to other parts of the country."
5. To ensure the social transformation of the Indian social hierarchy, Dr. Ambedkar had launched many a struggle and achieved partial success. Yet, his dream of 'annihilation of caste' could not be realized during his time. Thus, he had appealed to his fellow dalits to be part of a struggle for political empowerment so that their numerous problems could be addressed. Accordingly, his slogan of 'political power as master key' that was assumed by a few political institutions like the BSP can be contextualized with the prevalent urge of the dalits for empowerment.
6. Michael, S. M. 1999. *Dalits in Modern India: Vision and Values*, New Delhi: Vistaar Publications.
7. Ekta Singh, 2005. Caste System in India, Kalpaz Publications, Delhi.
8. Ambedkar, B. R., 1989. Dr. Babasaheb Ambedkar Writings and speeches. Vol. I, Education Dept, Government of Maharashtra, Bombay.
9. An Action Aid-conducted intensive survey of 555 villages in 11 states in 2000 provided the data on the subject. Denial of access to basic public services like water facilities, barbers' services, carpenters, potters, village shops/hotels, health centres and public transport has been observed quite glaringly
10. Of late, Anita's suicide in Tamil Nadu and Rohit Vemula's death in Hyderabad is fresh in our memories.

11. Thorat, Sukhdeo, 2013 op. cit
12. Chatrapathi Sahuji Maharaj was responsible for implementing certain reservation schemes whereby non-Brahmins were employed in his Kolhapur state for the first time.
13. Countercurrents.Org.dated August 14, 2005.
14. SukhdeoThorat and others (ed), op.cit
15. As part of the Poona Pact, Dr. Ambedkar, yielding to the hunger-strike pressure of M. K. Gandhi, had compromised on his earlier stand of 'separate electorate' on 24 September 1932.
16. Kanshiram's book, 'The Chamcha Age: An Era of Stooges'.
17. 10th Five Year Plan, Planning Commission, Govt. of India, New Delhi, 2001.

6

Digital Divide and Dalits: The New Media and Empowering the Marginal Communities

Korvi Vinayakala and Jenny Rowena P

ABSTRACT

Dalits in India are the one of the most oppressed communities in the world; their experiences with the media reflect the global experiences of the other oppressed communities. The media is recognised as the fourth pillar of democracy and oppressed communities across the world know its significance in their liberation struggle and are making efforts to make their presence felt through it; their efforts ending sometimes in failure and sometimes in success. The backward classes (SC, ST and OBC) constitute more than two-thirds of India's population and the conventional minorities make up another 17.2 per cent. Even amongst the backward classes, the scheduled castes and scheduled tribes form the hard core of India's backwardness. The people of these backward and minority communities, who form about 85 per cent of India's population, have no media of their own.

Dalits all through history have struggled for space in the media. The new media has come as a new-found platform for them to express their pain and also to develop their perspectives on important issues. It was in the 1970s that the New Media emerged, mainly fuelled by the growth in the internet, posing a challenge to existing television and newspapers and magazines in the print form. In the second wave and with globalization, new media digitization and the convergence of the media has changed the scenario. User-generated content, interactivity; audience participation and flexibility are the major features of the internet and new media today. Many believe that the new media is liberating, democratizing and empowering citizens and promoting egalitarianism and tolerance.

Dalits write blogs and create websites and showcase their views and thoughts to the public. Web portals such as Savari and Round Table India try to understand how dalits are using the new media for their emancipation. Savari is a women's web portal exclusively run by Adivasi, Bahujan and Dalit women. In this web portal, these groups of women are exposed to many detailed debates among non-upper caste women regarding their status in contemporary society. Most of their writings in these websites come from their individual experiences and therefore it carries collective experience. They also become the reading sources for a large dalit community. Dalits in these portals discuss and debate various problems that are their primary concern. Among the various subjects, caste and gender oppression are the main areas of my focus.

Key Words: media, marginal, caste system, internet, flexibility, exploitation

Introduction and Review of Literature

The caste system in its 5,000 years of existence resulted in a few castes becoming the dominant or upper castes while a larger number of castes were forced to remain backward. The backward classes (SC, ST and OBC) constitute more than two-thirds of India's population and the conventional minorities make up 17.2 per cent. Even amongst the backward classes, the scheduled castes and the scheduled tribes form the hard core of India's backwardness. All these people, who form about 85 per cent of India's population, have no media their own. Kenneth J. Cooper, an African-American and the then New Delhi bureau chief of *The Washington Post*, noted in the mid-1990s that "India's majority lower castes are minor voices in newspapers."[1] In 2006, the Centre for the Study of Developing Societies (CSDS), New Delhi, conducted a survey that found that "of the 315 key decision-makers surveyed from 37 Delhi-based (Hindi and English) publications and television channels, almost 90 percent of decision-makers in the English language print media and 79 percent in television were...from the upper caste". This fact has been highlighted by intellectuals from time to time. On a talk show, *Media Manthan* on the dalits and media, Kancha Illaih (2012), a dalit activist and an academician, answered a question as to why dalits are sidelined in the media industry. He says that from pre- to post-independence, almost all the Press has been with the Brahmins. Even if the owner of a newspaper organization is from the Shudras, the persons who worked in it were Brahmins, many a time in the majority. So, they avoided deliberately reporting issues concerning the dalits. Besides, the media was historically used against the dalits. One can trace back to Ambedkar the apathy shown by the nationalist press towards dalits. Ambedkar contested the claims of the Congress and Gandhi that they represented the dalits by citing the propagandistic nature of the national press. Pointing to the lack of representation of the dalits and their politics in the national media, Ambedkar noted: "The first and foremost circumstance for the spread of this view is the propaganda by the Indian press in favour of the Congress... [T]he second circumstance why the world outside believes that the Congress is the only organization which represents India, including even the untouchables, is because of the absence of propaganda on behalf of the untouchables to advertise their case against the Congress claim... [T]hey (Dalits) have no press and the Congress press is closed to them. It is determined not to give them the slightest publicity. They cannot have their own press." (Ambedkar, 1945). He carried on with his critique by focusing specifically on the Brahmin domination in the Indian press thus: "The staff of the Associated Press of India, which is the main news distributing agency in India, is entirely drawn from Madras Brahmins—indeed the whole of the press in India is in their hands and who for well-known reasons are entirely pro-Congress and will not allow any news hostile to the Congress to get publicity. These are reasons beyond the control of untouchables.[2] As a result, news about these communities never gained importance and issues pertaining to their pressing problems appeared in the press in a casual manner. Historically, dalits made several attempts to gain a hold in media space. The paper attempts to highlight the dalit efforts in this direction in Tamil Nadu and Maharashtra. Due to various historical reasons, these two states turn out to be the hub of the dalit movement.

Dr. Babasaheb Ambedkar

Babasaheb Ambedkar was born and brought up in a village. Caste had haunted him at every stage of his life. He faced the harsh reality of discrimination in his school, both from his school-mates and his Brahmin teachers. Babasaheb and his brother were usually made to sit in a corner of the class on a piece of gunny cloth which they carried to school; teachers would neither touch their notebooks; some teachers would not even ask them to recite poems or ask them questions for fear of being polluted. When these two boys felt thirsty in school, they opened their mouths and somebody would pour drinking water into them as if through a funnel. He also faced numerous problems in getting local conveyance, and even barbers refused to cut his hair. The cruel system of untouchability left a strong mark on his personality.

Ambedkar was the first highly-educated person from the dalit community. He identified his personal problems with the community's agony. His education helped him to turn his personal experience into words and to search for solutions. His education also provided him the strength to fight Brahmin exploitation. He turned his learned skill to strengthen the voice of the voiceless victims of the Brahmins. His commitment to the larger society can be found in his writings and movement. Babasaheb, as the Drafting Committee Chairman of the Constitution of India, paid utmost care to incorporate human experience from across the world for building a new and better society for everyone.

Babasaheb Ambedkar who had the opportunity to study abroad had seen the powerful role of the press. As part of his struggle spanning over four decades, Dr. Ambedkar always used print media as one of the instruments to achieve his goal of emancipating the untouchables. After he came back, he was greatly involved in several movements. Later, he realized that newspapers could be used to propagate his ideas in emancipating victims of the caste system. As part of the larger mission, his deep attention was to study the newspapers run by untouchables—non-Brahmins and Hindus. He came to know that newspapers run by Hindus had no commitment and sympathy to the worst victims of Brahminism, that is, the untouchables and marginalised communities. During the same period, untouchables owned or managed newspapers like 'Somavanshiya Mitra', 'Hind Nagarik', 'Vital Vidhwansak', 'Bahishkrit Bharat'. Their failure to generate adequate financial resources prompted Ambedkar to think seriously of launching his own newspapers.

In 1918, political reformation was sweeping the country. The Southborough committee was taking witnesses from various sections of society to implement the Montague-Chelmsford reformation. Babasaheb Ambedkar realized the importance of political power and he felt that to create awareness and public opinion in favour of political rights, a newspaper was a must. Raising funds for this noble cause not only included the common man, but also maharajas, employees and kind-hearted British officials. On 31 January 1920, the *Mooknayak* was launched from Bombay. In the first issue, Babasaheb Ambedkar observed that if subscribers gave good financial assistance, then only *Mooknayak* would shine like a star and serve the downtrodden masses. The first edition of *Mooknayak* ran under the title 'Good State does not have the necessity of Swarajya'. He observed that, "Swarajya becomes a weird apparition for the majority people. It is very natural that it should be so. It recalls to their mind the tyrannies, oppressions and injustices practised upon them by their fellow citizens. They fear that under Swarajya these violations may recur."[3] In the opinion of Babasaheb Ambedkar, Swarajya means "Establishing that social order to emancipate the masses from their problem."[4]

Realizing the fact Babasaheb Ambedkar said, "The interests of untouchables can be represented by the untouchables alone. They have their own distinct interests, and none else can truly voice them. Brahmin, a Mohammedan or a Maratha can vote for a free trade interest and were treated equally well. However, none of these can speak for the interests of the untouchables because they are not untouchables; untouchability constitutes a definite set of interests which the untouchables alone can speak for. Hence it is evident that we must find the untouchables to represent their grievances which are their interests and secondly, we must find them in such numbers as will constitute a force sufficient to claim redress."[5]

The discussion on Swarajya was continued even to the third edition of *Mooknayak* under the title, "It is not Swarajya but draconian rule for us." Babasaheb Ambedkar analysed the situation and traced the treacherous planning hatched by the upper castes to make backward classes powerless as a matter of political power as well as a concern. "You hate British because they are ruling you, but what morality you have to oppose the dignity of seven crore Untouchables."[6]

In *Mooknayak,* Babasaheb Ambedkar discussed in detail the communal representation of non-Brahmin communities. He gave evidence before the Southborough Committee on 27 January 1919. He advocated special representation for Untouchables. Hindus isolated the Untouchables from any kind of social participation. When Babasaheb Ambedkar returned to India in 1923, he made up his mind to be independent. However, he did not stop his crusade. He formed the Bahishkrit Hitakarini Sabha. The Sabha took another great step to establish the newspaper. Babasaheb Ambedkar wrote a pamphlet on 4 December 1924 which had plans to start the full-fledged Bharat Bhooshan printing press along with the newspaper. He appealed to the public to contribute Rs. 20,000 to materialize it. The public responded positively to Babasaheb Ambedkar's proposal and began contributing money. With the collected money, he started *Bahishkrit Bharat* newspaper on April 3 1927. Thirteen issues of *Bahishkrit Bharat* were published regularly. Then, the regularity could not be maintained. "Brahminism means not Brahmins"; "Just like imperialism, socialism, Bolshevism and capitalism, etc., Brahminism is also one of the traditions or isms."[7]

On 4 September 1928, the Samaj Samata Sangh was formed by B.V. Pradhan, D.V. Naik, R.D. Dalav along with many other members of Samata who were involved in the movement begun by Babasaheb Ambedkar. On behalf of the Samaj Samata Sangh '*Samata*' (Equality), a weekly newspaper, was started. Later, the title of *Bahishkrit Bharat* was changed to *Samata*. The song 'The Rise of Equality' was written on the first page of the copy of the first newspaper. The newspaper published 29 major editorials and most of them were written by the editor, D.V. Naik. It published these editorials on current affairs which were dynamic and in depth. Within one year he started *Janata* on 24 November 1930 as a monthly magazine from Mumbai. Babasaheb Ambedkar changed the name of *Bahishkrit Bharat* to *Janata* because people were not buying the newspaper because of its name. Although he was the founder of the newspaper,, he did not take the responsibility of editing it owing to his hectic work schedule. He contributed several valuable articles and letters to this journal. His speeches were also published in the *Janata* in detail. Above the editorial was the slogan 'Tell the slave he is a slave and he will revolt'. From the fourth year onwards, it was published the revolutionary message of Sant Tukaram who said that 'Whenever We Lived Under Your Rule and You Have Ridiculed us'. Some years later, an article on change of religion was published. The *Janata* extensively published reports related to labourers and farmers. Babasaheb Ambedkar suggested many remedies for the sustainable development of the agrarian economy. In 1935, he announced conversion for self-respect and self-development. The call given by Babasaheb Ambedkar was published in detail in the *Janata*. Babasaheb Ambedkar was subjected to severe criticism by the orthodox Brahminical press. However, he was never discouraged by their criticism. Babasaheb Ambedkar, while addressing the Scheduled Castes Federation, said, while referring on the need to counter the media's draconian role, "We have no press. The press never reported the crudest of tyrannies and oppressions, to which our people are subjected day in and day out all over India. Even our views on social and political questions are systematically suppressed by an organized conspiracy on the part of the Press. We have no funds to maintain machinery, to render help to our people and to educate, agitate and organize them." The name of *Janata* was changed to *Prabuddha Bharat* on 4 February 1956. Ambedkar, over a long period, had done a good deal of writing and research on journalistic aspects. His contribution in this area has become a subject of research. Two Ph.D.s have so far been awarded on the topic, 'Dr. Ambedkar and Journalism.' One was by Dr. Gangadhar Pantawane of Aurangabad University in the late 1960s. The second was by Dr. Shoraj Singh Bechain of JNU, New Delhi. Dr. Bechain's research topic was 'Effect of Dr. Ambedkar's Journalism on dalit Literature'. Numerous books like 'Patrakar Ambedkar' by Dr. Gangadhar Pantawane and 'Lokpatrakar Ambedkar' by Sukhram Hiwrale have been published. Dr. Ambedkar's editorials of B.B. were published in Marathi by Ratnakar Ganvir; as also small articles ('Sputh Lekh' in Marathi).

Minorities Falling Behind the Net

Against this scenario, where the "traditional media in India played a negative role in the construction of the dalit question" Robin Jeffrey states that the emergence of the new technology—the internet—has paved the way for the disenfranchised marginal to use it as an alternative to the mainstream media to write and respond to the rest of the world. The minorities and the marginalised in the world deem it a boon to express and share their pain and happiness with others. The advent of the internet has provided them the hope that it would make the previously marginalized actors and arguments more visible to a broader public. As we witness the rapid proliferation and availability of the internet, many marginal groups are making their presence felt in cyberspace. This phenomenon of "presence which the internet is producing is providing a unique forum for the dispossessed to find a voice in the public sphere that might have been otherwise denied to them in the real world" (Mitra, 2004). Mitra (2001) articulates that the internet serves as a medium where marginalized individuals can exercise discursive power and resist damaging representations. Socially marginalized groups speak to one another as they speak against authority. He says "On the Internet, the marginalized can call on the dominant and put the dominant in the difficult position of acknowledging the marginalized, or further distance the dispossessed by ignoring the call. Since the popularization of the internet in the early 90's, African-Americans have had ways to talk back to these negative stereotypes by using various forms of internet—blogs, videos, editorial websites and social media communities to combat negative image and to create new societal norms for African-Americans." There has never before been as much opportunity for conversation and participation as found in the internet, where the marginal not only speak but can expect a response as well. Blogs, an additional feature of the internet, which arrived in the 1990s has become a tool for the marginal to connect and share with others. Marginalized voices—the poor, the radical and even everyday people—are given little voice in the mass media news coverage. Blogs offer a chance to those voices and stories to be heard. In a study conducted by Pole (2006) on the use by Blacks of the blogosphere, it is found that the blogosphere is the place where more political participation by Blacks and other minorities takes place. Dalits all through history have struggled for space in the media. New media has come as a new-found platform for them to express their pain to the world and also to develop their own perspective on important issues. It was in the 1970s that the New Media emerged, mainly fuelled by the growth in the internet, posing a challenge to existing newspapers, magazines and television in print form. In the second wave and with globalization, new media digitization and convergence of media changed the scenario. User-generated content, interactivity, audience participation and flexibility are the major features of the internet and new media today. Many believe that the new media is liberating, democratizing and empowering citizens and promoting egalitarianism and tolerance.

The new media provides much more freedom and flexibility than the mainstream media to generate and disseminate ideas. Excluded communities and groups all over the world realized the scope, opportunities and possibilities of the new media and they started using them to express their experiences, thoughts, ideas and concepts. Dalits in India use the new media to promote their ideology and question the mainstream socio-political and cultural spheres. Dalits write blogs and create websites and express their views and thoughts to the public.

Two web portals, Savari and Round Table India, try to understand how dalits are using new media for their emancipation. Savari is a women's web portal exclusively run by Adivasi, Bahujan and Dalit women. In this web portal, these women were exposed to many engrossing debates among non-upper caste women regarding their status in contemporary society. Savari is basically devoted to building an alternative perceptive within the anti-caste movement. Since women from the entire South Asian region over a last five thousand years have been subjected to humiliation and oppression due to the caste system, the platform is open to all the women from the region. The present paper is exposed to many rich debates among non-upper caste women regarding their status in contemporary society. An article was written by one of the authors on a brutal gang rape that was done to a dalit woman in Jind, Haryana. The mainstream media had not reported this case and also did not report the protests against it. By bringing out a photo feature in Savari, I was able to draw more attention to the case. In the same way, Jenny and others wrote many articles against the whole feminist discourse during the infamous Delhi rape case. They pointed to the fault lines in the feminist discourse on rape and drew attention to the fact that it was the dalits and bahujans who bore the brunt of rape and they talked about the media ignoring this. This created a new conversation about caste and gender, and we saw how this was carried forward even in the mainstream space.

Round Table India is the web portal of the Ambedkarite movement. It is a forum of writers that aims for "an informed Ambedkar age" and sees caste as the primary fissure in Indian society. They aggregate news on politics, society and culture; they comment and critique and try to be a hub for dalit-bahujan voices. "Unlike mainstream media, we aren't casteist—we have many upper castes writing, at least as much as their share in the population." (Naren Bedide, one of the founders). The portal offers articles about dalit lives with images through which one can read India's history of caste-based discrimination. These portals represent new perspectives for dalit studies and turned out to be a larger platform for young dalit scholars and teachers. These groups have refused to accept the status quo as maintained by upper-caste Hindus. Most of their writings in these websites come from their individual experiences and therefore it carries collective experience. They also become reading sources for a large dalit community. Dalits in these portals discuss and debate various problems that are their primary concern. Among the various subjects, caste and gender oppression is one of the main areas of our focus. In our paper, we do not want to remain confined to two web portals. Here in this paper we would also like to say a few lines on a YouTube channel 'The Dalit Camera through Untouchable Eyes'. This channel began uploading videos depicting contributions of grass-roots activists and also covering various issues concerning the Dalits, Adivasis, Bahujans, Muslims and other minorities. B. Ravichandran started 'dalit camera' by making a documentary on the attack on a dalit woman who was a panchayat president. This channel aims to bring the unheard voices of the marginalized into the public domain, which is otherwise dominated by the corporate Hindutva mainstream media. There are, however, many challenges before us. There is the problem that we sometimes are seen as ghettoised within a limited audience without any reach to the mainstream. However, many dalit bahujans deny this argument saying that we are the mainstream. Another problem that we face is that much of our writing is borrowed and used by brahminical channels and media outlets and even academicians who do not attribute our work to us. So though we create the knowledge, it often becomes circulated as established knowledge in their own names. This is a huge challenge before us and there needs to be some discussion on this. Moreover, there is also the problem that we are often limited to talking about our own issues. There is a need to branch out and start conversations on issues outside the realm of our own world and we need to have a vibrant culture where we can come up with perspectives on all issues, and not only those that directly concern dalit-bahujan lives.

Methodology

In our paper we used the content and textual analysis method. The research methodology will also engage with an extensive and intensive study of the autobiographies, sociological accounts and web portals drawing upon the insights from contemporary critical discourse analysis. The approaches and strategies used in this exploration of dalit literature will be eclectic ones. There will also be relevant citations from secondary sources to support the argument of the paper which we are reading.

Findings

New Media has been widely accepted as the virus to check and counter challenges in the fraction of a second. And it also provides an opportunity for marginalised communities to raise their voices and draw attention in the public sphere. Savari and Roundtable India are worthy example of websites for dalit presence in cyberspaces. These two websites attempt to survey and critique the mainstream media perspectives and at the same time theorize the perspectives of dalits and marginalised communities in the New Media and attempts to initiate engagement with the specificities of their lives and struggles.

1. These websites intend to develop a perspective by expanding the existing theoretical works on dalits.
2. These web portals provide a free and unfettered space for dalits.

3. The contents of these web portals are pro-minority, pro-oppressors and pro-marginalised women.
4. Cultural and identity politics is among the content of these portals.
5. They bring out the art forms of different groups into the limelight to challenge the mainstream.
6. The content of each post carries images of the subject matter.
7. The posts also share details about fellowships, admissions and job advertisements related to marginalised communities

Conclusion

In our paper, we have attempted to analyze the historical background of dalits and how, historically, they have made several attempts to gain a foothold in media space. The media is also responsible to empower and enrich democracy by promoting pluralism and diversity. The media plays the role of the voice of the people and it must ensure that every section of society is represented without any bias. But despite such concepts on the role of the media, in India it has failed to properly represent the dalit cause against exploitation and oppression. Realizing this pathetic situation, dalits came forward to begin their own communication through newspapers and magazines. The conditions under which dalits have been living for ages illustrate the brutal face of the caste system. As part of understanding and assessing the present position of dalits, their literature proves to be most vital sources. Dalit writing represents newer discourses on caste and gender. These attempts have emerged in contrast to centuries of oppression combined with portrayals that have suited the oppressors. The paper aims for an engagement with the construction of dalit images in different historical accounts and how the oppressed themselves have begun to deconstruct and reconstruct their real images in the newer public spheres. This project attempts to survey and critique the mainstream media perspectives and at the same time theorize perspectives of dalits in the New Media and tries to look at how it engages with the specificities of their lives and struggles.

Ambedkar realized a need for the awakening of women, especially dalit women. He encouraged them to fight for dignity, self-respect and self-perception. Being highly educated, he understood the double exploitation of dalit women in the fact of being a dalit and a also a woman. He had realized the complexity of the caste system. It was the caste system that had dehumanized a certain category of people by naming them as untouchables. He initiated his struggle against the inhuman system known as the caste system. Since it was this system that had legitimized the exploitation of dalit women and recognizing the overlap of caste and gender, he tried to organize women through his movement. As a result of his encouragement, a good number of dalit women participated in the movements which he launched against the caste system. There was no other movement than Ambedkar's which attracted a large number of women. These participants, especially dalit women, stood at the forefront of the social, cultural and political programs of the Ambedkar movement. It is accepted that around 500 women participated in the historic Mahad Satyagraha (1927). Later, while addressing a meeting of more than 3,000 women of the Depressed Classes on 18 July, 1927, Ambedkar said:

> "I measure the progress of the community by the degree of progress which women had achieved. Never regard yourself as Untouchables, live a clean life. Dress yourselves as touchable ladies. Never mind if your dress if full of patches, but see that it is clean. None can restrict your freedom in the choice of your garments. Attend more to the cultivation of the mind and spirit of self-help."[8]

NOTES

1. Kenneth J. Cooper, 1996. 'India's Majority Lower Castes Are Minor Voice in Newspapers; Few Journalists Periodicals Advocate Interests of the Underclass', *The Washington Post*, 5 September.
2. Jeffrey, Robin, 2003. *India's newspaper Revolution Capitalism, Politics and the Indian Language Press*. New Delhi: Oxford University Press.
3. Khainnode C. B, 1989. Dr. Bhimrao Ramaji Ambedkar, Vol. 4, pp. 40, Pune: Sugava Prakashan,
4. Vasant Moon, *Dr. Babasaheb AmbedkarYanche Bahishkrit Bharat Ani Mooknayak*, op. cit, pp. 358.
5. Evidence taken before the Reforms Committee (franchise) (Southborough Committee) Vol. II, Calcutta, 1919, in C. B. Khairmode, 1978. Dr. Bhimrao Ramaji Ambedkar, Vol. L, (Bombay), Pratap Prakashan, pp. 100.
6. Vasant Moon, (Ed.), *Dr. Babasaheb Ambedkaryanche Bahishkril Bharat Am Mooknayak*, op. cit, pp.360.
7. Vasant Moon, *Dr. Babasaheb Ambedkar Writings and Speeches*, op. cit, pp. 352-353.
8. Katulkar, Ratnesh, 2008. 'Dr. Ambedkar on Women Liberation,' Countercurrents.org, 31 August.

7

Caste or Reservation: Who is Damaging Society?

An Analytical Study of Caste-Based Reservation in India

Pallavi Devi

ABSTRACT

It is no longer wise to rationalize the worst form of injustice based on the caste system as a part of tradition by taking recourse to historical argument. What matters most for our present concerns to eliminate the worst forms of caste-based injustice is that a particular tradition as a whole should be subjected to reasonable assessment. Reservation is a temporary and make-shift arrangement so that resources are distributed in such a way that all castes get something. The present Indian scenario, specifically after independence, provides a relevant context of ever-increasing recognition and progressive understanding of democratic values and the ideal of equal dignity of all human beings. This paper attempts to discuss the following points:

1. *Reservations should not be mixed with the welfare activities of the State.*
2. *Reservations are not meant for conferring benefits to the poor.*
3. *Caste is what primarily damages society, not reservation.*

Key Words: caste-based injustice, positive discrimination, reservation

Introduction

> *"So long as you do not achieve social liberty, whatever freedom is provided by the law is of no avail to you."*
>
> *—B.R. Ambedkar*

Affirmative actions are those measures—executive, administrative or legislative—that benefit or create privileges for needy and eligible claimants from vulnerable groups like children, women, Scheduled Castes[1] and Scheduled Tribes[2] or those of the backward classes.[3] The affirmative action sanctioned by the Indian Constitution and implemented by various governments is called the Reservation Policy. The objective of Affirmative Action or Positive Discrimination or the Reservation Policy is 'to redistribute resources and opportunities to those who enjoy the fewest advantages owing to historical and traditional reasons.'[4] Though affirmative action and reservations are not the same, yet they resemble each other in that they both strive to accommodate members of historically-disadvantaged communities by a deliberate relaxation of standard norms.

The Directive Principles are guidelines laid down in the Constitution to the State as defined in Art. 12 (central, state, local government and local bodies) to achieve the goal of a welfare state. The State should keep these principles in mind while framing laws, policies, passing ordinances, etc. Thus the State, according to the directions set in Art 38, shall strive to promote the welfare of the people by securing and protecting as effectively as it may, a social order in which justice—social, economic and political—shall inform all the institutions of national life. The Constitution of India also directs the State via Art. 46 to take special care to promote the interests of the weaker and disadvantaged sections of society, in particular the Scheduled Castes (SCs) and Scheduled Tribes (STs), and protect them from social injustice and all forms of exploitation. The Constitution enjoins the State vide Art. 16(4) to make special provisions for the advancement of SCs and STs and the socially and educationally backward classes[5] and also for reservation/affirmative action in jobs in which they are not adequately represented in the government services. An outstanding feature of the reservation policy in India is the reservation for the SCs and STs in the Lok Sabha, in Legislative Assemblies and in elected councils of local government. The number of jobs, seats and political positions for SCs and STs is fixed in proportion to the population of the respective groups. The Constitutional scheme of compensatory discrimination towards backward classes are Art. 15(1), Art. 15(4), Art. 16(1), Art. 16(4), Art. 29(2), Art. 338(1), Art. 338(3), Art. 340(1), Art. 342(2) and Art. 340(3).

The first Backward Classes Commission was appointed under Art. 340 under the chairmanship of Kaka Kalelkar in 1953 but it ended ignominiously. The Janata Government in 1979 appointed the Second Backward Class Commission with Bindeshwar Prasad Mandal as chairman to report on the socially advanced sections or the creamy layer. It recommendations were implemented in September 1993.

It is not that the policy of positive discrimination is designed to bring about the total elimination of inequality. While inequalities will persist in spite of such policies, they will largely be the result of individual differences, uncomplicated and unburdened by historical handicaps. It is in this sense that positive discrimination/reservation and affirmative action will lead to a truly liberal society. This also implies that the measures instituted in favour of deprived communities are time-bound in character. This is the way the Indian Constitution devised reservations for the ex-untouchable castes and for the tribal population. The Indian Constitution advocates positive discrimination and reservations in the spirit of 'fraternity'. This paper attempts to discuss the following points:

1. Reservations should not be mixed up with welfare activities of the State.
2. Reservations are not meant for conferring benefits on the poor.
3. Caste is what is primarily damaging society, not reservation.

Methodology

This paper adopts the doctrinal method of research. It will involve an in-depth study of source materials, text review and case studies.

Caste through the Ages

In India, caste is the most important basis of social categorization. Though caste is believed to have originated in a division of people on the basis of their natural inclinations and occupations, it has turned out in course of time to be hereditary. It has created social groups based on kinship and ethnicity. The hereditary occupations have created vested interests in the form of socio-economic monopolies and have bred an extreme form of exploitation. The caste system is overburdened with considerations of ritualistic purity and this, in turn, has engendered inflexibility, rigidity and feelings of superiority and inferiority. The Brahmins occupy the top position and the Shudras occupy the last one. The privilege of the twice-born is denied to the Shudra who is therefore called *ekajati* (once-born). Jati[6] is also a vernacular term for caste. The statement that God created the Shudra to be the slave of all the others is repeated and he is given the name 'padaja' (born from the feet). He is supposed to be fed and clothed with the remnants of food and raiment of the higher castes. He is contrasted with the Arya who, though younger than him, must be respected by him and rise in his presence.[7] A Shudra cannot perform sacrifices, could not listen to or recite the Vedic texts, nor practise austerities. He was categorically denied the right of initiation and, consequently, the first stage of an individual's life (*ashrama*) that is, studentship. Of the other sacraments, marriage is the only one, which is explicitly applicable to the Shudras. Apastamba opines that the Shudra is not entitled to the rite of initiation, the study of the Vedas and the kindling of the sacred fire. His works (rites) are declared by implication to be unproductive of reward either in this world or in the next. For a Brahmin to eat the food given by a Shudra is a sin that must be expiated and to avoid taking it is one of the few things that assures a Brahmin of bliss in heaven. The great nineteenth century Indologist, Max Mueller, the scholar-missionary, Abbe Dubois, and even the sociologist, Max Weber, were not very certain if India would ever succeed in modernizing itself as they felt that the caste system would continue to frustrate all attempts towards social and economic progress. Their understanding of the caste system was largely conditioned by Hindu sacerdotal texts that are heavily biased in favour of the Brahminical point of view. The belief that Brahmans alone can speak on behalf of Hindu society continues to dominate even contemporary scholarship on caste.[8] This is the kind of exploitation, humiliation and deprivation they faced.

Thus, post Independence, the Indian Constitution is first and foremost a social document where the majority of its provisions are either directly aimed at furthering the goals of social revolution or attempt to foster this revolution by establishing the conditions necessary for its achievement. The concept of socio-economic justice broadly embodies the distribution of political and administrative power among the various social sections through constitutional means.

The Policy and its Rationale of Reservation Policy

Social, educational and economic inequalities have existed in different social segments of Indian society. The SCs, STs and OBCs (broadly known as backward classes) represent the social groups that suffered through the ages due to caste prejudices, economic inequality, educational backwardness and lagging in educational and economic development in comparison with certain advanced or forward castes. To minimize these social and economic deprivations, many social provisions were made to safeguard their interests along with the provision of equality before the law and prohibition of discrimination on grounds of race, religion and caste The Constitution of India permits the State to adopt such affirmative action or reservation as it deems necessary to uplift the backward classes to levels of equality with the rest of the countrymen. In the past, the backward classes have been denied access to government services on account of their inability to compete effectively in open selection on the basis of merit. It is, therefore, open to the government to reserve a certain number of seats in places of learning and in the public services in favour of the Scheduled Castes and Tribes and Other Backward Classes to the exclusion of all others, irrespective of merit. Therefore, reservation policy is meant to eradicate the present social, educational and economic disparities caused by purposeful societal discrimination in the past. Reservations are part of a much larger policy package. It comprises a series of legislations, ameliorative programmes and preferential schemes designed to benefit the weaker sections of society. The package has evolved over a long period of time and has been administered by the Central as well as the State governments.[9]

The overall package, as it operates today, is addressed to three sets of policy goals. First, to remove social and religious disabilities of certain specified groups suffering disabilities on account of their social segregation and spatial and cultural isolation; namely, the Scheduled Castes (SCs) and Scheduled Tribes (STs). Second, to facilitate and promote equal participation with others, of all socially disabled and disadvantaged groups, in the organized sectors of the country's economic and political life. This is sought to be achieved through provisions for preferential treatment in education, in government employment, in parliament, State legislatures and local bodies and through other ameliorative measures and schemes designed to improve their life. Third, to protect, if necessary through legislative action and executive orders, all these groups, also described in the Constitution as weaker sections of society, or simply, the backward classes, from all forms of social injustice and exploitation.

Reservations, along with other measures of protection and upliftment of the weaker sections of society, should thus be viewed as an instrument of a larger social policy of the State addressed to a long-term goal of creating a civil society through extending effective citizenship rights to vast sections of the population that have been historically deprived and marginalized.

In articulating these goals, the policy has acquired multifarious content of which reservations is one. Thus, we have a series of laws that aim at removing disabilities such as the Untouchability Offences Act of 1955, the subsequently amended and tightened protection of the Civil Rights Act of 1976, the legislation to prevent forced labour and the amended Criminal Tribes Act of 1952 removing the legal disabilities suffered by the so-called criminal tribes. We also have protective laws preventing alienation of tribal lands, regulating money-lending and providing debt-relief and legal aid to the weaker sections. Besides, there are schemes and programmes for land allotments, housing, scholarships, subsidies, etc., aimed at providing physical security and promoting occupational mobility of these groups. The five-year plans have a special feature in the form of tribal sub-plans and scheduled caste components of plans The most significant and now a controversial aspect of the policy is however the provision of reservations. Although these provisions are based on the same values and rationale that inform other parts of the policy package, their impact is felt adversely and directly by those outside the beneficiary groups and that too in the vital area of social mobility where the means of mobility are always scarce and the competition is intense.[10]

The Mandal Commission

The extension of reservation beyond the SCs and the STs is based on the premise of identifying such OBCs who can be given reservation under Arts. 15(4) and 16(4). The identification of such backward classes was left to the State by setting up a commission to enquire into the conditions of socially and educationally backward classes (SEBCs) under Art. 340 of the Constitution. The second backward class commission headed by Bindeshwar Prasad Mandal adopted 11(eleven) criteria to identify the socially and educationally backward classes, which can be grouped under three major headings: social, educational and economic. Of these three groups, separate weightage was given to indicators of each group. A weightage of three points each was given to all the social indicators. Educational indicators were given two points each. And economic indicators were given one point each. In addition to social and educational, economic indicators were considered important as they directly flowed from social and educational backwardness mainly to highlight the fact that socially and educationally backward classes are economically backward also. The commission proposed the following over-all scheme of reservation for OBCs:

1. Candidates belonging to OBC and recruited on the basis of merit in an open com-petition should not be adjusted against their reservation quota of 27 per cent.
2. The above reservation should also be made applicable to the promotion quota at all levels.
3. The reserved quota remaining unfilled should be carried forward for a period of three years and de-reserved thereafter.
4. Relaxation in the upper age limit for direct recruitment should be extended to OBC candidates in the same manner as done for SCs and STs.
5. A roster system for each category of posts should be adopted by the concerned authorities in the same manner as presently done in respect of SC and ST candidates.

These recommendations are applicable in total to all recruitment to public sector undertakings, both under the Central and State governments, as also to nationalised banks. All private sector undertakings that have received financial assistance from the government in one form or the other should also be obliged to recruit personnel on the aforesaid basis. All universities and affiliated colleges should also be covered by the above scheme of reservation.[11]

Contradictions in Mandal Report

At the heart of the Mandal approach is the strong correlation between *jati* status and economic and social deprivation. By taking *jati* as the principal indicator of deprivation, it excludes non-Hindu sections of the Indian population. Muslims are an obvious omission and until the recent report of the Sachar Committee, the social and economic deprivation among them was not investigated, much less addressed. The frequent problem of Christian dalits or neo-Buddhist dalits indicates the omission which is consequent to making *jati* a quintessential Hindu category the basis of affirmative action. Around a fifth of the population is thus excluded. This violates the principle of equality of all citizens before the law which is essential to liberal and social democratic traditions.[12]

Thus, if we were to classify people by, for instance, measuring only income and wealth there would be poor among the population of all *jatis*, not just the SCs/STs or the OBCs. Thus, there can be poor Brahmins and rich dalits. The average income/wealth of a *jati* may be higher than that of another, yet individual members of even households of a 'rich' *jati* may be poorer than an individual member of a backward *jati*.[13]

Caste and Class

In Max Weber's phraseology, caste and class are both status groups. While castes are perceived as hereditary groups with a fixed ritual status, social classes are defined in terms of the relations of production. A social class is a category of people who have a similar socio-economic status in relation to other classes in society. Individuals and families who are classified as part of the same social class have similar life chances, prestige, style of life, attitudes, etc.

In the caste system, the status of a caste is determined not by the economic and political privileges but by the ritualistic legitimating of authority. In the class system, ritual norms have no importance at all but power and wealth alone determine one's status.[14]

The class system differs in many respects from other forms of stratification—slavery, estate and caste. While 'class' represents a 'democratic society' having equality of opportunity, 'caste' is the opposite of it.

Judicial Interpretation of the Criteria for Backwardness

The 'Special Provisions' for Backward Classes has been a subject of serious controversy since the First Amendment to the Constitution of India came into effect in 1951. Candidates of the forward castes and upper classes have been challenging the reservation policy of the state governments before the High Courts and the Supreme Court of India as a denial of equal protection of law, denial of equality before law, and discriminatory and violation of Fundamental Rights guaranteed to citizens under Arts. 14, 15 and 16 of the Constitution.

In the early years, the Supreme Court of India in the cases of Balaji vs. State of Mysore[15] and Chitralekha vs. State of Mysore took a rigid stand in refusing to accept caste as a factor of backwardness, treating social backwardness as a result of poverty and not recognising class and caste as synonymous and directing that the Other Backward Classes should be comparable to Scheduled Castes and Scheduled Tribes. Lastly, objected to reservation above 50 percent in educational institutions and government service as excessive.

However over the years, the Supreme Court of India has been taking a liberal attitude, specially after 1968, towards caste as a factor for social backwardness, accepting class and caste as synonymous. 'Caste-cum-means' tests became factors for the identification of socially and educationally Backward Classes and this has been reflected in cases like P. Rajendran vs. State of Madras, Peria Karuppan vs. State of Tamil Nadu, S.V. Balaram vs. State of Andhra Pradesh, K.S. Jayashree vs. State of Kerala and K.C. Vasanth Kumar and Others vs. State of Karnataka.[16]

The main point of dispute in this controversy has been between 'social backwardness as represented by 'caste' and 'economic backwardness' as represented by 'poverty' as the determinants of socially and educationally Backward Classes or Other Backward Classes under Arts. 15(4) and 16(4) of the Constitution. Finally, the issue seemed to have been resolved by the Supreme Court of India in the case of K.G. Vasanth Kumar and Others vs. State of Karnataka delivered by the Constitutional five-judge Bench. All the five judges delivered separate judgements, but there was general agreement among the majority of them that 'Caste-cum-Means' must be the main criteria for identification of socially and educationally backward classes or other backward classes.[17]

Judicial Interpretation of Special Provisions as Enabling Provisions

It is equally important to know that for a long time the judicial view regarding the 'Special Provisions' has been that Arts. 15 and 16(4) of the Constitution are 'exceptions' to Arts. 15(1) and 16(1). According to this view, the claims of the Backward Classes could be recognised and implemented only through 'exceptional clauses'.

However, in the case of State of Kerala vs. N.M. Thomas, the Supreme Court, by majority, rejected this notion of 'exceptions' and observed that the State was free to choose any 'means' to achieve equality for the Other Backward Classes. As per the judgement, these special provisions are in the nature of enabling provisions because of the discretionary power of the State under Arts. 15(4) and 16(4) to adopt any measure for the advancement of socially and educationally backward classes.

Accordingly, in the light of the views expressed by the Supreme Court, the State can make any special provision for the advancement of socially and educationally backward classes under Art. 15(4) of the Constitution. Similarly, under Art. 16(4), the State can make any provision for the reservation of posts in the services of the State in favour of Backward Classes. This discretionary power given to the State by the Constitution and now recognized by the Supreme Court will enable the State and Central governments to take whatever measures are necessary for the advancement of the socially and educationally backward classes or Other Backward Classes.[18]

Self-proclaimed Backwardness: Reverse Discrimination

There is a growing demand by some castes[19] to get themselves included in the Other Backward Classes (OBCs) category, and by some OBC's to be considered as STs (for instance, Jats in Haryana and Rajasthan; Gujjars of Rajasthan; Moran, Muttock, Tai Ahom, Koch Rajbongshi, Sootea and Tea Tribes in Assam). Very recently, the Haryana Jats once again agitated demanding OBC status. Nowhere else in the world is there is competition to assert backwardness. It has become counter-productive and reverse discrimination. Thirty years after the Patidars or Patels of Gujarat took to the streets protesting against reservation for dalits, adivasis and Other Backward Castes in government jobs and educational institutions, they are agitating again. This time, the Patels want to be counted as one of the socially and economically weaker communities in the State.[20] In December 2012, the SC/ST quota for promotions in government jobs was also implemented. It has created a competitive culture among traditionally dominant castes to be categorized as OBCs.

Mandal, Liberty and the Caste System

The Mandal Commission sparked off a still-raging debate on public policy for underrepresented and underprivileged sections of the population of India. In its recommendations,[21] reservation in Government services and educational institutions for Other Backward Classes (OBCs) candidates was suggested to cure the historical discrimination and its continuing ill-effects in public employment.[22] It was based on the argument that every community has equal rights and legitimate aspirations to participate in ruling this country, and the social conditions, denying nearly 52 per cent of the population an opportunity to fulfil those aspirations, call for urgent rectification. In view of the legal constraints, a 27 per cent reservation was recommended not only for recruitment but also for promotion and selection in universities.

In addition, educational concessions given by the Government did not make a substantial impact and, hence, strong emphasis was placed on two fronts. Firstly, intensive and time-bound educational programmes in high OBC population areas were necessary. Secondly, free residential schools, and even government hostels, were to be launched to attract backward students to an environment conducive for studies. Further, institutional finance and technical assistance was found to be necessary for helping OBC communities, especially the village vocational communities involved in cottage industries. Structural changes, Central Government assistance to the States, setting up of a separate ministry for OBCs and land reforms are among the many suggestions given by the Commission.

Positive liberty strongly advocates the creation of opportunities for all to excel. Many attacked the Mandal Commission for adopting caste as the criteria for determining social and educational backwardness. The caste system rejects the very roots of foundational equality, where it claims equal moral worth of all humans. It assigns people different social worth, based on their occupations. By denying people the freedom to switch occupations, the system has led to a stagnant society, perpetuating the supremacy of the upper castes. The caste system in Indian society, more than any other phenomenon, has had a greater hand in influencing the destinies of Indians.

It is undeniable that equality is intrinsic to the fulfilment of important values such as justice. The caste system brings bias and prejudice to the rule of law, not only in the realm of the judiciary but in all aspects of governance. In addition, it has deprived millions, over the years, of a chance to possess self-respect. Many do not even think twice before discriminating people on the basis of caste.

Reservation and Equality

Unless and until an individual, however much disadvantaged by circumstance, can realistically hope to maximise his liberty, neither he nor the nation can realise its true potential. It is within this ambit of reservation and equality that reservation on the basis of caste has been propagated. Reservation is among a host of policies aimed at ensuring social justice, equality of resources and equality of opportunity. The actual evil of the caste system has two facets—one is the real inequity in the distribution of resources and the other is the active discrimination of the backward classes, which constrains them and denies them fundamental rights and equality of opportunity.[23]

The Question of Identity

Had the politics and social restructuring revolved not just around caste/ identity-based politics after the Mandal Commission and targeted other areas of universalistic appeal like healthcare, education and implementation of social welfare programs, a uniform ground would have been set up for all to compete, thereby instilling more confidence in the hearts and minds of the oppressed classes.

Therefore, the mere representation of the under-privileged in the legislature cannot bring about social transformation. The lack of integrity amongst our elected representatives, cutting across party lines and cast spectrums, is the only equality we observe. Indian voters, in recent years, have understood this and have forced politicians to accept the new paradigm of developmental politics.

Structural Changes

Reservations in government employment institutions, as also all possible financial assistance, will remain mere palliatives unless the problem of backwardness is tackled at its root. The bulk of small land-holders, tenants, agricultural labour, impoverished village artisans, unskilled workers, etc., belong to the Scheduled Castes, Scheduled Tribes and Other Backward Classes. Apart from social traditions, the dominance by the top peasantry is exercised through recourse to informal bondage which arises mainly through money-lending, leasing out of small bits of land and providing house sites and dwelling space to poor peasants.[24] As most of the functionaries of government are drawn from the top peasantry, the difficulties of the marginalised groups remain firm. This also tilts the socio-political balance in favour of the top peasantry and helps it in having its dominance over others.[25] The net outcome of the above situation is that notwithstanding their numerical preponderance, the backward classes continue to remain in mental and material bondage of the higher castes and the rich peasantry.

Conclusion

Reservations in the long run would certainly ruin society because it is only the second choice and certainly not the best one. The remedy is not to abolish reservations but transform the caste society into a homogenised and egalitarian one so that reservations become redundant. This means that the State should initiate measures in order to bring all castes onto a level playing ground, particularly through uniform and universal education so that within a stipulated time-period, reservation becomes useless. Therefore, as long as caste exists, reservations also would exist, and if one wants to remove reservation, one should first remove caste; most of those who want to remove reservations speak either directly or indirectly for the preservation of caste-privileges and remove the little benefits that go to the relegated castes. Caste is what is primarily damaging society and not reservation.

NOTES

1. The SCs were denied education, and could only perform menial and polluting jobs, besides suffering from a variety of other deprivations as defined in Dipankar Gupta, *Towards Affirmative Action,* India International Centre Quarterly, Vol. 33, No. 3/4, India 60 (WINTER 2006-SPRING 2007), pp. 150-161.
2. In the case of the STs, it was their physical isolation that puts them at a disadvantage with respect to others in society, *supra* note.
3. The OBCs, on the other hand, are politically powerful on account of the fact that many of them are self-sustaining farmers and owner-cultivators, *supra* note.
4. Marc Galanter, 1984. *Competing Inequalities: Law and the Backward Classes in India.*
5. For the purpose of Art. 16(4) in determining whether a section forms a class, a test solely based on caste, community, race, religion, sex, descent, place of birth or residence cannot be adopted because it would directly offend the Constitution as expressed in Triloki Nath vs. State of J & K AIR 1969 SC1 (p. 171).
6. A rigorous demarcation of meaning between 'varna' and 'jati', the former denoting the four large classes and the latter only their sub-divisions, cannot, however, be maintained. The word 'jati' is sometimes indiscriminately used for 'varna'.
7. G. S. Ghurye, 2014. *Caste and Race in India,* Popular Prakashan, Reprinted, pp. 59.
8. Dipankar Gupta, 2000. *Interrogating Caste: Understanding hierarchy and difference in Indian Society,* Penguin Publishers, p. 54.
9. D. L. Seth, 1987. 'Reservations Policy Revisited', *Economic and Political Weekly* November 14.

10. Ibid.
11. A. Ramaih,, 1992. 'Identifying other backward classes', *Economic and Political Weekly*, June 6.
12. Meghna Desai, 2008. 'Reservations; Compulsions & Contradictions', *Indian Journal of Industrial Relations*, Vol. 44, No. 2, Oct., pp. 149-153.
13. Ibid.
14. Louis Dumont, 1966. *The Homo Hierarchies.*
15. (1963) Supp. 1 SCR. 439.
16. A. I. R. 1985 S. C. 1495.
17. K.H. Gheluva Raju, 1986. 'Backward Classes in India: Issues and Trends', *The Indian Journal of Political Science*, Vol. 47, No. 4, October–December, pp. 473-485.(
18. Ibid.
19. Asian Centre of Human Rights, http://www.achrweb.org/Review/2008/217-08.html as assessed on 20.12.2015.
20. http://www.ndtv.com/india-news/the-real-story-of-what-hardik-patel-21-wants-and-why-1210424 as assessed on 20. 12. 2015.
21. Aruna Singh, August 1984. A comment on the recommendations of the Mandal Commission.
22. Satija Kalpana and Patel Mohan, 2012. 'Mainstreaming Women Employment and Human Development in Kheda District India—Sustainable Livelihood Approach to Poverty by UNDP', *I. Res. J. Social Sci.*, Vol. 1, No. 3, pp. 26-35.
23. Jha, G. M., Trehan, S., Rao G., Vishwanath, B., Sarin, R. and Monga, A., June 2013. 'Mandal Commission: Equality and Liberty', *International Research Journal of Social Science*, Vol. 2, No. 6, pp. 35-38.
24. Ibid.
25. Pradhan M Prasad.1980. 'Rising Middle Peasantry in North India', *Economic and Political Weekly*, Annual Number.

SECTION III

Status of Dalits: Experience of States

8

DALIT MOVEMENT FOR SOCIAL JUSTICE: POLITICS OF ACCOMMODATION IN TELUGU REGION IN INDIA

H. Srikanth

ABSTRACT

Dalits in India, officially recognized as Scheduled Castes, occupy lowest status in the caste hierarchy. Despised by others as untouchable castes, for centuries the Dalits were subject to various kinds of discrimination and violations of basic human rights. Although caste system was by-product of Hinduism, the practice of untouchability has spread to all communities in the Indian sub-continent. It was only during the colonial period that some members of the Dalit communities could get access to modern education and respectable jobs. Since then the Dalits in all linguistic and religious communities have been organizing themselves and leading movements to articulate their demands for social justice. The paper focuses on the trajectory of Dalit movement in Telugu speaking provinces in India. It shows how the autonomous Dalit movements that laid bare the caste blindness of the mainstream political parties and declared annihilation of the caste as their goal, are gradually becoming prey to philistinism and exclusionary politics, and getting absorbed into the mainstream politics, allowing the ruling class parties and governments to become final arbitrators and dispensers of social justice.

Key Words: Dalit movement, social justice, caste oppression, scheduled castes, Andhra Pradesh, India

Introduction

The concept of Social Justice, like ideas of Freedom and Equality, has no single accepted definition or interpretation. Social Justice means different things to different people (Finn & Jacobson, 2017; Witcher, 2013, pp. 1-30; Burchardt & Craig, 2008, pp. 1-16). Demands made in the name of Social Justice differ depending on whether the peoples fighting for it are workers, peasants, women, indigenous peoples, homosexuals, ethnic minorities, or Dalits. The people invoke Social Justice to demand equal treatment and equal opportunities for the marginalized; upholding of identities and self-respect of the hitherto neglected communities; respect for human rights and recognition of one's unique problems and rights; imposition of progressive taxation and creation of safety nets, and implementation of positive discriminatory policies and programmes (Giddens, 1999, pp. 51-54; T.M.D., 1960, pp. 70-74). Despite the variations in demands made in the name of Social Justice, what appears to be common to almost all movements seeking Social Justice is that all these movements exert pressure on the state and expect the state to initiate social policies for bringing about the desired changes within the system (Piachaud, 2008, pp. 33-52). In this respect, Social Justice movements are different from those movements aiming at Social Revolution seeking change in the very nature of the state. The movements for Social Justice seek accommodation without radically changing the nature of the power relations within the system. It is possible that some movements for Social Justice can be prelude to Revolution. But many do end up as reform movements that would be content with some changes in power equations within the system. With this understanding, an attempt is made in this paper to study the trajectory of Dalit movement in the erstwhile composite state of Andhra Pradesh and see how far the Dalit movement for social justice could address the issues that are vital to annihilation of caste system in India.

Dalits' Quest for Social Justice

The Dalits, legally recognized as Scheduled Castes (SCs), are the most exploited, subjugated and discriminated community that occupy the lowest status in the traditional caste hierarchy. For centuries the Dalits, derided by others as untouchable castes, were denied of basic human rights. Compelled to live in the outskirts of the villages, the Dalits were forced to do menial and unhygienic jobs. Some Dalit communities were engaged in agricultural activities as marginal peasants, sub-tenants and forced labourers. Deprived of the right to education and dignified jobs, they remained passive victims of the feudal oppression and exploitation for centuries. Although the casteist notion of purity and pollution originated first in Hindu society, in course of time, it has affected almost all communities in the Indian sub-continent.[1] As such the Dalits are visible in all linguistic and religious communities in the mainland India (Stalin, 2007; Aloysius, 2010).

There were several religious and cultural movements in ancient and medieval India challenging the brahminical notions of caste (Iraqi, 2009; Omvedt, 2003, Teltumbde, 2017). However, these anti-caste movements could not bring any qualitative change in the lives of the Dalits, as they failed to target the economic base of the caste that had roots in the division of work in traditional village economy. It was only during the colonial period, by attacking decentralized self-sufficient village economy and exposing them to vagaries of market, the British rule gave a big jolt to caste division of labour. The colonial rulers, in their own interest, opened up modern education and modern jobs to people of all castes and communities. The opportunities thrown open to them enabled a section of the Dalits to study in schools and college, and seek take up jobs other than the ones imposed by the caste division of labour. Christian Missionaries and social reformers also played positive roles in initiating changes in the lives of the lower castes, including the Dalits. These changes in social and economic spheres facilitated the emergence of leaders, social activists and reformers among the Dalits. Leaders like Jyoti Rao Phule and B.R. Ambedkar attacked the hierarchical and oppressive nature of the traditional caste system and exposed the hypocrisy of the religious and nationalist elite (O'Hanlon, 1985; Omvedt, 2004; Ambedkar, 1936). They appealed to the Dalits to get educated, organize and agitate for their rights. Apart from the movements led by Phule and Ambedkar in Bombay Presidency, other provinces and princely states in the subcontinent also witnessed Dalit movements under the leadership of different leaders and organizations (Rodrigues, 2008; Patankar & Omvedt, 2004; Geetha & Rajadurai, 1998). These leaders and organizations representing the lower castes brought pressure on the colonial government and also on the nationalist leaders fighting for independence from the colonial rule to make concessions for the depressed sections of the society. After independence, Government of India abolished the practice of untouchability and provided constitutional and legal provisions for protection and development of the Dalits. On their part, the Dalits are organizing themselves at national and provincial levels and forming different pressure groups and political parties to defend their rights and dignity as citizens of India (Teltumbde, 2017).

Dalit Movements in Telugu Region

Telugu is a distinct language spoken by majority of the people in the southern states of Andhra Pradesh and Telangana. During the colonial period, Telugu inhabited areas were in Madras Presidency and also in the princely state of Hyderabad.[2] In Hyderabad State the Telugus lived in Telangana region. In Madras Presidency majority of the Telugu people lived in coastal Andhra and the ceded districts of Rayalaseema. There were quite a few Telugu speaking people in Madras city also. In Madras Presidency the Telugus had to share space with Tamil people; whereas in Hyderabad State they lived alongside the Kannada, Marathi and Urdu speaking people. As Telugu speaking Dalits were living under two different kinds of political and administrative jurisdictions, the history of Telugu speaking Dalits took different trajectories during the colonial period.

Dalit Movement in Hyderabad State

In the princely state of Hyderabad, the Dalits were subjected to different kinds of feudal oppression and discrimination. Initiative to address the socio-economic problems of Telugu speaking Dalits in Hyderabad State was initiated by one Madari Bagaiah, who later became popular as Bhagya Reddy Verma (1888-1939). Influenced by Jyoti Rao Phule, Bhagya Reddy started *Jagan Mitra Mandali* in 1906 to educate and organize the Dalits, using folk song and theatre traditions. In 1911 the *Mandali* was renamed as Adi-Hindu Social Service League. He started 34 schools for educating Dalit boys and girls. Aiming at internal reform, he spoke against child marriages, *devdasi* system[3], black magic and other social evils prevalent among the Dalits. To resolve internal differences within the Dalit community, he advocated the revival of panchayat court system. To showcase the craftsmanship of the Dalit artisans, he organized the exhibition of handicrafts. At his initiative Adi-Hindu Bhavan was built at Chaderghat in Hyderabad, which later became the centre for many political activities and programs. Long before Ambedkar opted for Buddhism, Bhagya Reddy Verma began organizing Buddha Jayanthi to popularise the ideas of Buddha among the Dalits. He offered guidance to Dalit movements in neighbouring states, including in Andhra region of Madras Presidency. He insisted on not using the term *Panchamas* to denote the Dalits. Responding to his demands, in 1931 Census, the Nizam government enlisted the Dalits as Adi-Hindus. He was given awards for his services by Nizam government. He was made an Advisor to government in social matters (Rajesh, 2015, pp. 27-31; Chinna Rao, 2015, p. 119).

Other important personalities associated with Dalit movement in Hyderabad State were Arigay Ramaswamy, J.H. Subbaiah and B.S. Venkat Rao. Ramaswamy who worked with Bhagya Reddy for several years, broke with him in 1921 and started Adi Hindu Jatiyonnati Sabha and Shabari Sangham to work for the Mala and Madiga communities. Later he initiated Arundhateeya Mahasabha in 1936 exclusively for welfare and development of the Madiga community (Rajesh, 2015, 36-40; Muthaiah 2004). With the help of J.H. Subbaiah, Ramaswamy revitalized Hyderabad State Adi-Hindu Mahasabha. J.H. Subbaiah later became president of the Hyderabad unit of Scheduled Caste Federation (SCF). Another known Dalit leader, B.S. Venkata Rao started Youth League of Ambedkarites and Hyderabad Depressed Classes Association (DCA) in 1938. As President of DCA, he demanded separate electorate for the Dalits. Acclaimed as "Hyderabad Ambedkar", Venkat Rao established Hyderabad State Adi Hindu Mahasabha in 1941 which was later renamed as Hyderabad State (Adi Hindu) Scheduled Caste Federation and worked under the advice of Ambedkar. B.S. Venkata Rao was nominated to Hyderabad Municipal Corporation in 1937, to the defence council of Nizam in 1943, elected unconditionally to the Nizam's Legislative Assembly in 1946 and became Education Minister under the leadership of Mirlaik Ali in 1947. As

Education Minister in Nizam government, he worked to create more avenues for the Dalits in education and public employment.

The Nizam's government which eyed on converting the Dalits to Islam showed soft corner for the Dalits by establishing schools and providing scholarships for the Dalit students. As Gandhians sought reform of Hindu society and Ambedkar started advocating Buddhism, there was intense debate in Hyderabad State as to whether the Dalits should continue as Hindu or become Buddhists. Some Dalit leaders like P. Veerani, Shyam Sunder, Kusuma Dharmanna and even B.S. Venkat Rao expressed their solidarity with Islam and supported the Nizam state (Chinna Rao, 2015). Here it is also necessary to keep in mind that several Dalits who suffered as bonded labourers, landless agricultural labourers and sub-tenants supported the communists and actively participated in Telangana peasant struggle (Dhanagare, 1979; Benbabaali, 2016). The Dalit movement got weakened because of caste rivalries within the Dalit communities and also because of personal ego clashes among the leaders. After Hyderabad state was integrated with Indian Union, the autonomous Dalit movement lost its momentum, as most Dalit leaders joined Congress party.

Dalit Voices in Madras Presidency

Most dominant narratives project Justice Party as the pioneer of anti-brahminical movements in Madras Presidency. It was true that Justice Party fought against the Brahmin domination in social, economic and administrative spheres and initiated policy reforms that facilitated representation of non-Brahmin castes in politics and public employment. But it was also fact that Justice Party was a party of the non-brahmin landlords, zamindars and traders loyal to the British, and it opposed nationalist movement on the pretext that it was led by Brahmins. It lost the support and sympathy of lower castes because of its elitist character (Blecha, 2012, pp. 20-25). The mantle of fighting against Brahminism was later taken over by the more radical Dravidar Kazhagam movement, which sought to unite all Shudra castes by invoking Dravida identity. Its leader, Periyar Ramaswamy did try to attract the Dalits under its hold. However, Dravidar Kazhagam while evolving as a political party, ended up becoming an organization of the upcoming middle castes and left little space for the Dalits (Blecha, 2012, pp. 41-43). Hence Tamil speaking Dalits had to choose their own path defend their rights after India became independent.

The Dalit movement among the Tamils in Madras Presidency was initiated by leaders like Pundit Jyothee Thass (1845-1914), Rettamalai Srinivasan (1860-1945) and M.C. Rajah (1883-1943). Jyothee Thass from Paraiyar community was a renowned scholar well-versed in different languages and philosophies. It is interesting to note that long before Ambedkar took cudgels against Hinduism and embraced Buddhism, Jyothee Thass had appealed to the Dalits in Madras Presidency to enrol themselves as casteless Dravidians, not as the Hindus. He embraced Buddhism and propagated it among the Dalits. Rettamalain Srinvasan established Adi-Dravada Mahajana Sabha and started newspaper 'Paraiyan' to propagate his ideas. He led different movements asserting the rights of the Dalits to walk on the streets and drink water from common wells. He worked with Ambedkar in Round Table Conference and with his assistance established Madras Province Scheduled Caste Federation. As nominated member of Legislative Assembly he ensured passage of different bills that benefitted the depressed castes. The colonial government acknowledged his services to the untouchables and gave him different titles. M.C. Rajah, another Dalit leader, was Secretary of Adi-Dravida Mahajana Sabha. He was also a member of Justice Party and served as member of Legislative Assembly. He quit the Justice Party in 1923 over Party's treatment of Dalits. He worked with B.R. Ambedkar in different forums. However, on the issue of Communal Award, M.C. Rajah took a stand in favour of the joint electorates with reserved seats and expressed solidarity with Mahatma Gandhi.[4] He became the President of All India Depressed Castes Association and then became member of Imperial Legislative Assembly (Geetha & Rajadurai, 1998). The Dalit movement in today's Tamilandu takes inspiration from these pioneers.

Dalit Movement in Telugu Districts of Madras Presidency

The trajectory of Dalit movement in Telugu Districts was, however, different from that of the Tamil Dalits in Madras Presidency. Socio-economic development of Dalits in Telugu Districts was influenced to a considerable extent by religious, cultural and educational activities of the Christian Missionaries and the social reformers sympathetic to lower castes. The Dalits in Andhra region were benefitted by the colonial government initiatives to open up schools and administrative positions for the lower castes (Chinna Rao, 2015, pp. 115-119). First political initiative to organize the Dalits in the region came from Guduru Ramachandra Rao, a social reformer who organized First Provincial Panchama Conference in Vijayawada in 1917. At the instance of Bhagya Reddy who presided over the Conference, the word Panchama was replaced by Adi-Andhra and the conference was renamed as Andhra Desa Adi-Andhra Conference. The conference demanded removal of untouchability, better opportunities for education of the Dalits and political representation of the Dalits in Legislative Assembly. Responding to its demand, the British nominated three Dalit leaders from Telugu districts as members of Legislative Assembly in Madras Presidency. The Dalit leaders in Andhra took initiative to establish schools for their kids and started periodicals to rouse the consciousness of the Dalits. Realizing the need for unity of Dalit communities, Boyi Bheemanna coined the term "Ma-Malu", wherein the 'Ma' refers to Madigas and the 'Malu' refers to Malas, two important Dalit communities among the Telugus. [5]

Some Dalit activists like Sundru Venkaiah, Kusuma Dharmanna, B.S. Murthy, Buldas Swamy, etc., were attracted towards Ambedkar's thoughts. Inspired by Ambedkar, they started a unit of Scheduled Caste Federation. However, unlike in Hyderabad State, Ambedkar's influence on Dalits was nominal in Andhra region. Most Dalit leaders in Andhra region in Madras Presidency were attracted towards Congress Party or Communist of India (CPI). Boyi Bheemanna was a prominent Dalit figure in Congress Party. Harijan Sevak Sangh, initiated by Congress Party made attempts to convince the caste Hindus to allow the Dalits to draw water from community wells and enter the temples. The socialists and communists recruited Dalits in their peasant and Agricultural labour unions. Vundru Subba Rao and Konda Surya Prakash Rao, hailing from Dalit community, were elected as leaders of the agricultural workers (Chinna Rao, 2015, pp.120-125; Chinna Rao, 2016). Despite the hegemonic influence of the upper castes, most Dalits in Andhra districts of Madras Presidency supported and actively participated in the activities of in Congress and CPI.

Dalit Politics in Composite Andhra Pradesh (1956-1985)

Acceding to the popular demand for linguistic reorganization of the states in India, the state of Andhra Pradesh (AP) was formed in 1956 uniting the Telugu speaking districts of Madras Presidency and Hyderabad State. The emergence of a single composite state of Andhra Pradesh for all the Telugu speaking people brought a new trajectory in Dalit politics in the region. By the time, the Congress party had succeeded in overcoming the challenge of the communists and consolidated their political position both in Andhra and Telangana region. Republican Party unit started by Amebdkarites like Bali Vadapalli and B. Jagannatham failed to take off. Congress Party which formed the government used reservation policy, land reforms and land distribution to neutralize the discontent among the Dalit masses. It attracted the Dalit leaders in various organizations by offering them positions in the party and government. The constitutional safeguards allowed fixed number of SCs in every election. This apart the Congress leadership saw to it that every Ministry symbolically included certain number of Ministers from Dalit community. In 1960 Damodaram Sanjeeviah, a Dalit leader, became the Chief Minister of Andhra Pradesh. Although his rule continued only for about two years, the Congress Party claimed credit for making a Dalit the Chief Minister of the State. The provision of reservations in education and employment did help some educated Dalits to enter bureaucratic jobs, although it should be said that many reserved positions for SCs, especially at higher levels of bureaucracy, were never filled fully on the pretext that there were no SCs who fulfilled the necessary qualifications for the job. Implementation of land reforms benefitted the middle castes more than the Dalit castes. Land redistribution programs enabled some Dalits get one or two acres of land which was barely sufficient to sustain decent livelihood. There was simmering discontent among the Dalits in some rural areas, which led them to join Maoist movements. Many poor Dalits were active in *Ryotu Coolie Sanghams* (Association of Peasants and Agricultural Labourers) spearheaded by Naxal parties. Several Dalit leaders and artists like K.G. Satyamurthy, Gaddar, Vangapadu Prasad Rao, etc., were actively involved in Naxal movements in the state (Ratnam, 2008, pp.15-17). Rural unrest in the state as a whole was however to some extent neutralized by the then Prime Minister, Indira Gandhi's initiatives taken as part of her "*Garibi Hatao*" program. The Dalits became vote banks of the Congress Party. The Party could survive and retain power in the state in 1977 elections, when the rest of the country was swept by Janata Party wave. The Dalits then voted for the Congress Party. It was only in 1980s that there was shift in the Dalit support to the Congress Party.

New Momentum in Dalit Politics since 1980s

In 1983 the Congress Party was swept off from power by Telugu Desam Party (TDP), a party established by Telugu film icon, N.T. Rama Rao barely six months before the Assembly elections. It was in the elections, for first time, majority of the seats reserved for the SCs were won by a non-Congress party. The assassination of Mrs. Indira Gandhi in 1984 weakened the hold of Congress over the Scheduled Caste voters. However, TDP failed to retain the support of the Dalits and take advantage of the declining hegemony of Congress, because of the domination of the Kamma community in the party. TDP relied more on the Kammas and other upcoming rural castes, than on the Dalits and the tribals. Killing of Dalits in Padirikuppam (1983) and Karamchedu (1985) by upper caste people roused the Dalits against the TDP government and led to the birth of Dalit Mahasabha in 1985 under the leadership of left leaning Katti Padma Rao and Bojja Tharakam, who believed in fusing Marxism with the thoughts of Ambedkar (Ratnam, 1997; Jamanna & Sudhakar, 2016). During this period the state witnessed the publication of several Dalit periodicals, books and literature (Ratnam, 1997; Satyanarayana, 2000; Gundieda, 2009b; Kumar, 2011).

In Andhra Pradesh all left parties expressed their concerns over the plight of the Dalits and tribes in their political and cultural platforms. However, the parliamentarian left parties like CPI and CPI (M) lost the sympathy of the Dalits because of their truck with Telugu Desam Party. But different Maoist factions continued to enjoy grassroot support among the Dalit youth in rural areas. However, even the Maoist parties faced crisis, when some Dalit leaders and cadres associated with them began to feel discriminated within the parties. The perception that despite all their sacrifices, the Dalits were looked down upon and not allowed to take leadership positions made the leader of a stature of K.G. Satyamurthy leave the Peoples' War Group (PWG) and form *Samatha* Volunteer Force (SVF) to organize the Dalit youth against the upper caste atrocities (Srinivasulu, 2017; Gudavarthy, 2005). This was also the time, when at national level Bahujan Samaj Party (BSP) started emerging as a force. The victory of Mayawati in Uttar Pradesh inspired the Dalits all over the country with a new hope. In Andhra Pradesh the leaders associated with Dalit Mahasabha joined BSP. It then appeared for a while that autonomous Dalit movement has come of age, and is there to stay forever in the State (Srinivasulu, 1994).

Rifts in and Decline of Dalit Movement

The hopes of reviving autonomous Dalit movement were however belied with rifts appearing soon in the Dalit movement. BSP failed to take off in AP, as Bojja Tharakam left the party within a couple of years, accusing the BSP national leadership of opportunism and highhandedness (Mehta, 2015, 17). Katti Padma Rao also became inactive and later joined Praja Rajyam Party, started by Telugu actor, Chiranjeevi. Meanwhile, the Madigas began raise their voice against monopolization of the benefits of reservations by more advanced Mala community. Mala–Madiga rift has a long history dating back to 1920s when Arigay Ramaswamy denounced Bhagya Reddy Verma for his Mala bias and started Arundhateeya Mahasabha for promoting the welfare and development of the Madiga community (Rajesh, 2015, pp. 39-40; Muthaiah, 2004). The Madigas always complained that the Mala community always looked down upon the Madigas who occupied lower position in the hierarchy of Dalit castes and avoided treating them as equals. These old animosities and grievances came to the fore once again as the Madigas began to feel that all the advantages that the Constitution has given to the SCs in matters relating to politics, education and government jobs are monopolized by the Malas, leaving little for the Madigas. This growing awareness led to the formation of Madiga Reservations Porata Samithi (MRPS) under the leadership of Krishna Madiga (Gundimeda, 2009b). MRPS organized the Madigas and spearheaded the movement for sub-categorization of the reservation quota. The Malas who are the beneficiaries of Reservations opposed the demand of the Madigas and started their own organization named Mala Mahanadu (Jamanna & Sudhakar, 2016).

With the two major Dalit caste constellations fighting with each other over the issue of reservation quotas, the possibility of building a united front of all Dalits began to wane. The Mala-Madiga division was exploited by major political parties in the state. While TDP sided with the Madigas, Congress Party supported the Malas. With the court striking off the TDP government's move to sub-categorize the quota, the issue is still hanging (Nageshwar, 2016; Gundmeda, 2010). Apart from this Mala-Madiga rift, the rise of regional movement for separate Telangana divided the Dalit voices along regional lines. While some sections of the Dalits supported the formation of separate state of Telangana, some others felt that the Dalit cause would be served better in united Andhra Pradesh (Thirumali, 2013; Iialiah. 2013). In order to woo the support of the Dalits for Telangana movement, K. Chandrasekhar Rao (KCR), the leader of Telangana Rashtra Samithi (TRS) initially proclaimed that a Dalit would be the Chief Minister of Telangana. But once the demand for Telangana materialized in 2014, KCR forgot his promise and himself became the Chief Minister of Telangana. Much to the frustration of BSP, a couple of MLAs who won in Telangana with its support in the 2014 elections subsequently joined TRS and assumed ministerial positions in KCR ministry. After the TRS formed the government, the left leaning Dalit youth, artists and political activists who lent support the Telangana movement were either co-opted or were completely side lined. Like his counterpart Chandrababu Naidu in Andhra Pradesh, KCR expressed his helplessness over the Madiga demand for classification after the Supreme Court verdict and wrote to the central government to do the needful.

Towards Conclusion

Trajectory of Dalit movement in Andhra Pradesh, for that matter in India as a whole, shows a particular pattern. Autonomous Dalit movements took shape in the country during the colonial period accusing the nationalist / communist parties for being caste blind. Reluctance of the nationalist and communist leadership to address the issue of caste discrimination led B.R. Ambedkar to devise a different course for welfare and development of the Dalits. Instead of joining the nationalist and socialist movements, he chose to work with the British for getting legal and constitutional concessions for the depressed classes. His preoccupation with caste question and neglect of the issue of class, made him suspect all upper caste Hindus and drove him to seek salvation for the Dalits by demanding separate electorates and later advocating religious conversion (Shourie, 1997; Jaffrelot, 2016; Ranganayakamma, 2001). This pattern was replicated in the anti-Brahmin movements in South India also. Justice Party that came out strongly against the domination of the Brahmins in Madras Presidency and initiated reforms accommodating non-Brahmin upper castes in administration and politics did not join the freedom struggle. Justice Party, dominated by non-Brahmin upper caste landlords, zamindars and traders, remained loyal to the British Raj. In contrast, the Dravidar Kazhagam which started as a radical rationalist movement advocated the unity of all Shudra castes giving them a distinct identity as Dravidians. Fighting the Brahmin-Bania domination was so crucial to the leaders of Dravidar Kazhagam that they became sceptical of the nationalist movement and demanded secession from the Indian Union. Once the middle castes leading the movement grabbed positions of power in economy and politics, the movement neglected the Dalit castes down below, forcing Dalits to chart out their own path (Geetha & Rajadurai, 1998).

Similar developments were visible in Hyderabad State wherein Bhagya Reddy and his associates took up different programs for the welfare of the Dalit communities. These reformist leaders articulated the interests of the Dalits, but they never questioned or challenged the feudal rule of the Nizam. Unlike the Congress and the communist party who fought against the Nizam, the Dalit leaders like Bhagya Reddy Verma, Venkat Rao, etc., supported and relied on the Nizam to seek concessions for the Dalits. Like the British, the Nizam also found an opportunity for legitimizing his authority by offering awards to Dalit and other depressed caste leaders and initiating certain constitutional and economic concessions to co-opt them (Sreenivas 2010; Srinivas 2010). In this respect, the Dalit movement in Telugu districts of Madras Presidency was little different. The domination of Congress and communists prevented the growth of autonomous Dalit movement in these districts. Anti-Brahminical movements in Tamil dominant areas in Madras Presidency had little impact in Andhra region. The influence of Ambedkar was minimal. Most Dalit leaders worked through Congress and CPI. But these regional variations disappeared once Andhra State merged with Telangana region of Hyderabad State and formed the state of Andhra Pradesh in 1956.

The working of one-party dominant system[6] that was in vogue in the state till mid-1980s and the emergence of India as a welfare state brought in a new kind of political dynamics within the State, with educated Dalit leaders showing eagerness to associate themselves with the Congress Party and government. The urban SCs who benefitted from the policy of reservations became the vote bank of the ruling Congress (Pushpendra 2005, pp. 363-64). Contrarily, the poor Dalits in rural areas who were left untouched by development policies of the government supported the extreme left-wing parties (Ratnam, 2008, pp. 7-17; Srinivasulu, 2017). Although some Dalit leaders tried, autonomous movement of the Dalits could not take shape in Andhra Pradesh for first three decades. But the killing of Dalits during the Telugu Desam regime, decline of the hegemony of Congress, the rise of BSP at national level and frustration with left parties created necessary conditions for the revival of autonomous Dalit movement in mid 1980s and early 1990s. However, very soon the momentum fizzled out following the Mala-Madiga conflict over categorization of reservation quota, personality clashes between Dalit leaders, and growth of Telangana movement and the divisive politics of the dominant parties in the State.

Trajectory of Dalit politics in India in general and Andhra Pradesh in particular clearly points out certain weaknesses in Dalit movements that rely only on caste identities. The Dalit movements that emphasized more on reservations and ignored the importance of agrarian reforms have ended up as educated middle class movements seeking co-option within the system. Far from uniting the poor Dalits, their over emphasis on the caste differences led to the rise of competing identities from within the Dalit castes. The movement no doubt united the Dalits in their fight against the domination and exploitation of the upper castes. But the Dalits are not a homogenous community; one can see hierarchy of castes and sub-castes within the SCs. The Dalits who accuse upper castes often tend to forget that they themselves are victims of Brahminical ideology of purity and pollution, and in their own domain the Dalit castes who are better off, look down upon other Dalit castes and sub-castes placed below them, by invoking the ideas of purity and pollution and by practicing endogamy (Muthaiah, n.d.). As long as their fight against the upper caste domination goes hand in hand with democratization of the Dalits from within, the Dalit movement for annihilation of caste remains a dream. It is difficult to ensure the unity of all Dalit castes, as long as the feelings of superiority and inferiority exist among its members and the fruits of development are not shared equitably.

Further, it is observed that the governments and the ruling parties have enough power and resources to appease and corrupt the Dalit leaders and activists, and absorb their protests within their political fold. As stated, instead of confronting those in power, most movements seeking social justice for one or the other communities often rely on the governments to deliver justice to them. During the colonial period, in the name of seeking benefits for the depressed castes, Justice Party leaders and even Ambedkar avoided confrontation with the colonial government. Similarly, Dalit leaders of Hyderabad State such as Bhagya Reddy and B.S. Venkat Rao sought the help of the feudal government of the Nizams to seek justice for the Dalits. Today leaders like Krishna Madiga, fighting in the name of justice to the Madigas, are looking toward Chandrababu Naidu or KCR to help him in ensuring sub-categorization of the reservation quota. These instances indicate that there is every possibility that the movements for social justice end up as opportunities for the ruling elite to legitimize their authority by providing certain concessions to particular communities within the system.

As long as the Dalit movements remain exclusive, view all members of other castes as enemies; shy away from bonding with progressive elements in other castes, parties and movements and continue to patronize opportunist elements within the movement, there is always a possibility of Dalit movement becoming parochial and getting co-opted by the system. By posing themselves as peace makers and dispensers of social justice, the ruling parties and the governments intervene in the caste conflicts and perpetuate caste divisions among the masses. Consequently, the autonomous Dalit movements end up becoming pressure groups seeking petty concessions within the system, without any emancipatory agenda.

NOTES

1. In India caste system is not visible in north-eastern region inhabited by Mongoloid tribes.
2. During the colonial period, apart from the territories which were under the direct political control of the British, there were also several princely states in the subcontinent which accepted the suzerainty of the British, and was allowed to enjoy internal sovereignty. Whereas Madras Presidency was a province in British India, Hyderabad was a princely State ruled by the Nizams. Both were multi-lingual and multi-cultural states. Telugu speaking people were there in both territories.
3. Devadasi system is a practice among the lower castes where the young women were married to local deities and designated as servants of gods. Such women were sexually exploited by the men from upper castes.
4. B.R. Ambedkar's demand for separate electorate was opposed by Mahatma Gandhi, who believed that such a demand would divide the Indians and weaken the Indian nationalist movement. Opposing Ambedkar's demand, Gandhi went on fast and brought pressure on Ambedkar to give up the demand and accept instead reservations as means for development of the SCs. Subsequently, after India became independent, the Constitution of India provided provision for reservations for Scheduled Tribes and Scheduled Castes in education, jobs and in state assemblies and the parliament.
5. In Telugu the word, "Mamalu" means uncles. The slogan "Ma-Malu" is strategically used to unite the Malas and the Madigas, two major constellations of Dalit castes among the Telugus, indicating that they are related to each other by blood relations.
6. Although there were several political parties in the country, scholars like Rajni Kothari considered India as One-Party Dominant System, as Congress Party continued to dominate the politics in the first three decades after independence. See, Kothari, 1970/2015, pp. 158-227.

REFERENCES

Aloysius, G. (2010). *The brahminical inscribed in body-politic.* New Delhi: Critical Quest.

B.R. Ambedkar, B.R. (1936/ 2016). *Annihilation of caste.* Verso.

Balagopal, K. (2006, July 22). Maoist movement in Andhra Pradesh. *Economic and Political Weekly,*

41(29), 3183-3184.

Benbabaali, D. (2016). From the peasant armed struggle to the Telangana State: Changes and continuities in a south Indian region uprisings. *Contemporary South Asia*, 24(2), 184-196.

Blecha, V. (2012). *Political movements of dalits in South India: Dalit movement and affirmative action in the context of dravidian politics*. Retrieved from https://is.cuni.cz/webapps/zzp/download/140015373

Burchardt, T., & Gary C. (2008). Introduction. Craig, G., Burchardt, T., & Gordon, D., (Eds.)., *Social justice and public policy: Seeking fairness in diverse societies*. Bristol: Policy Press, University of Bristol.

Chaudhary, S. K. (2011, August 16). Sub-classification of dalits: Law and politics. Retrieved from www.countercurrents.org/chaudhary160811.htm

Chinna Rao, Y. (2015). History of dalit movement in Andhra Pradesh: History outline of a hundred years. *Indian Historical Review*, 42(1), 113-139.

Chinna Rao, Y. (2016). Caste and Class in late colonial Andhra: Dalit and communist mobilization. *Studies in People's History*, 3(1), 89-99.

Craig, G., Burchardt. T., & Gordon, D (Eds). (2008). *Social justice and public policy: Seeking fairness in diverse societies*, Policy Press, University of Bristol.

Desai, A.R. (Ed). 1979. *Peasants Struggles in India*. Bombay: Oxford University Press.

Dhanagare, D.N. (1974/1979). Social origin of the peasant insurrection in Telangana 1946-51. Desai, A.R. (Ed). Bombay: Oxford University Press.

Finn, J. L. & Jacobson, M. (2017, March 25). What is social Justice? Retrieved from https://blog.oup.com/2017/03/what-is-social-justice/

Geetha, V., & Rajadurai, S.V. (1998). Towards a non-brahmin millennium: From Jyothee Thass to Periyar, Calcutta: Samya.

Giddens, A. (1999). Six notes on social justice and the welfare state. Plant, R. (Ed). Bristol: Policy Press, University of Bristol.

Gudavarthy, A. (2005). Dalit and naxalite movements in AP: Solidarity or hegemony. *Economic and Political Weekly*. 40(51), 5410-5418.

Gundimeda, S. (2009a). Madiga dandora: A social movement for rationalization of dalit reservations. Retrieved from https://socialjusticeanddemocratization.wordpress.com/2009/12/29/madiga-dandora-a-social-movement-for-rationalization-of-dalit-reservations/

Gundimeda, S. (2009b). Madiga sahityam: Telugu sahitiphalakampaikotta daruvu, (Madiga literature: A new beat on Telugu literary drum), *Veekshanam*, 7(4, 5 & 6).

Gundimeda, S. (2010). Supreme court and categorization of scheduled castes list. Retrieved from https://socialjusticeanddemocratization.wordpress.com/2010/01/02/supreme-court-and-categorisation-of-scheduled-castes-list/

Ilaiah, K. (2013 September 28). *Pranteeya Fundamentalism* (Regional Fundmentalism). *Andhrajyothy*.

Iraqi, S. (2009). *Bhakti Movement in Medieval India: Social & Political Perspectives*. Delhi: Manohar Publishers and Distributors.

Jaffrelot, C. (2016, April 14). Ambedkar against nationalism. *The Indian Express*. Retrieved from http://indianexpress.com/article/opinion/columns/ambedkar-birth-anniversary-ambedkar-against-nationalism/

Jamanna, A., & Sudhakar, P. (2016). *Dalits struggle for social justice in Andhra Pradesh (1956-2008)*. New Castle upon Tyne: Cambridge Scholars Publishing.

Kothari, R. (1970/2005). Politics in India. New Delhi: Orient Longman.

Kumar, K. P. (2011, May 15). Voice of protest: A study of dalit song in Telugu. Retrieved from http://untouchablespring.blogspot.in/2011/05/voice-of-protest-study-of-dalit-song-in.html.

Mehta, V. (2015). Caste, urban spaces and the state: Dalits in Telangana. Policy Report No. 9. Hyderabad: The Hindu Centre for Politics and Public Policy. Retrieved from http://www.thehinducentre.com/multimedia/archive/02626/Policy_Report_No_9_2626189a.pdf

Muthaiah, P. (2004). Dandora: The madiga movement for equal identity and social justice in A.P. *Social Action.* 54 (2), 184-209.

Muthaiah, P. (n.d.). Sub-caste conflict and dalit movement in Andhra Pradesh. Retrieved from xa.yimg.com/kq/groups/13359347/1172507441/name/sub-caste

Nageshwar, K. (2016, July 20). Categorising SCs: To be or not to be. *Hans India.* Retrieved from http://www.thehansindia.com/posts/index/Editors-Desk/2016-07-20/Categorising-SCs-To-be-or-not-to-be/243352

O'Hanlon, R. (1985). *Caste, conflict and ideology: Mahatma Jotirao Phule and low caste protest in nineteenth century western India.* Cambridge: Cambridge University Press.

Omvedt, G. (2003). *Buddhism in India: Challenging Brahminism and Caste.* New Delhi: Sage India.

Omvedt, G. (2004). *Jotirao Phule & the ideology of social revolution in India.* New Delhi: New Delhi.

Patankar, B., & Omvedt, G. (2004). *The dalit liberation movement in colonial period.* New Delhi: Critical Quest.

Piachaud, D. (2008). Social justice and public policy: a social policy perspective. Craig, G., Burchardt. T., & Gordon, D (Eds). Bristol: Policy Press, University of Bristol.

Pushpendra. (2005). Dalit assertion through electoral politics. Shah, G.S. (Ed). Delhi: Permanent Black.

Rajesh, K. (2015). Dalit movement and left politics in Telangana (Unpublished Ph.D. Thesis). Osmania University, Hyderabad. Retrieved from http://shodhganga.inflibnet.ac.in:8080/jspui/bitstream/10603/176714/7/07_chapter_1.pdf

Ramaswamy, G. (2016, September 22). Bojja Tharakam, red star in a blue sky. *TheWire.* Retrieved from https://thewire.in/67493/bojja-tharakam-obituary/

Ranganayakamma. (2001). *For the solution of the caste question Buddha is enough, Ambedkar is not enough either, Marx is a must.* Hyderabad: Sweet Home Publications.

Ratnam, K.Y. (1997). The dalit movement in Andhra Pradesh: A study of political consciousness and identity (Unpublished Ph.D. Thesis). Jawaharlal Nehru University, New Delhi.

Ratnam, K.Y. (2008). The dalit movement and democratization in Andhra Pradesh. Working Paper No. 13. Washington DC: East-West Centre. Retrieved from https://www.files.ethz.ch/isn/95902/EWC_WP_13.pdf

Reddy, D.N. (1985). Karamchedu – A dialectic without development. *Economic and Political Weekly,* 20(37), 1546-49.

Rodrigues, V. (2008). *Dalit-bahujan discourse.* New Delhi: Critical Quest.

Satyanarayana, S.V. (Ed). (2000). *Dalitavada vivadalu.* Hyderabad: Vishaalandhra Publishing House.

Shah, G.S. (Ed). (2005). *Caste and democratic politics in India.* Delhi: Permanent Black

Shastri. (2016). Telangana history aborigin downtrodden (adi-dalit) movements in Telangana. Retrieved from http://www.recruitmenttopper.com/telangana-history-aborigin-downtrodden-adi-dalit-movements-in-telangana/4186/

Shourie, A. (1997). Worshipping false gods: Ambedkar and the facts which have been erased. New Delhi: ASA Publishers.

Sreenivas, J. (2010, November). Granted the Nizam's despotism: What about ARASAM's. *Anweshi*, 1(1).

Srinivas, A. (2010, November). The attempt to dilute facts. *Anweshi*, 1(1).

Srinivasulu, K. (1994, October 1). BSP and caste politics. *Economic and Political Weekly*, 29(40), 2583-86.

Srinivasulu, K. (2002). Caste, class and social articulation in Andhra Pradesh: Mapping differential regional trajectories. Working Paper 179. London: Overseas Development Institute, London. Retrieved from https://www.odi.org/sites/odi.org.uk/files/odi-assets/publications-opinion-files/2692.pdf

Srinivasulu, K. (2017). Caste question in the naxalite movement. *Economic and Political Weekly*, 52(21), 48-52.

Stalin, K. (Director) (2007). *India untouched* (Documentary on caste discrimination in India). Drishti. Retrieved from https://www.youtube.com/watch?v=iz_ehD92C-s

Teltumbde.A. (2017). *Dalits: Past, present and future*. New York: Routledge.

Thirumali, I. (2013). *Telangana-Andhra: Castes, Regions and Politics in Andhra Pradesh*. New Delhi: Aakar Publications.

T.M.D. (1960). *Life of the Spirit (1946-1964)*. 15(170/171), 70-75.

Walker, R. (Ed). (1999). *Ending child poverty: Popular welfare for the 20th century*. Bristol: Policy Press, University of Bristol.

Witcher, S. (2013). *Inclusive equality: A vision for social justice*. Bristol: Policy Press, University of Bristol.

9

Social Justice and Women Empowerment through Reservation in PRIs: SCs in Uttar Pradesh

Sangita Yadav

ABSTRACT

The 73rd Amendment of the Constitution of India is a step forward that provided the space for those who were excluded for centuries from all social, cultural, economic and political processes due to their vulnerable identity in Indian society. They got an opportunity to participate in grass-root level political processes by the government ensuring them accessibility to the decision-making through constitutional commitment to decentralization of power. It is relevant in the case of marginalised women, especially from the Scheduled Castes, who are 'the most oppressed bottom'. This amendment is an important move in the political arena as it provides 33 percent reservation in PRIs to women at all levels of the Panchayat system conceived as the real notion of social justice. But this brief study of Uttar Pradesh proves that unless reservations are accompanied by voting rights, literacy and change in their status in society and family, women would remain mere namesake representatives of their male counterparts and will still not be given justice in decision-making.

This paper will question the idea of social justice and women empowerment, especially in the context of SC women. It includes three major aspects. The first deals with the concept of Panchayti Raj Institutions in general and Uttar Pradesh in particular. The second deals with the idea of social justice and decentralisation of power in the context of both the icons, Ambedkar and Gandhi, respectively. The third deals with SC women's participation in Panchayati Raj in Uttar Pradesh.

Key Words: social justice, empowerment, SC women, reservation, Panchayati Raj Institutions

Introduction

The 73rd Constitutional Amendment Act, 1992 that provides one-third reservation to women in the *Panchayati Raj* system has supported them to engage in the process of decision-making and participate in discussions in the public sphere.[1] But still, their presence at society and family levels are not very noteworthy; they are fighting unjust tyrannical forces and are restricted by the typical biased attitude of society which is controlled by patriarchy.

The Uttar Pradesh Panchayat Raj Act was passed in 1947.[2] It was the first state to introduce panchayat legislation. After India's independence, the Act has been amended repeatedly. In accordance with the provisions of the 73rd Constitutional Amendment Act, the Uttar Pradesh Panchayat Act, 1994, was passed.[3] This step was considered a significant milestone in Indian history. With this step, one-third reservation has been given to women at every level of the panchayat system.

Uttar Pradesh is a large state with a huge population. The total population is 199,812,341 as per Census 2011. There are 79.73 percent Hindus and 19.26 percent Muslims.[4] The Scheduled Castes constitute nearly 22 percent of the total population. Among them, approximately are SC women.[5] They are the most neglected, discriminated and marginalized section of Indian society. They play a very crucial role at the household level as wife and mother and participate equally in economic activities with their male counterparts. Yet, they are excluded when it comes to political participation or decision-making. They have been kept away from the political sphere for centuries even after independence.

History of the Panchayat System

The Panchayat system is an age-old institution that played a very crucial role in public life from ancient times. It has always been a basic entity of administration in Indian villages. In ancient times, there were four forms of village councils, namely, *Samiti, Sabha, Gana* and *Vidhata.* Women were acknowledged to be present in two councils only; *Sabha* and *Vidhata*; in the others they were not allowed. Chanakya's *Arthashastra* also mentioned that villages were the basic units of administration at that time.[6]

During the period of Buddha too, the panchayat system was important. The traditional panchayat system and effective attendance of common folk in the decision-making practice by voting, discussion and dialogue were continued. The kinship system became hereditary then. But most decisions of the day-to-day life of the people with regard to administration were taken through village assemblies. The judgments or decisions appropriated by the village councils were also appreciated by the king. Here, it is important to note that decentralization of power was not from top to bottom but it was from the bottom upwards, where the actual power remained in the hands of the people and not with the king. The majority of the population was living in villages and therefore, the panchayat system was the symbol of popular sovereignty. But, in the medieval period, the panchayat system withered under the military authoritarianism of the Mughal empire. In the British era, it was eclipsed by the administration. Nonetheless, the British administrators were attentive about the relevance and importance of local-level politics. Therefore, Charles Metcalfe, the then interim governor-general of colonial India, in his renowned Minute of 1860, wrote "India's village communities are little republics, having nearly everything they want within themselves, and almost independent of any foreign relations."[7] But soon, during the British rule itself, the panchayat system began to lose its sovereignty in the villages.

After independence, the government showed efforts to endorse the formation of village panchayats to build them as potent entities of regional politics. Article 40 of the Indian Constitution stated: "The state shall take steps to organise village *panchayats* and endow them with such powers and authority as may be necessary to enable them to function as units of self-government."[8]

Gandhi and Ambedkar on Decentralization of Power

Gandhi had dealt with the long and varied experiences of the state system during his stay in Asia, Europe and Africa. He witnessed the harsh cruelty of the state in his own life and in the lives of the people as well. He was not happy with the state's way of dealing with situations of the people. In his book 'Hind Swaraj' he envisioned a different system. This was a kind of village-regulated way of life and administration that Gandhi named 'Inner Swaraj.'[9] He perceived that if we have to increase 'Inner Swaraj' then it was necessary to minimise Outer Swaraj (state). He was always in favour of the minimal role of the State to ensure people's liberty but he was never against the importance of the state or Outer Swaraj. It will save the primary notion of democracy by equipping proper space to Inner Swaraj or local governance or panchayats.

He forms an image of a model village that would be self-sufficient and self-reliant in its essence. According to him, freedom necessarily commences at the bottom and Indian villages would be republics with adequate powers. Thus eventually it will be a single unit. It necessarily will be highly cultured. It will be based on truth and non-violence.

But Ambedkar was against the idea of Gandhi because he was aware of the problems of villages through his own sufferings of being a dalit. According to Ambedkar, villages were cesspools of cruelty, communalism and caste prejudice. No human rights would be protected if left to predominant groups that had denied minorities for a long time in the most brutal form. While participating in the general discussion on the reconsidered draft of the Constitution in the Constituent Assembly in 1948, Ambedkar, the chairman of the Drafting Committee, did not conceal his virulent scorn for the traditional system of village and administration when he stated, "A population which is hidebound by caste; a population which is infected by ancient prejudices; a population which flouts equality of status and is dominated by notion of gradations in life; a population which thinks that some are high and some are low; can it be expected to have the right notion even to discharge bare justice? Sir, I deny that proposition, and I submit that it is not the way to expect us to submit our life, and our liberty, and our property to the hands of these panchas."[10] He was very much justified when he expressed his views on the caste system in his famous work 'Annihilation of Caste.'[11] This was the work that led to exchange of thoughts between Gandhi and Ambedkar in the 1930s.[12]

Ambedkar's observation about decentralization of power continues to be true seven decades later even though there have been numerous constitutional safeguards, laws and political speeches. In Punjab, Haryana and western U.P., village assemblies known as *khap panchayats* behave like actual courts and negotiate on all kinds of family and village conflicts from matrimony and murder to land and cattle. While addressing such disputes, they break all human rights or legal provisions. Their decisions include restrictions on women from wearing Western clothes, using mobile phones and supporting child marriage and sanctioning the lynching of couples in the name of so-called 'honour killings'." This is not only in the northern states of India but also common in other Indian states.

Ambedkar was against Gandhi's idea of village life and morals. He considered the idea of a village republic undemocratic which violated the basic human rights given by the Constitution of India to every citizen. How relevant are Ambedkar's observations today? Perhaps, they are as relevant as they were in the 1940s. Even now, 68.84 percent of India's population lives in the villages.[13] In 2000, about two-thirds of rural dalits were landless and close to half depended solely on farm labour for their livelihood.[14]

Gandhi's idea of a village was empirically mistaken and politically unviable. Even when he recognised untouchability as a 'problem' and sincerely worked for its eradication, he did not want the caste system to go away because, for him, it was merely a moral system. However, as Ambedkar had relentlessly argued for those lower down in the caste hierarchy, it had always been a source of humiliation, violence and deprivation.[15] As argued by Jodhka, Indian villages have always been unequal, materially, socially and politically and continue to be so even today. Though Gandhi never recognized this fact, and even when he did, he attributed it to a kind of moral corruption which, for him, was a symptom of colonial enslavement.[16]

SC Women in India

India, popularly known as a country of diversity has its own pros and cons. On one hand, it is the home of people from diverse religions and ethnicity but at the same time society is divided in a very exploitative system of caste and gender discrimination. The status of women is not equal in society and people from the most oppressed community, i.e., Scheduled Castes, are treated badly. Women from the SC community are the most exploited group in society and face both caste and gender based discrimination; hence, they are oppressed among the oppressed. They are victims of multiple exploitation—religious, social, economic and cultural—as well. SC women experience patriarchal domination of a more severe form than that of non-SC women. Even after seven decades of Independence and Constitutional provisions, women from the SC community cannot dress like other Hindu women nor could they wear jewellery of their choice. They were exploited sexually by upper caste men and as domestic hands by upper caste women. This way, they are doubly exploited by the men and women of the upper castes. Dr. Ambedkar also mentioned it very clearly in his article titled 'The rise and fall of Hindu woman' that the root cause of the poor status of women in India is the Hindu religious books. Works like the Manusmriti divide individuals into a graded caste framework. According to it, women are not given the right to education, independence or wealth.[17]

In Indian society, SC women carry an overlying identity of caste, class and gender. Owing to poverty, they have to engage in menial work to earn a livelihood from a very early age. Due to the caste framework, they are denied access to education, public places like markets, temples, wells, etc., and forced to live on the fringes of the village. Being SC women, they have always been in fear of abuse and violence and this fear erodes their self-confidence and dignity.

Social Justice

Social justice is a very broad term and cannot be defined in a single sense. Social justice has a multidimensional significance. Social justice, in reality, is the core of the wide thought of justice. It is predominantly concerned about the development of a just and reasonable society, parallel circulation of commodities and assets to all sections of society, equal opportunities to all, etc. The term 'justice' embraces three different forms; social, economic and political. Social justice ensures proportionate treatment to all individuals without any kind of social discrimination based on religion, caste, class, gender, colour or race. There are various intellectuals and scholars who considered the thought of justice in various ways. Plato suggests justice as a 'deserved treatment' particularly awarding all citizens their due. Robert Nozick defines it as a 'historical entitlement' like an imperative component of distributive fairness where people know about their wrongs and get them redressed through remuneration. John Rawls defines justice as fairness. For David Miller, it is the sharing nature of equity.[18]

Empowerment of SC Women through Reservations in PRI

Women empowerment involves various factors that include opportunities to exercise their economic and political rights at the household and community levels. The principle objective is to challenge the man-centric idea of society, exchange the structures and establishments that encourage gender discrimination and social imbalance and empower poor people and women by access and control of both material and instructive assets.[19] As defined in the Jakarta Declaration, "Empowerment of women is not only an equity consideration; it is also a necessary pre-condition for sustainable social and economic development, involvement of women in the political arena and in the decision-making process."[20]

Empowering women belonging to the most oppressed community (Scheduled Castes) of Indian society is the biggest challenge. The Gram Panchayat, which is the smallest unit of governance in Indian democracy, was thought to be the most important unit for the empowerment of SC women to exercise their political rights. Hence, the panchayati raj system provided a platform for them. The 73rd Amendment to the Constitution and the provision of inclusion under Article 243 can be seen as one of the milestones of state initiative to provide political opportunity to women from rural areas. It had shown a change in the approach towards women's motivation. Earlier women were, by and large, seen as an object of development only. Nonetheless, the amendment has given women the right to exercise their decision-making power at the community level. Due to reservation of seats in PRI, participation of women in general and SC women in particular in local politics has increased considerably.[21] However, there are examples that show that its achievement and progress is limited in the genuine political participation and empowerment of women. In 1995, a workshop of elected women panchayat individuals from many states made a humiliating disclosure that most women were overwhelmed by their male family members. The decisions taken by women representatives were the decisions of the males. Elected women representatives hardly exercise their power in the decision-making process due to the dominance of their male counterparts.

In Uttar Pradesh, it is challenging for SC women to work as PRI representatives at every level of the Gram Sabha. In Indian society, SC women have to face dual challenges of both caste and patriarchy. Sudha Pai's work on three villages of Meerut district of Uttar Pradesh proposes that the provision of reservation has been unsuccessful in creating the expected outcome. The investigation uncovers those women *pradhans* who are just for 'name'. The women also said that they had contested for the panchayat election not by choice but rather because of family pressure and that of their community. When asked questions related to the gram sabha they said they did not have any idea and asked their male counterparts. This prompted the ascent of the idea of '*panchayat pati.*'[22]

The same was observed during fieldwork in Bishunpur Gram Panchayat of Balrampur District, Uttar Pradesh. The present *pradhan* is a female. She is literate but when one asked the name of the *pradhan*, people from the community said it was a male. However, the actual name of the *gram pradhan* is X. Y is her nephew and working as a clerk in ITI college near the village. The lady *pradhan* X lives in Balrampur city with her husband who is a government employee in a hospital. When the researcher went to her house to interview her, *gram pradhan* X and her nephew were present. The irony here is that the post of the *gram pradhan* is held by the lady X whereas all important decisions are taken by male member, Y. The lady does not know anything about the ongoing works; she comes only to sign[23] papers.

Another instance relates to A belonging to the SC category who is the *gram pradhan* of Pachhiyana Chhetra Panchayat, Faizabad district of Uttar Pradesh. She is an illiterate housewife. In the last *panchayat* elections of 2015, she stood for the post of *gram pradhan* and was elected because the seat was reserved for an SC woman. Her husband had already been the *pradhan* in the panchayat elections of 2005. He is completely influenced by the previous *pradhan* who is a Verma by caste and had been *pradhan* for two terms. The area is OBC-dominant and *Kurmis* (Verma) are in a majority. Therefore, they have always been dominant in local politics and play the role of king-maker when seats are reserved for SC males or females. Subsequently, they influence the decision-making.[24]

The above examples show that caste discrimination and patriarchy in society is prevalent to such an extent that the provision for reservation proves insufficient for women (SC and Non-SC) empowerment and social justice. These shortcomings were exacerbated by the way many of the lady *pradhans* owed their positions to their male members or other influential people. In order to genuinely fulfil the provisions of the reserved seat, political specialists need to convey different procedures to persuade women and one of them is to influence women through their relatives. Subsequently, women politicians are 'leaders through' their spouses or some other male members. In this way, they might be named latent spectators who are not able to actually take up *panchayat* leadership and decisions. This phenomenon is considerably clearer in the case of women having a place with SC identity.

Despite all the above limitations, the Panchayati Raj system has made a significant contribution in strengthening the *gram sabha* and local politics. Through the implementation of PRIs, people got a positive voice in local-level politics. Hence, the village *panchayat* framework had taken the democratic spirit to local-level politics by raising the level of the credibility of women from all groups.

Conclusion

Women constitute half the country's population; however, their voices have always been ignored due to the patriarchal nature of society. Due to long periods of exploitation and oppression based on caste and gender, the status of women is not satisfactory. They have limited opportunities to exercise their decision-making power, both at the household and community levels. The provision of reservation for women in PRIs has definitely encouraged them to participate and lead at every level of decision-making. But they are not participating freely in the decision-making process. There are many examples where women are working as proxies for their husbands or any other male of the family. These examples show the real character of Indian society which is completely patriarchal in nature and restricts women from exercising their political power. The age-old problem of patriarchy and caste discrimination cannot be changed in just one-and-a-half decades; however, the reservation for women in PRIs has led to a new beginning for them in grass-root level politics and has shown a significant impact on women's participation in the panchayats. The objective of women empowerment, especially for SC women through reservation in PRIs is not a disappointment. But a change is needed and an effort should be made to accomplish the higher objective to achieve the planned goals. To achieve this and make society free from discrimination based on caste and gender issues, the provision of reservation for women has to take a milestone initiative to get social justice in the long run.

NOTES

1. S.K. Pradhan and G. Dutta, Empowerment of Women in India through Panchayati Raj System, 2008, *The Indian Journal of Social Work*, p. 559.
2. B.S. Baviskar and G.Mathew, *Inclusion and Exclusion in Local Governance*, 2009, Sage Publications, p. 355.
3. Ibid.
4. Census, 2011, GOI.
5. Ibid.
6. R.C. Pradhan and Siby K. Joseph, Panchayat Raj and Gandhis Vision of Village Governance, 2013, http://siby.iecit.in/wp-content/uploads/2014/09/Dia_Oct-013.pdf, DIALOGUE, Volume-15 No. 2. p. 56.
7. http://www.sociologyguide.com/rural-sociology/village-community-in-india.php
8. The Constitution of India, Government of India, Ministry of Law and Justice, 2015, New Delhi, http://lawmin.nic.in/olwing/ coi/coi-english/coi-4March2016.pdf, p. 22.
9. Gandhi's inner swaraj means traditional system of governing villages like Panchayats and Outer Swaraj means state system of ruling people. In current scenario central and state government can be count under Outer Swaraj.
10. S.A. Aiyer, "Ambedkar vs Gandhi: The risks of village empowerment", Times of India, 9 Feb 2014, http:/blogs.timesofindia.indiatimes.com/Swaminomics/ambedkar-vs-gandhi-the-risks-of-village-empowerment/
11. B.R. Ambedkar, Annihilation of Caste, http://ccnmtl.columbia.edu/ projects/mmt/ambedkar/web/readings/ aoc_print_ 2004.pdf
12. Ambedkar was against the caste system but Gandhi had complete faith in the caste system. Gandhi had believed that caste system is the base of Hindu religion which is natural and also necessary. According to him untouchability is not the part of caste system, therefore, it is the

stigma on the forehead of caste system. He was against of abolition of the caste system but Ambedkar was against the idea of Gandhi and wanted to abolish it as it was the main cause of untouchability.

13. Census, 2011, GOI.
14. S.Waghmore, "Shaking up our village culture", *The Hindu*, 18 March 2015.
15. S.S. Jodhka,"Who will speak for the village?", *The Tribune*, 9 June 2015, http://www.tribune india.com/news/comment/who-will-speak-for-the-village/91267.html
16. Ibid
17. B.R. Ambedkar, The Rise and fall of Hindu Woman, 1980, Bheem Patrika Publications, Jullundur, pp. 17-19.
18. S.K. Darokar, "Social Justice and Social Development of Scheduled Caste and Scheduled Tribes in Maharashtra" 2014, Indian Journal of Dalit and Tribal Studies and Action, pp. 1-23.
19. M.P. Borain, Empowerment of Rural Women: Towards Reversal of Gender Relations', 2003, The Indian Journal of Social Work, p. 521.
20. Kuldeep Fadia, Women's empowerment through political participation India, 2014, Indian Journal Political Administration, Vol. LX, No. 3, pp. 537-548.
21. P. Datta, Women in Panchayats, Kurukshetra, 2001, p. 30.
22. P. Datta, Women in Panchayats, 2001, Kurukshetra, p. 32.
23. Information collected by researcher herself during her fieldwork in sep-oct, 2017.
24. Information collected by researcher herself.

REFERENCES

Aiyer, S. A. "Ambedkar vs Gandhi: The risks of village empowerment," *Times of India*, 9 Feb 2014, http:/blogs.timesofindia.indiatimes.com/Swaminomics/ambedkar-vs-gandhi-the-risks-of-village-empowerment.

Awasthy, S. S. Indian Government and Politics, New Delhi, 2006, Har-Anand Publications Pvt. Ltd.

Borain, M. P. 'Empowerment of Rural Women: Towards Reversal of Gender Relations', 2003, *The Indian Journal of Social Work*, Mumbai: Tata Institute of Social Sciences, 64(4), 521–32.

Census 2011. Government of India.

Darokar, S. K. 'Social Justice and Social Development of Scheduled Caste and Scheduled Tribes in Maharashtra,' *Indian Journal of Dalit and Tribal Studies and Action*, 2014, Vol. 2, Issue 1, No.1, pp. 1-23.

Datta, P. 'Women in Panchayats', 2001, *Kurukshetra*, 50(2), 30–33.

Fadia, K. 'Women's empowerment through political participation India', 2014, *Indian Journal of Political Administration*, Vol. LX, No. 3, pp. 537-548.

Hashemi, S., Schuler, S. R. and Riley, A. P. 'Rural Credit programs and women's empowerment in Bangladesh', 1996, *World Development*, Vol. 24(4), pp. 635-53. http://www.sociologyguide.com/rural-sociology/village-community-in-india.php

Jodhka, S. S. "Who will speak for the village?" *The Tribune*, 9 June 2015, http://www.tribuneindia.com/news/comment/who-will-speak-for-thevillage/91267.html

Lal, S. K. "A Study of Issues and Challenges in Empowerment of Women through Their Participation in the Panchayati Raj Institutions: A Case Study of Allahabad District of Uttar Pradesh", http://www. isical. ac. in/ wemp/ Papers/ PaperShivaLalRevised.doc and http://www. un. Org/ womenwatch

Mahanta, U. and Sinha, S. "The Political Empowerment of Women through Panchayati Raj Institutions: A Critical Assessment of India's Experiment with Affirmative Action", 2007, Paper presented at the Third International Congress of the Asian Political and International Studies Association (APISA), New Delhi.

Marx, Karl. "The British Rule in India" 1853, originally appeared in the New York *Daily Tribune*, See http://www.marxists.org/ archive/marx/works/1853/06/25.htm

Pai, S. 'Pradhanis in New Panchayats: Field Notes from Meerut District', 1998, *Economic and Political Weekly*, pp. 1009-1010.

Panda, K. K., 'Women in India: A Study of the Process of Empowerment', *Mainstream*, 2007, 45(12), 8-10.

Pradhan, R. C. & Joseph, Siby K. 'Panchayat Raj and Gandhi's Vision of Village Governance', http://siby.iecit.in/wp-content/uploads/2014/09/Dia_Oct-013.pdf, 2013, *Dialogue*, Vol. 5, No. 2.

Pradhan, S. K. & Dutta, G. 'Empowerment of Women in India through Panchayati Raj System', *The Indian Journal of Social Work*, 2008, Vol. 69, Issue 4, pp, 559-577.

Rajan, M. C. 'In Tamil Nadu, after caste violence Cupid enters political discourse,' *India Today*, 20 Nov 2012. http://indiatoday.intoday.in

Saini, G. S. & Singh, M. 'Panchayati Raj: A Micro View,' *Kurukshetra*, 2001, 49(6), 28–29.

Satapathy, S. 'Women's Empowerment and Panchayati Raj: A Case Study from Orissa (India), Bangalore: Research Project, 2002 ISEC.

Singh, I. & Kumari, U. 'Rural Development and Women Empowerment,' *Kurukshetra*, pp. 3-4.

Singh, I. & Usha Kumari. 2007, 'Rural Development and Women Empowerment,' *Kurukshetra*, 55(5), 3-8.

The Constitution of India, Government of India, Ministry of Law and Justice, 2015, New Delhi, http://lawmin.nic.in/olwing/coi/coi-english/coi-4March2016.pdf, p.22.

Waghmore, S. 'Shaking up our village culture,' *The Hindu*, 18 March 2015.

SECTION IV

Empowering the Dalits in North-East India

10

Issues and Challenges of Scheduled Caste Population in Nagaland: Select Case Studies from Kohima

Visakhonü Hibo and Visi Yhokha

ABSTRACT

Nagaland had witnessed heavy presence of scheduled caste population after it attained statehood in 1963. Their entry into Nagaland was mostly to earn through construction work as legal migrant workers. The tribal Nagas knew no caste system but racism did exist towards outsiders, irrespective of caste or creed. However; as a consequence of living and working together, many migrant workers blended with the local population. The presence of coolies, water carriers and petty shopkeepers was not uncommon in the 1970s and 1980s. The migrants became important customers for the local wine sellers and immorality was not an issue. There was no undue harassment or taxation as long as they possessed permits to enter Nagaland. The tribals did not feel felt threatened by the migrants believing them to be harmless in profession and character, especially prior to the factional killings of the Naga underground groups. The issues and challenges of SCs has changed drastically in the present Naga society. On one hand is unabated taxation and on the other hand are the illegal Bangladeshi immigrants (IBIs) who provide cheap labour for construction works. Therefore, the need to research on them has become pertinent today. Their fears, aspirations and instability vis-à-vis continuity need to be addressed. Suggestions and measures for policy makers for protection, cordial co-existence and systematization of legal permits is a matter of urgent deliberation in Nagaland. This paper will be limited to select case studies of Scheduled Caste Population confined to the capital, Kohima.

Key Words: scheduled castes, Angami coolies, water carriers, shopkeepers, Athis, deshwali

Introduction

Scheduled caste groups are basically migrants in Nagaland. Their socio-economic status varies as some are placed highly while the majority falls under the category of marginalized groups. The Government of India, through the Constitution, has conceptualized the Scheduled Caste groups following the principle of positive discrimination. However, in a Scheduled Tribe-dominated State such as Nagaland, negative discrimination is often attributed to such groups. The present paper will dwell on the issues and challenges faced by scheduled caste migrant workers in Kohima town. Naga society is in a state of transition towards an unfocused, unknown future fuelled by turbulent factional clashes among the national workers, in which the migrant workers bear the brunt of legal and illegal taxes among others. Multiple identity cards both from over-ground and underground organizations exact monetary taxes from them. The uncontrolled influx of illegal Bangladeshi immigrants (IBIs) with their offer of cheap labour poses a threat to the migrant workers. The increasing identity consciousness among the Naga tribes is alienating these groups. In spite of varied problems and difficulties, the population of the scheduled caste migrant workers is increasing in both the rural and urban areas of Nagaland as the indigenous inhabitants continue to mostly aspire for white-collar jobs. Other indicators in relation to this paper will be examined for an analytical study of the issues and challenges faced by migrant workers in a rural village while the scenario of being a scheduled caste in a tribal society will remain the overall backdrop. Intergenerational and intra-generational mobility vis-à-vis social discrimination will also be examined.

Nagaland is basically a tribal society. In the past, Nagas had little contact with the outside world and neither were outsiders keen to wander into Naga land as head-hunting was rampant. Head-hunting was not a brutal sport but a way of earning honour, prestige and prosperity for the little segmented democratic Naga villages. The question of scheduled castes in Nagaland or their presence was totally absent in the past until colonisation of the Nagas by the British. However, it may be noted that during British rule, many Nagas acted as porters and coolies for the white people but when the British left, the manual work was left for outsiders. The Nagas might have felt that they were inferior to the whites who were more able-bodied than them but superior to the migrant workers who strayed into their land for work. The feeling of subjective inferiority and superiority complexes might have made menial work unappealing for the Nagas who were also being fed with the ideas of freedom and sovereignty at that point of time. It was after Independence in India that scheduled castes, or *deshwalis*, as they are referred to by the locals, came and made their presence known as migrant workers in Nagaland towns like Dimapur and Kohima. Dimapur, the present business hub of Nagaland with the only airport and railway station was and continues to accommodate the bulk of scheduled caste migrant workers who are engaged in varied menial manual work. In Kohima, the capital of Nagaland, the scheduled castes were engaged in low-grade jobs such as water carriers, coolies, small street hawkers and vegetable vendors, particularly in the mid-Seventies. They live in cheap housing quarters located near wine shops and were habitually found drinking alongside local alcoholics after their daily job were completed; the locals drank from dawn to dusk. Their jovial adaptation to local languages and habit of immediate payment of their drinking bills were and are popular amongst *Angami* women local wine handlers known as *Athis*. These *Athis,* perhaps, gave a sense of belonging, acceptance, accommodation and maximum work to the scheduled caste migrant workers apart from their work as coolies and as manual labourers in the erstwhile Kohima Town Committee presently upgraded to Kohima Municipal Council. A unique feature of the migrant workers in is that they came alone and went back alone. There are no inter-marriages between them and the locals and neither do they bring their wives and families to Nagaland, excepting in some stray cases. Some striking aspects that made them reliable are their sense of morality, their honesty and maintaining constant rates for their services.

Over the years, Kohima town has witnessed a floating, fluctuating inflow and outflow of migrant scheduled caste workers in Nagaland. They floated back and forth between Nagaland and their native places according to the ferocity and peace phases of the Naga movement. After the formation of the state of Nagaland in 1963, the influx of such migrant workers increased. The demand for construction workers on building sites accelerated their inflow as the government was required to setup administrative infrastructures and meet the housing needs of its employees. But the issue of the infamous Shillong Accord of 1975 in Naga history ushered intense internal conflicts, confusion and fratricidal killings amongst the various Naga underground split groups. There were rampant broad daylight killings even in civilian-dominated areas and fear became a daily experience for all categories of people in Nagaland. The population of outsiders in Nagaland decreased to a large extent in the mid-Eighties except for a sizeable number of scheduled caste migrant workers who had established a sense of belonging in spite of the ongoing violent political conflict. The demand for them, especially those involved in masonry work, increased as salaried locals could afford to build concrete houses for themselves. The demand started in towns and trickled down to villages. Many builders became affluent and established close relationships with pioneer Naga leaders. Some of the conceptual ritualistic aspects and limited existential cases are presented for analytical reference.

The Scheduled Castes are those groups of people who have been discriminated against by the superior castes down the ages and were never socially accepted by the majority upper castes. The term 'Scheduled Caste' relates to those groups of people that were out of the caste system or the varna hierarchy in the past. They comprise the bulk of untouchables. D.N. Majumdar writes "the untouchable castes are those who suffer from various social and political disabilities, many of which are traditionally prescribed and socially enforced by the upper castes." In fact, he uses the term 'Scheduled Caste' mainly to refer to the 'Untouchable Castes'. However, it should be noted that all Scheduled Castes are not untouchables. The list of Scheduled Castes also includes some 'touchable' castes. They occupy the bottom-most rung of the social ladder and nowhere in India have they occupied the top position in the social, political and economic field. Caste has been an important element of the Hindu social order. In fact, even today, the Scheduled Castes constitute an integral part of Indian village life. They are spread over the entire nation rendering menial services to the upper castes. M.N. Srinivas in 'Social Change in Modern India' (1972) writes, "They perform certain essential tasks in agriculture, they are often village servants, messengers and sweepers, and they beat the drums at village festivals and remove the leaves on which people have dined at community dinners." Everywhere there are Brahmins, untouchables and peasant, artisan, trading and service castes. 'Rural Development: Scheduled Castes and Scheduled Tribes' (2005) by Khali Sahoo mentions that Scheduled Castes still suffer from unprecedented miseries not because they do not have the motivation to develop but because the ecology and culture are not yet conducive to the removal of poverty and ignorance as the caste system is deeply entrenched in the social structure as a whole. Questions of inclusion, exclusion and understanding the scheduled caste migrant workers in Nagaland are particular because questions of untouchability, ritual barriers and ideas of pollution and purity do not arise in it. Social inclusion is based more on existential dimensions. For better clarity, the cases of two scheduled castes *Thikadars* from Uttar Pradesh and other workers from mainland India are placed alongside illegal Bangladeshi immigrant (IBIs) workers for examining cases of inclusion, exclusion and implications vis-à-vis complications.

CASE I

A Scheduled Caste contractor or *Thikadar* known as Ramdhani from Uttar Pradesh worked hand in hand with prominent leaders like Vizol, who was a former chief minister of Nagaland and member of Parliament in the Rajya Sabha. Ramdhani also worked extensively for John Angami, an illiterate contractor during British times who funded and was part of the Naga delegation that went and met Mahatma Gandhi asking for complete sovereignty for the Nagas on 19 July 1947. Ramdhani constructed house after house for area leaders like Vizol and John Angami. It was due to his close proximity with high-ranking leaders and their children that all good residential houses of affluent persons, community houses and commercial complexes were assigned to him. The *Deshwali* factor with a negative connotation was ousted to a great extent as a result of Ramdhani who was hardworking, honest and humble, and thereby, accepted favourably. Ramdhani ate, drank and socialized in Nagaland without any prohibition or inhibition shadowed by his scheduled caste status. However, with increasing hostility and factional conflicts after the mid-Nineties, the population of the reliable scheduled caste migrant workers is dwindling. Their population is decreasing day by day due to rampant taxation, loss of value for life and influx of IBIs with their offer of cheap labour despite increasing potential for criminal acts. The IBIs came to Nagaland with their wives and children with no intention to leave. They were regular in their work and this kept their employers happy.

CASE II

Another prominent scheduled caste builder named Porban Chauhan came to Nagaland and worked as a labourer in 1980; he too was from Uttar Pradesh and had followed following his maternal uncle who was employed as a mason in the Public Works & Housing (PWD) department, Government of Nagaland after it attained Statehood. In 1985, Porban Chauhan shifted to southern Angami area at Kezocha as a carpenter under a *thikadar* from his native state. Back then, constructions were not multi-storeyed buildings but low-cost cottages built often with wood, thatch or tin sheets. The scheduled caste migrants were given shelter by a school master called Meziho from Kidima village. On gaining familiarity with the residents, Porban Chauhan soon became a *thikadar* himself in 1988. His raised status as a *thikadar* was initiated at the mission centre of Japfüphiki Baptist Church Council (JBCC) Kipfüzha, Kigwema, Kohima where a mission school was being set up. It was a half brick, half bamboo walled school with tin sheet roofing. But as the JBCC comprised 14 Baptist churches in southern Angami area, Porban Chauhan got frequent opportunities to meet church pastors, leaders and affluent persons in the area. Thus, by 1988, he was existentially established and won the confidence of the leaders. In 1996, Porban Chauhan got a major breakthrough in his career when JBCC decided to establish a secular under-graduate school at its mission centre instead of a school that it was previously managing. The setting up of Japfü Christian College was a real boon for him because as the college grew more and more concrete buildings were contracted to him. Porban Chauhan has four daughters and a son who was the youngest.

He earned a substantial amount of money as a *thikadar* but continued to live a very simple life which was necessitated due to the dowries that he had to pay for marriages of his four daughters. He took to drinking alcohol which has disadvantaged him and affected his health negatively at 57 years. His drinking sprees often land him in dire circumstances and he often gets beaten up by street miscreants. In spite of the problems that he creates for himself and also those arising out of the troubled Naga society, he preferred to still stay and earn his livelihood in Nagaland because he tends to save more money. He pre-supposes that if he worked in his native place in Uttar Pradesh, there will be so many social obligations arising out of deaths, marriages and festivals which are often expensive; therefore, it is more economical and logical to earn, live and save in Nagaland. Porban Chauhan continued to be a Hindu and wishes to remain faithful to his ancestral faith. On queries of sudden death, he said the Hindu Samaj at Chandmari, Kohima, can cremate his mortal remains in Nagaland itself.

As Porban Chauhan nears old age, labourers working under him often become insecure, particularly because of his addiction to alcohol. The insecurity felt by his labourers has affected him severely as many had left him for greener pastures. His loyalty, his expertise and his good relations with the locals have ensured a continuous work flow. Despite the influx of *Miyas* claiming to be residents of Assam with their offer of cheap labour, Porban Chauhan manages to survive as he can complete his works on time by sub-letting them. On the other hand, the *Miyas* are snatching the jobs of the scheduled caste migrant workers with offers of more manpower, cheaper rates and settled families which do not require long-distance travel like the scheduled caste migrant workers. However, the *Ramdhani* factor for Porban Chauhan has decreased immensely in the new millennium. He has insecurities, distrusts practically most people and local acceptance has lessened as the reliability factor has dipped below expectations.

CASE III

Porban Chauhan's workers are basically scheduled caste migrants but are dwindling in number. A study was made on those working under Porban Chauhan in order to examine their socio-economic status; the Christian converts vis-à-vis Hindus. The Christian converts were previously Hindus and belonged to the lowest caste. As Hindus from the lowest caste, they were subjected to the practice of untouchability and engaged in impure occupations. They were also prohibited from entering the village temple or draw water from public wells. They were restricted from approaching the wards inhabited by the 'clean' castes and prohibited from following any other occupation other than their own. In response to these challenges, they converted to Christianity. One of the workers, a father of two from Assam, ran a bakery ten years ago but discontinued because of a financial setback. After that he took up masonry work in and around Dimapur. He revealed that finding work had never been a problem in Nagaland which made him financially stable and enabled him to buy his own plot of land on which he resides. He said that in spite of their improved financial condition, the attitude of the upper caste Hindus never changed; not sparing even high-ranking officers belonging to the Scheduled Castes. They said untouchability in its visible and invisible forms continues to affect inter-personal and social relationships with upper castes Hindus. Another worker said that conversion to Christianity has made him give up alcohol which enabled him to find work more easily. Inequalities within the Christian community are least felt and this makes them more determined in their new-found religion. On the other hand, the lone Hindu working under Porban Chauhan felt that even in the present-day, the caste structure is making life difficult for him and his family. In Nagaland, the alienation that arises out of caste does not pose any problem, especially in relation to ideas of untouchability or the polluted. Festivals like Durga Puja are celebrated by all Hindus irrespective of caste differences which relaxes the ancient ritualistic caste strictures. Hardly anybody knows each other's original caste and it is not uncommon to claim lineage of upper castes in a tribal social setting. However, life in Nagaland is tough with the immense presence of multiple factions from the underground and over-ground taxations, both legal and illegal. Many of the scheduled caste migrant workers were sad owners of three-four different identitycards issued by different sources.

CASE IV

About 100 migrant workers were interviewed from Case I to IV using the survey method. However, a group of 11 scheduled castes from different fields of work was intensely quizzed and included exclusively as Case IV in order to study their aspirations, fears and contentment factors vis-à-vis suggestions. The 20 questions with the responses are presented in pie charts and bullet points for inclusion of all responses:

1. The respondents were mostly in the 21-30 and 41-50 age groups.

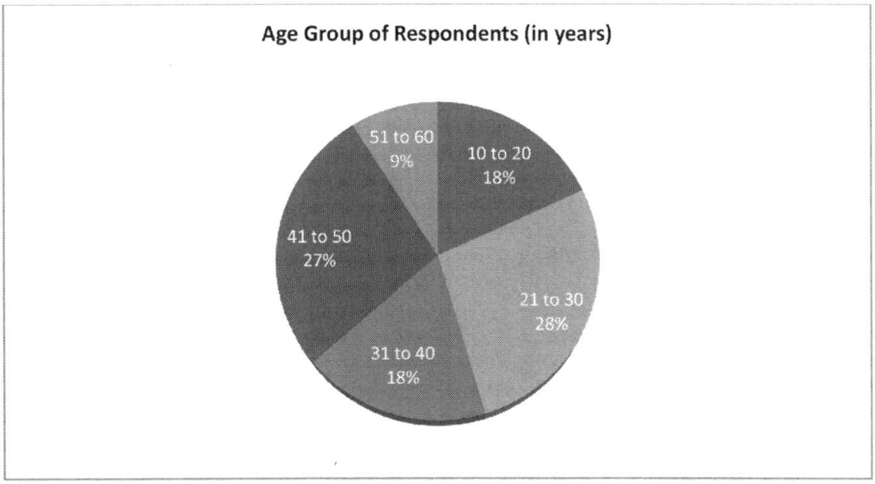

2. All the respondents, when about the purpose of their migration, answered that it was to find work and a means of livelihood.

3. On being asked why they chose to settle in Nagaland, these were the factors they cited:
   - Good climate/weather
   - Availability of clean water
   - Better environment
   - Presence of already-settled family/relatives
   - People here are good
   - Been in Nagaland since birth

4. The average period for which the 11 respondents had lived in Nagaland is 20 years. Some of them have settled in Nagaland for 33 years and some for as little as 6 years.

5. The majority of the respondents have migrated to Nagaland leaving their families in their village/hometown.

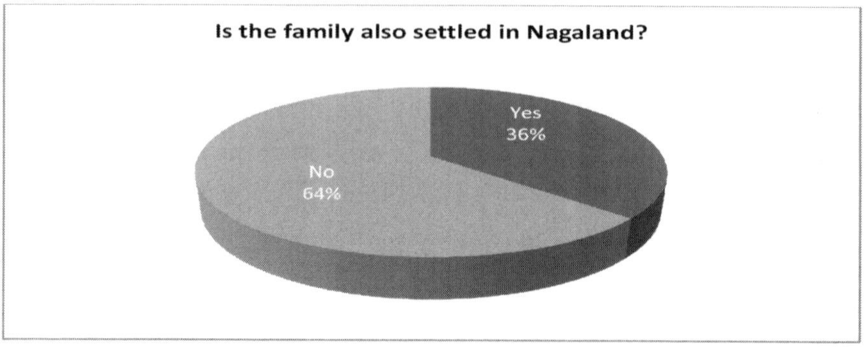

Some of the respondents answered that they had left their family back home. On being asked why, they cited the following reasons:

- Extra expenses when there are more people living with them
- Some family members had to stay back and look after their aged parents
- Some family members had to look after their property and also cultivate the fields in their villages

6. All the respondents, on being asked about their relationship with the locals, answered positively that they generally shared 'good' relationship with the local people of Nagaland.

· The positive reply may also be read as being courteous to the host for fear of being isolated /chided.

7. On being asked if they felt safe in Nagaland, the majority of the respondents had answered that they did.

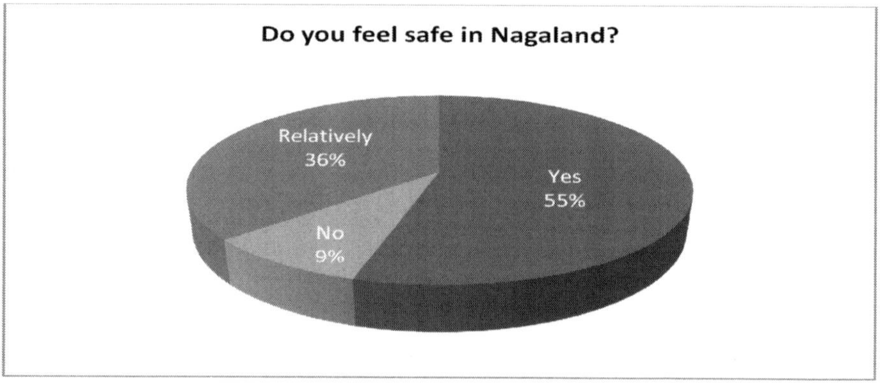

8. On being asked to identify their 'feeling of safety' on a scale of 1 to 10, the average was found to be 6, ranging from as high as 8 and 3 on the lower side.

   Some of the measures suggested by the respondents to improve their state of safety in Nagaland are as follows:

   - Better understanding between locals and non-locals
   - Changing public perspectives toward non-locals
   - Locals supporting non-locals when the latter are in need
   - Good house owner
   - Good landlord/tenant relations
   - Validity of legal permit to be extended
   - Fairer treatment from the police

9. On being asked if they faced any form of physical abuse while living in Nagaland, a majority responded negatively.

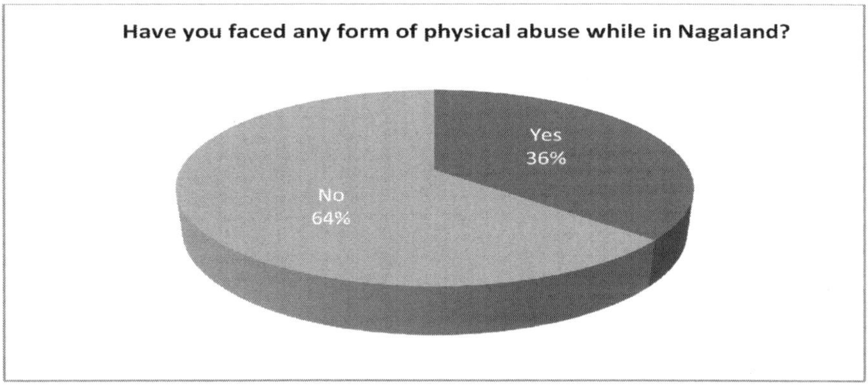

10. On being asked if they faced any form of verbal abuse while living in Nagaland, a majority responded that they did.

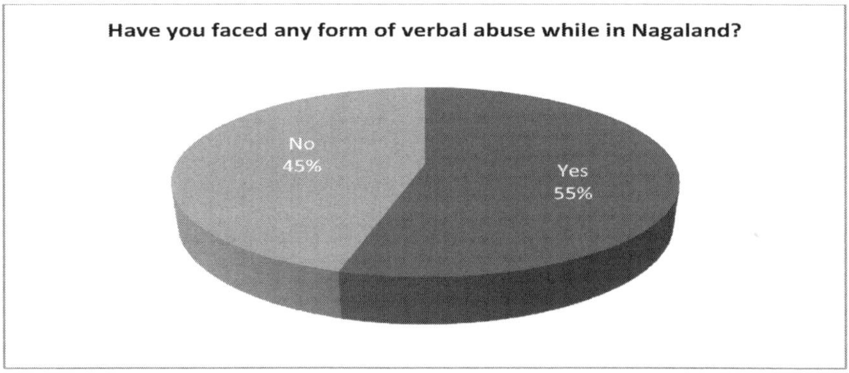

11. On being asked if they faced any form of casteism in Nagaland, all the respondents answered negatively.
    - Hints of racism rather than casteism prevail more in Nagaland but not to the point of intolerance.
12. More of the respondents were second-generation migrants to Nagaland.

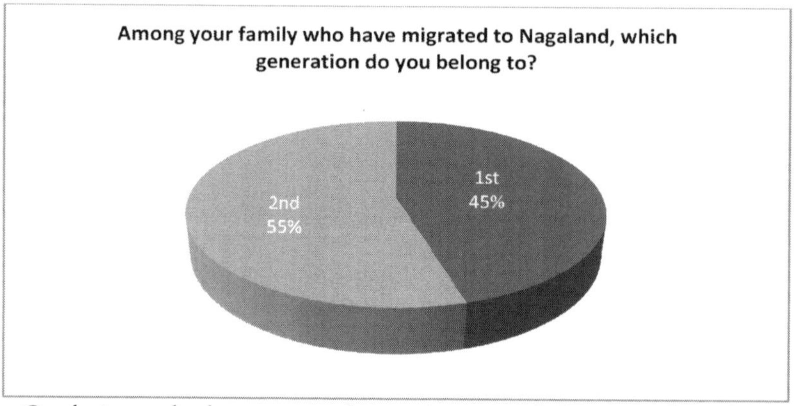

13. On being asked to name the underground factions that they have most commonly heard of, they included the following:
    - NSCN (I-M)
    - NSCN (K)
    - Federal
    - NSCN (U)
14. A majority of the respondents were also found to be paying taxes to each of the mentioned factions on an annual basis.

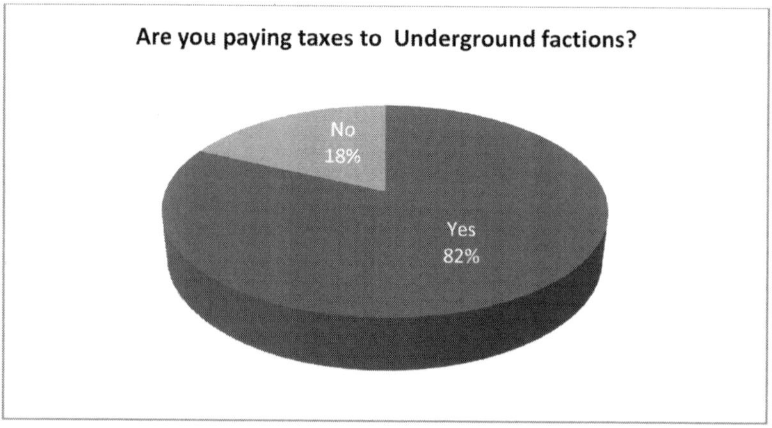

15. 10 out the 11 respondents stated that their average monthly income is around Rs. 10,000 or less.
16. 10 out of the 11 respondents also mentioned that their earnings in Nagaland is better than what would have been in their native village/town/city.
17. On being asked if they faced any problems while obtaining a legal permit in Nagaland, more than half answered that they did.

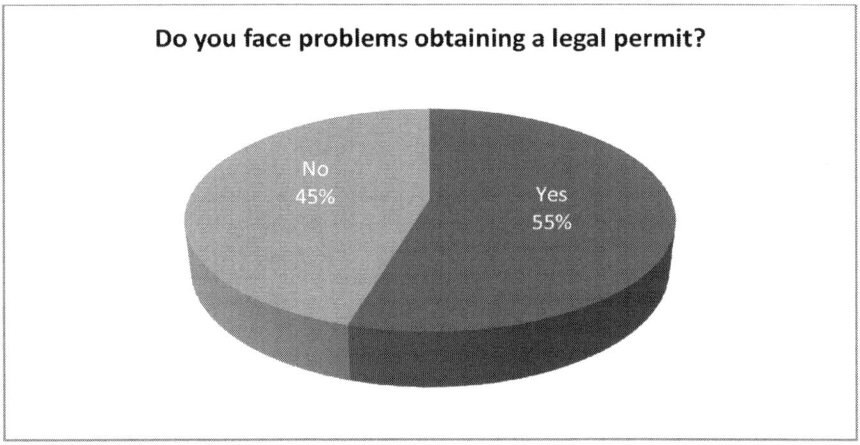

Some suggestive measures they cited in order that these issues relating to legal permits be addressed are:

- Office timings should improve
- Fair treatment from officials
- Pre information circulation when checking of permits is to take place
- Improve connectivity in offices
- Three months permit should be replaced with a card whose validity is for at least one year
- Legal permits for those born in Nagaland should not be made mandatory
- Local citizenship should be allowed for non-locals who have settled here for a long duration

18. On being asked if the respondents would send their children/relatives to study or work in Nagaland, a majority said they would.

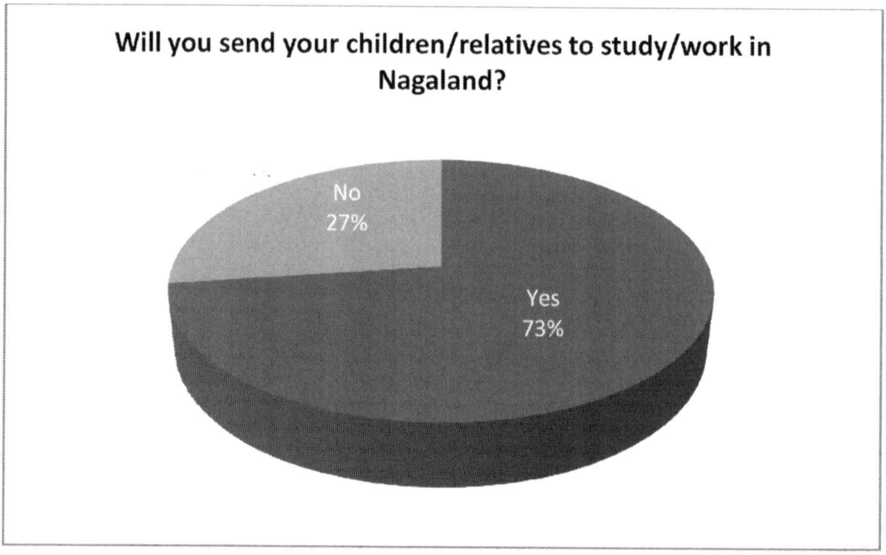

19. On being asked if their sacrifice of leaving their hometown and their family/relatives/friends was worth coming to Nagaland and finding a livelihood, they responded positively.
20. The respondents were asked to generally cite their aspirations/future plans in Nagaland:
    - To get their children educated while in Nagaland as they can learn English well
    - To ultimately leave Nagaland and settle in their hometown
    - To save money and gradually start a small business in Nagaland
    - To continue living in Nagaland
    - To continue working in Nagaland and sending back remittances to dependent members back in their hometown/village
    - To gradually bring the family to live with them in Nagaland
    - To continue working in Nagaland as long as their health permits

Conclusion

The issues and challenges faced by scheduled castes migrants in Nagaland are many. Yet, they are more readily accepted by the Naga people when compared with the illegal Bangladeshi immigrants (IBIs) as the former has no interest to settle permanently while the latter seeks to settle along with their respective families within it. Nagaland with its Article 371(A) and

Inner Line Permit (ILP) is theoretically becoming stricter but practically very porous as a result of rampant corruption at every corner. The land and, more particularly, the people are developing a complacent stance on menial work which is why Nagaland is turning into an employees' and employers' paradise just for the present generation as the future looks bleak. It is evident that the scheduled castes as migrant workers or *Deshwalis* were quite common in the 1970s and 1980s in Nagaland as street vendors, porters, water carriers and cleaners. In the 1990s and beyond, the shift towards massive multi-storied constructions have propelled many of the earlier scheduled caste workers to the status of *thikadars, dukan maliks* and other higher occupations as the locals favoured white collar jobs which got them higher earnings. The elevation of scheduled castes migrant workers to higher occupations is in sharp contrast to their assigned castes and, therefore is a clear indication of occupational mobility in the realm of caste studies. The scheduled caste migrant workers are also reluctant to reveal their true caste and claim a higher caste even when they respond to queries.

Social inclusion of scheduled caste *thikadars* have no barriers in Nagaland. They are invited to marriage celebrations, important festivals of the Nagas and other social gatherings. However, in the churches, their presence is almost totally absent because Christian converts, particularly from the scheduled castes from Uttar Pradesh and Bihar, are hardly seen except in the rarest of the rare cases. Christian converts of the scheduled castes from other states are seen more; they are currently daily wagers of affluent scheduled caste *thikadars.* The scheduled caste Christian converts are, however, excluded often from social gatherings of the host community, not on the basis of ritualistic barriers but on existential limitations in terms of relation-building or even of materialistic limitations that often bars social recognition. Nagas are a casteless but class defined society which is determined by economic and social connections for social acceptance.

Nagaland is increasingly developing into a salary-dependent State with employment opportunities taken through proper and improper channels for white-collar jobs which make blue-collar jobs unacceptable to the locals. The demand for manual workers is on the rise. The shift to concrete house construction is becoming more demanding day by day which is being fulfilled by the IBIs rather than the Scheduled Caste migrant workers. The locals are aware that safety and reliability are found more in the scheduled caste migrant workers but this manpower is dwindling because of the increasing atrocities, extortions and violations of their basic human rights. The few who remain face the threat of being replaced gradually by the cheaper IBIs. The *thikadar's* job is yet to be learned properly by the IBIs but once they do so they will be in control of major blue-collar jobs in Nagaland. The borders of Nagaland are so porous that many IBIs have entered and are desperate to be included into the social fabric of Naga society. Their labour charges and willingness to do any type of manual work, any time, anywhere may fast replace the scheduled caste migrant workers from mainland India which will bring in more social problems. It is evident that scheduled caste migrant workers with valid permissions hardly get involved with law and order in Nagaland whereas IBIs have raped, robbed and killed even locals on many occasions; however, their availability is becoming convenient for the locals irrespective of the lurking dangers.

There is an urgent need to educate locals on the dignity of labour and to earn their livelihood honestly. In the process of the requirement of workers from any part of the world, a proper mechanism should be set up and adhered to strictly. A replay of the situation in the 1970s and 1980s of peaceful relations with scheduled caste migrant workers, legally, is the need of the hour. The Government of Nagaland must re-structure an effective and stable work permit system so that legal migrant workers can work in peace sans harassment and poor system. Unabated multiple taxations should be curbed and the presence of IBIs diminished as more crime and unhealthy syndicates often rise with them. The legal scheduled caste migrant workers can be an antidote for illegal immigrants who are infusing fear and discord in Naga society. Development should not be impeded but should be accelerated in tune with the globalization that is impacting the world with social, political and economic inclusions. Legal migrant workers, irrespective of caste, creed and race should be brought to the state alongside local workers but it should be those who have no other ulterior motives except to work and earn and go back to their deep-rooted families in their native places. The scheduled caste workers/petty businessmen have no intention to pollute or displace the local population, reduce them to a minority or create an imbalance in the social environment. Therefore, fair pay, fair treatment and an equally efficient system should be a prod for their growth. They must also be given their fair due of human rights and privileges as expected from a just society. On the part of the state, protection should be ensured to legal migrant workers and measures should be taken to ban illegal action and multiple taxes against them. A favourable working environment should be systematically and strongly activated so that both the employer and the employee are benefitted equally. The social environment and the political environment must improve to bring about progressive social change. To enable such a social change, healthy social inclusions are a necessity; therefore, systematic accommodation without fear of assimilation by all groups concerned are urgent steps that need to be taken. The issues and challenges arising for legal scheduled caste migrant workers in Nagaland are indicative of a deteriorating Naga society that requires major structural and functional changes.

REFERENCES

Beteille, Andre. 1998. *Caste, Class and Power*, New Delhi: Oxford University Press.

Dumont, Louis. 2010. *Homo Hierarchicus: The Caste System and its Implications*, New Delhi: Oxford University Press.

Ghurye, G. S. 2011. *Caste and Race in India*, Mumbai: Popular Prakashan Private Limited.

Khali, Sahoo. 2005. *Rural Development: Scheduled Castes and Scheduled Tribes*, New Delhi: Classical Publishing Company.

Majumdar, D. N. 1961. *Races and Cultures of India*, Bombay: Asia Publishing House.

Rawat, Gyanendra Singh. 2005. *Dalits in the Past and Present*, New Delhi: Sumit Enterprises.

Srinivas, M. N. 1995. *Social Change in Modern India*, New Delhi: Orient Longman Limited.

11

CASTE, TRIBE AND RESERVATION IN MANIPUR: A CRITIQUE

Vijaylakshmi Brara

ABSTRACT

According to Padmanabh Samarendra, "Caste, as conceived in contemporary academic writings or within the policies of the State, is a new idea produced during the second half of the 19th century in the course of and because of the census operations....

"The history of caste enumeration in the Indian census illustrates how difficult it is to capture indigenous social hierarchies and identities under the term 'caste'." (EPW, Aug.13, 2017). Manipur too grapples with this issue. In this state too, caste is not part of the indigenous social construction. Both among the valley Meitei and the hill tribes, there were clans which were not hierarchical as we conceive it in the case of the caste system. Power equations have been based on proximity to the ruler but not hierarchical as every clan is an exogamous unit with no exclusions on the basis of the ascribed status.

The second issue which this paper will try to argue is what happens when we postulate Dumont when he says, "without caste there is no Hindu." It will discuss the historical antecedents of the conversion of the Meitei into the Vaishnav Hindu fold.

Thirdly, it will critically analyse the creation of the SC category to fulfil the policy of reservation as, to continue with Dumont, the SCs in Manipur are not even part of the Hindu religion! It will also discuss the impact of reservation on the ST population.

The idea of reservation was to 'uplift' the backward categories with the idea of social justice.

The scenario today is what prevails all over India; the forward castes and social categories like the Jats, the Marathas and now even the Meitei are demanding reservation. Today, the Meitei are bringing forth the indigenous discourse by 'recalling' their tribal identity.

Fourthly, has reservation really benefitted all the people in the selected list or are we seeing a new elite emerging within the marginalised?

Therefore, has the time come to review the reservation policy?

This paper will try to develop on these arguments and attempt to bring in some suggestions on this policy.

Key Words: caste, tribe, reservation, Manipur, Hinduism, identity, indigenous

Introduction

According to Padmanabh Samarendra, "Caste, as conceived in contemporary academic writings or within the policies of the State, is a new idea produced during the second half of the 19th century in the course of and because of the census operations....The history of caste enumeration in the Indian census illustrates how difficult it is to capture indigenous social hierarchies and identities under the term 'caste'." (EPW, Aug.13, 2017). Manipur too grapples with this issue. In this state too, caste is not part of the indigenous social construction. Both among the valley Meitei and the hill tribes there were clans, which were not hierarchical as we conceive it in the case of the caste system. Power equations have been based on proximity to the ruler but not hierarchical as every clan is an exogamous unit with no exclusions on the basis of the ascribed status. The second issue which this paper will try to argue is what happens when we postulate Dumont when he says, "without caste there is no Hindu." It will discuss the historical antecedents of the conversion of the Meitei into the Vaishnav Hindu fold. Thirdly, it will critically analyse the creation of the SC category to fulfil the policy of reservation as, to continue with Dumont, the SCs in Manipur are not even part of the Hindu religion! It will also discuss the impact of reservation on the ST population. The idea of reservation was to 'uplift' the backward categories with the idea of social justice. The scenario today is that all over India, the forward castes and social categories like the Jats, the Marathas, the Patels and now even the Meitei are demanding reservation. Today, the Meitei are bringing forth the indigenous discourse by "recalling" their tribal identity. Fourthly, has the reservation really benefitted all the people in the selected list or are we seeing a new elite emerging within the marginalised? Therefore, has the time come to review the reservation policy? This paper will try to develop on these arguments and attempt to make some suggestions on this policy.

The Idea of Social Justice

What do we mean by social justice? It's an important question—the way it's used as a cry call on social media, one would think that some level of agreement has been reached regarding its meaning. No, it hasn't. In fact there are many varieties of senses of social justice perspectives and often even conflicting ones. But the good thing is that the world is accommodative to such varieties and viewpoints. Concepts such as 'fairness', 'opportunities', 'equality' and 'rights' are never too far away from discussions of justice in whatever form, and these are all concepts that have seen their fair share of disagreement over the years. These inter-connections and associated disagreements can be witnessed in a variety of approaches to social justice, including the work of one of the major intellectuals in justice theory, John Rawls, whose 1971 book, *A Theory of Justice*, is considered a cornerstone of the field. He developed and revised two principles of justice:

- Liberty Principle—which establishes equal basic liberties for all citizens
- Difference Principle—The Difference Principle regulates inequalities, only permitting inequalities that work to the advantage of the worst off.

Rawls held that social justice depended on having just institutions, whereas Amartya Sen thinks that good social outcomes are what matter. Strictly, both could be right. The practical brunt of Sen's criticism, however, is that just institutions do not ensure social justice. You can, in addition, recognise social injustices without knowing how a perfectly fair society would arrange or justify itself.

No society in the world is equal and just. Hence, trying to achieve social justice is trying to reach the ideal and therefore not real and yet a correct thing to do. It is human endeavour to hold these principles high.

In the dual classification of caste and class we have been taught that one is ascribed and the other one is achieved. It is the ascribed status which brings out societal guilt. It is considered morally and ethically wrong to ascribe a status to an individual on the basis of his birth for which he has no choice. Although how much the class status being an achieved status can be argued if we take a relook at C. Wright Mills 'Power Elite' or dig into Pareto's 'Circulation of Elites' and Robert Michel's, 'Iron Law of Oligarchy'.

Reservation and the Idea of Social Justice

The idea of social justice in India has been predominantly seen through the prism of ascribed hierarchy of castes and the marginalised society of tribes. It was understood by the Constitution-makers that certain sections of society had been deprived of privileges to acquire education and jobs because of the continuous denial to them of such opportunities because of their birth and the region where they were born. They needed to be uplifted to come at par with the rest. Hence, certain impetus like reservation of seats in educational institutions, in jobs and also exemption from income tax to the tribals in the north east were introduced.

Today, it has been more than seventy years since we have had our Constitution. And it is an appropriate time to assess this provision and present a critique. This subject is very complex in the sense that it has multiple facets, like particular histories, the country's diversity differential hierarchies and also societal dynamics. At the same time, there has not been any assessment study on the impact of reservation in bringing forth social justice in the societies at large. There are still questions like have the marginalised been uplifted? How many of them? Has there been another set of marginalised groups which has emerged over a period of time? Has it changed the perspective towards them? Are inequalities disappearing? Is caste consciousness disappearing? And then, was reservation enough or we needed to do something more? Also do we need to continue this legislation or bring in some amendments? And so many more.

'Caste' itself is a foreign word, probably relating to the Portuguese origin 'casta'. In the traditional parlance, we had *varna* and *jati*. Translating them as 'caste' is a serious fallacy. Secondly *jati* is more identifiable than caste. *Jati* categories had regional differences in their hierarchies and compositions. The heterogeneous nature of what we call India has somewhere been missed out.

The Manipur Context

Manipur too grapples with this issue. In this state too, caste is not part of the indigenous social construction. Both among the valley Meitei and the hill tribes, there were clans which were not hierarchical, contrary to what we see in the case of the caste system. Power equations have been based on proximity to the ruler and not hierarchical as every clan is an exogamous unit with no exclusions on the basis of the ascribed status. The second issue that comes to the fore is what happens when we postulate Weber when he says, "without caste there is no Hindu." The historical antecedents of the conversion of the Meitei into the Vaishnav Hindu fold challenges this statement somehow. The community got converted to Hinduism only in the 17th century. Conversion necessitated assigning caste. And they had to be given a higher caste in the ladder. Nobody would agree to be converted to a caste lower in the hierarchy. Hence, all of the Meitei got Kshatriya status and those who did not embrace the Hindu fold were sent to *loi* areas where traditionally all those people went who disobeyed the king's orders. They were therefore outside the matrix of the caste system. And among the four categories of Brahmins, Kshatriya, Vaishya and Shudra, there are no Vaishyas and Shudras.

The Lois (means banishment and not low caste)

These non-converts to Hinduism, when it was declared a state religion, were sent to the peripheral areas like Andro, Khurkhul, Awang Sekmai, Phayeng, etc. Other lesser-known *Loi* villages are Leimaram, Leimaram Khunou, Koutruk, Kwatha, etc. Andro, famous for its coiled technique of pottery, is situated near the Nongmaijing hill, Khurkhul near the Koubru hills and Phayeng at the foot of the Kangchup hills. Awang Sekmai, the second largest scheduled caste village in Manipur, is situated near National Highway No. 39 (the Imphal-Dimapur road).

Since these communities were part of the larger Meitei community before the advent and influence of Hinduism, they too have the seven *salai* structure like the Meiteis.[1]

According to some, those who got *Loi* status after Hinduism were the Chakpas who were the earliest settlers of Manipur. They believe that they did not come from anywhere; they have been here since time immemorial and are the actual descendants of Soraran/Asiba (the Sky God) at the Koubru hill. Koubru hill is considered the first settlement even by other Meiteis.

According to the myth of their origin, the ancestors of the Chakpas and Andros were two brothers who once occupied *Kangla.*[2] They were driven out by the *Pakhangba.*[3] Before leaving, they decided to have a meal. The Phayeng Chakpa's ancestor cooked *ngakra* (a kind of fish) and his younger brother cooked *khajing* (prawn). The *khajing* took a long time to cook, so the Andro ancestor told the Phayeng ancestor to go ahead and said he would follow him later. But when the Andro ancestor finally followed, he was unable to locate his elder brother and returned. Thus he got his name Andro, a derivation from *Handros* (who returned). The Andro settlements are in the east while the Phayangs live in the west.

In the traditional ancient text *Chakparol,*[4] there is a detailed account of the origin and later migration of the *Loi/Chakpa* settlements. The Sekmais derive their name from Sengmai, which comes from 'Sengba', meaning 'pure'.

Khurkhul is the only *Loi* community that does not claim to be the original settlers of the present place. They trace their origin to the story of *Khamba* and *Thoibi.* In this epic, Thoibi (one should notice the fact that she was in fact a princess) was exiled (*loi-thaba* in Manipuri) to Kabo (in Burma, Now Myanmar) for refusing to marry Nongban (the son of a nobleman), the villain of the story. When she was called back from exile (*loi-koukhatpa*), the chief of Kabo presented her 15 slaves. She and the slaves proceeded on a journey after the ritual throwing of an egg which fell and broke in the area belonging to *Ichum lairembi* at Khurkhul, where they had stopped. Their descendants have continued to stay here up to the present day and celebrate Lai-Haroaba to please Ichum lairembi.

The term *loi* has got several meanings when used as an independent word or, as a prefix or suffix. For example, *Loi thaba* means to be exiled to a *Loi* village or outside Manipur and *Loi hanba* means to return from exile. *Loi chanba* means to conquer a country, while *Loi kaba* means to pay tribute to the conquering power. *Loi pot* means a tribute in addition to the *lallup* services that were compulsory for everybody except for the nobles and privileged classes.

There are some scholars who say that the *Lois* were people who were sent into exile as punishment. Thanga, Sugnu, Ithai, Chairel, Kumbi, Arong, etc., were some of the places where offenders were exiled.

As mentioned in the myths of Phayeng and Andro, they were driven out by Pakhangba from Kangla and were pushed to the periphery of the valley where they continue to reside.

Probably, these people who were *Lois* at the time of Pakhangba became outcasts during the time of Pamheiba when they refused to embrace Hinduism and retained their original identity.

People of Sekmai, Khurkhul, Andro, and Phayeng mainly belong to the Ningthouja, Angom and Khuman *salais*. Some people who now want to adopt Hinduism go through the 'purification' rite called *penathokpa* after which they are allowed to marry within the Hindu Meitei fold.

The conversion of *Loi* into the scheduled caste status came only as a consequence of the formation of the Kakasaheb Kalelkar Commission in January 1953. Some *Lois* of Manipur, under the aegis of the 'Loi Association' began efforts to gain recognition as 'Scheduled Caste' but only a few *Loi* villages responded to the Association's mobilisation due to their apprehension of suffering from the stigma of a low caste or untouchables (Chaoba, 1993). Thus, 1953 marked the beginning of the demand for Scheduled Caste status among the Lois. In response to their demand, the Kakasaheb Kalelkar Commission visited Manipur from 29 November to 1 December 1953 and after observing their socio-economic backwardness and different lifestyle from the Hindu Meiteis, the Commission agreed to enlist the seven Loi villages, i.e., Sekmai, Khurkhul, Phayeng, Leimaram, Tairenpokpi, Andro and Kwatha as scheduled caste villages of Manipur.

Later, an official notification in 1956 recognised the above seven/eight villages as SC villages of Manipur (Devi, p. 137).

So, these groups of people are the ones who did not embrace Hinduism. But if, according to Weber, without caste there is no Hindu, then how did these people who were out of the ambit of Hinduism become a caste and subsequently a scheduled caste? At the same time, can they be equated with the untouchables or shudras? As stated above, in 1953, many of the *lois* did not want to be enlisted as scheduled castes in apprehension of being branded as low caste or untouchables. This is a very important marker to the fact that the *lois* have not been seen as untouchables as in other parts of India. If we look into the dynamics of this group today, they are not at all categorised as lowly. There have been intermarriages between them and the Hindu Meitei. There is commensality and neither is occupation ascribed. I think Manipur is the only place where such a mass conversion to Hinduism took place. And those who did not convert to Hinduism and retained their original faith, the *lois,* were given scheduled caste status.

This is very confusing to sociologists. While it is understandable to give certain privileges to them since they were sent out of the state apparatus, to call them castes when they are not even part of the caste system points to a major fallacy, according to me. Secondly, when there is so much fluidity in the ascription of castes in society, how can one have rigidities of hierarchies within them?

Therefore, in Manipur, there is not much social value ascribed when one describes scheduled castes, as they do not suffer from the indignities that are heaped upon such communities in other societies.

In contrast, assigning scheduled tribe status to tribes of Manipur has much more clarity. Although the majority of them have converted to Christianity, they still dwell on their ancestral land and many of them still follow their traditional occupations. But now, many have joined senior-level positions in bureaucracies in Delhi and other government departments. Over a period of time, there has emerged a class of very rich and powerful. But here, as well as in the scheduled caste reservation issue, the benefits of reservation seem to be moving within the beneficiaries and not seeping down to the more marginalised. Has reservation really benefitted all the people in the selected list or are we seeing a new elite emerging within the marginalised?

Here what we see is a strong 'power elite' growing, the benefits of reservation being used only by a privileged few. While the idea of reservation was to 'uplift' the backward categories with the idea of social justice, it is not creating a ripple effect but forming concentric circles, one inside the other. Probably if the concept of 'creamy layer' is also introduced in the reservation of both SCs and STs, the benefit may seep down to the lesser privileged among them. Another point of dissension is that the tribals of this state are exempted from paying income tax which, I feel, should be based on income and not on ascribed constitutional status.

The scenario today is prevails all over India; the forward castes and social categories like the Jats, the Marathas and now even the Hindu Meitei are demanding reservation. Today, the Meitei are bringing forth the indigenous discourse by 'recalling' their tribal identity. And if the Meitei manage to get the tribal status, then reservation of scheduled castes will have no rationality, as by ethnic construction the scheduled castes of Manipur are as much Meitei as any other. Reservation was, to use John Rawls's *The Difference Principle of regulating inequalities, only permitting inequalities that work to the advantage of the worst-off,* in fact, working to the advantage of the best-offs and also desired by them.

Why is this happening?

May be, we may have to think of a new model or mechanism to work out reservation so that the benefits percolate down amongst the underprivileged. Secondly, policies have to be framed keeping the heterogeneous societies with their own contexts and histories in mind. Every state in India has its own systems of exclusion and inclusion, based on caste, class, gender and region.

NOTES

1. The seven *salai* of Meitei are Ningthouja, Khuman, Moirang, Chenglei, Angom, Khaba-ngangba and Luwang.
2. The ancient capital of Manipur is situated in the middle of Imphal, the present capital of Manipur.
3. Believed to be the ruler of Manipur in 33AD.
4. The stories of Chakpa.

REFERENCES

Bino Devi, Lairenlakpam. 2002. *The Lois of Manipur*, New Delhi: Mittal Publications.

Brara Vijaylakshmi. 1998. *Politics Society and Cosmology in India's North East*, New Delhi: Oxford University Press.

Chaoba, Sekmai. 1993. *Manipurda Scheduled Caste*, in the Souvenir of the Silver Jubilee Camp of All Manipur Scheduled Caste Students Union.

Laishram, Simon. https://www.academia.edu/8639776/Dual Religious Identification ofThe Meities of Manipur? Accessed on 21-03-2017.

John Parrat. 2005. *Wounded Land: Politics and Identity in Modern Manipur: Cultural Renaissance and Political Awakening*, New Delhi: Mittal Publications.

Kunj Bihari Singh. September 1963. 'Manipur Vaishnavism: A Sociological Interpretation,' *Sociological Bulletin*. Vol. 12, No. 2, pp. 66-72.

Lairenmayum Ibungohal. 1987. *Introduction to Manipur*. The Saraswati Printing Works, Imphal, Manipur, third edition.

Mayanglambam Lilee Devi. June 2015. 'Juxtaposing Social Inclusion and Exclusion of Lois In Manipur', *International Research Journal of Human Resources and Social Sciences*, Vol. 2, No. 6, pp.136-141.

Padmanabh Samarendra. Aug.13, 2017. 'Religion and Scheduled Caste Status,' *EPW*, Vol.51, No. 31.

Parratt, Saroj Nalini. 2009. *The Court Chronicle of the Kings of Manipur The Cheitharon Kumpapa*, Vol. 2, 1764-1843 CE, Cambridge University Press Pvt. Ltd.

12

Constitutional Justice to Lois of Manipur: Comparative Village Profiles

M. Lilee Devi

ABSTRACT

Under Article 341(1) of the Indian Constitution, the Lois community in Manipur, Northeast India, was for the first time declared as a Scheduled Caste with reference to the Scheduled Castes and Scheduled Tribes Order, 1950. Thereafter, the population of Scheduled Castes in Manipur has been increasing. Constitutional justice to the Lois on the demand for Scheduled Caste status is one of the ongoing issues of exclusion and inclusion in the State. The constitutional status of the Lois, as found in many research papers, has been in a transitional phase as more and more Loi locales are being gradually notified as Scheduled Castes. Against this backdrop, this paper explores a comparative profile of Scheduled Caste and Non-Scheduled Caste Loi locales in Manipur. More precisely, this paper gives a sociological insight into the similarities and differences between SC and non-SC Loi locales of Manipur.

Key words: Constitutional Justice, Exclusion, Inclusion, Scheduled Caste, Non-Scheduled Caste, Lois Locale, Manipur

Introduction

Village studies attract many social scientists that serve as repositories of social phenomena. Rural sociology studies all the 'statics and dynamics' of village society. After independence, the need for a systematic study of Indian villages was felt as an urgent necessity to understand rural socio-economic organisations, their structure, functions and evolution. Due to some historical reasons, existing society in India has become a veritable mosaic of rural societies and hence reveals a diversified cultural pattern (Desai, 1994). Like every village society, each *Loi*[1] village of Manipur in Northeast India also has a unique history, socio-economic significance and cultural life. Though caste-based hierarchy reflects the social ordering of different communities in India, the scenario in the North-Eastern part of the country depicts a multifarious social system. Meanwhile, there is a prolonged dialogue on the issues of exclusion and inclusion of particular communities into the list of Scheduled Castes (SCs), Scheduled Tribes (STs), Other Backward Castes (OBCs), Socially and Educationally Backward Classes (SEBCs), etc. In post-independent India, based on certain criteria, many castes or communities were identified and were then notified as Scheduled Castes. The *Lois* of Manipur is also one such community which was notified as SC in the Constitutional Notification during the 1970s. Nevertheless, despite their common historical identification as *Lois*, it was found that some *Loi* villages are yet to be recognized as SC (Devi, 2013, 2015a[2], 2015b, etc.). It means the question of constitutional justice to the *Lois* on their demand for Scheduled Caste status is a pertinent case as one of the ongoing issues of exclusion and inclusion in the state. In this connection, the main objective of this paper is to explore a comparative profile of Scheduled Caste and Non-Scheduled Caste *Loi* locales[3] in Manipur. More precisely, this paper gives a sociological insight into the similarities and differences between *Loi* locales of Manipur. Before we discuss the comparative profiles of *Lois* locales in detail, it becomes imperative to clarify some conceptual problems and operational definitions of the term 'Constitutional Justice'.

On the Concept of 'Constitutional Justice'

The notion 'constitutional' means relating to the constitution of a particular country or organisation and the concept of 'constitutional justice' implies substantive power rather than informal activities. It involves an external upper-level agency to grant justice rather than people below seizing it in the course of struggle. Above all, this concept is a part of the Constitution or the 'rule of law' in the new democracy of the Western world. It has diverse or varied meanings and usages across countries. For instance, in a seminar[4] on 'Constitutional Justice,' it highlighted the rule of law as is defined and understood in the OSEC Human Dimension, that it requires constitutional justices to interpret their national constitutional provision in the spirit of what the OSEC's Copenhagen Document of 1990 termed "the supreme value of human personality". However, in this seminar, special emphasis was placed on access to and accessibility of constitutional justice. The European Commission for Democracy through Law[5] (2010)—better known as the Venice Commission, studied individual access to constitutional justice. Here, it is possible to distinguish between direct individual access in which individuals are given the possibility to challenge the constitutionality of a given norm or act directly and indirect individual access, in which the constitutionality can be challenged only through state bodies. Many countries have a mixed system, both with direct means of access to constitutional justice and with indirect means. Further, it explains that individual access to constitutional justice means the various different mechanisms that enable violations of the constitutionally guaranteed rights of individuals, either separately or jointly with others, to be brought before a constitutional court or equivalent body. Given the context of contemporary Australian Constitutional, the phrase 'access to constitutional justice' can be understood as no more and no less than access to the courts to seek judicial review of the constitutional validity of laws (Holland, 2010). He reassessed how procedural rules impact people who seek 'access to constitutional justice'. Christopher (1997) claimed that history has a useful role to play in constitutional interpretation, but not, as is often thought, at the expense of our commitment to moral principles or justice. History should figure in constitutional interpretation as an aid to the pursuit of justice, not as a constraint. The term 'fidelity problem' in constitutional justice therefore is a long-running debate among constitutional interpreters, especially on the extent to which constitutional meaning depends upon political theory (*ibid,* 1997:1612).

The Constitution of India has entered into the 68th year of its operation and undoubtedly, being the Constitution of the largest democracy in the world, it embraces the goal of achieving social equality in expressive terms.

The Constitution is fundamentally the supreme law of India laying down basic objectives of a polity and procedures of institutional functioning to facilitate the attainment of goals and fulfilment of objectives. The judiciary under our Constitution is its watchdog (Misra, 2013). Here, the concept of 'social justice' under the Indian Constitution implies more than the term 'constitutional justice' in ensuring a substantial degree of social, economic and political equality. However, some writers (Baxi, 2010; Chandrachud, 2010; Agnes, 2011; Misra, 2013; Bohra, 2015, etc.) refer to constitutional justice in relation to caste census, social justice, constitutional democracy/judiciary, concubine, etc., while struggling to pledge justice in each citizen equally at respective courts. Hence, for want of a consensus, the operational definition of the concept 'constitutional justice' for this paper basically denotes justice delivered to any section of society, through any law-court in India as a State apparatus by abiding with the country's Constitution.

Constitutional Status of *Lois*

Under Article 341(1) of the Indian Constitution, the *Lois* community of Manipur was for the first time declared as a Scheduled Caste with reference to the Scheduled Castes and Scheduled Tribes Order, 1950. However, in the Presidential notification of 1956 regarding Scheduled Castes, it only mentioned *Lois*, but did not define it (Devi, 2016:140). Astonishingly, Article 341 of the Constitution of India deals with Scheduled Caste but there is no clear definition of the term 'Scheduled Caste'. Meanwhile, the population of Scheduled Castes in Manipur has been increasing. According to Census 2011, the Scheduled Caste population, including the two indigenous communities, i.e., *Lois* and Yaithibi and other in-migrants castes, i.e., Dhopi, Muchi, Sutradhar, Patni and Namasudra, constitute 3.8 percent of the total population of Manipur. However, the *Lois* alone, both Scheduled and Non-Scheduled Castes, constitute 6.56 percent of the total population (Devi, 2013:155).

After the constitutional amendment in 1976, claims and counterclaims among the *Lois* in Manipur for recognition as a Scheduled Caste entered into legal cases like Representative of *Lois* (RoL) vs State of Manipur,[6]

RoL vs Supreme Court of India (Assam High Court), Shri Heikham Surchandra Singh & others vs The Representative of *Lois* (RoL)[7], etc. Subsequently, many other court cases regarding reservation-related issues in admission, recruitment, etc., are still going on. Due to the constitutional justification made by the respective authorities, conflict among the *Lois* has heightened but many *Lois* villages in Manipur are still excluded from the list of Scheduled Castes. Though Non-Scheduled Caste *Lois* began to claim and earn SC status, there is a long way to go to achieve equal constitutional status as many *Loi* villages remain excluded to some extent.

Background: Regions under Study

According to Census 2011, the population of Manipur is 27,21,756 and it constitutes nearly 0.24 per cent of the total population of India. The sex ratio of the state is 987 while the overall literacy rate is 79.85 per cent against the national average of 74.04 per cent. The percentage population of SC and ST in the state is 3.8 and 35.1, respectively.

Historically, as mentioned in the Royal Chronicles, there were 34 *Loi* villages and towns in Manipur but seven villages are no longer recorded in the 2001 Census as well as in the 2011 Census on the ground that there were no longer any inhabited villages/towns as such (Devi, 2013). All the 27 inhabited *Lois* locales are scattered in valleys as well as in hill areas. For the purpose of the present comparative study, two *Loi* village/towns (*Loi* locales) were selected only from the Imphal West district where both SC and non-SC *Loi* locales are available.

This paper does not attempt to give comprehensive details of all SC and non-SC *Loi* locales. It only deals with the descriptions of the sampled two *Loi* locales (one SC and one non-SC) selected from the most populous district, i.e., Imphal-West District of Manipur. The Scheduled Caste town Awang (North) Sekmai of Lamsang sub-division and the non-Scheduled Caste village Phoubakchao of Wangoi sub-division were selected for the present research. Profiles of these selected two *Loi* locales will be put side by side in order to understand the similarities and differences between *Lois* in different social set-ups.

Imphal-West District

Censuses of 1991, 2001, and 2011 show Imphal West as the most thickly populated district in the State, bearing the highest density of population (855 per sq. km.). Out of the total population of 4,44,382, the number of males is slightly higher than females. There are 79,078 households in Imphal West district and it is the largest valley district with an area of 519 sq. km. Imphal West district has four sub-divisions—Lamsang, Patsoi, Lamphelpat and Wangoi.

Awang Sekmai: A Scheduled Caste Loi Locale

Sekmai is one of the largest scheduled caste towns in Manipur. It is located at a distance of about 12 miles to the north of Imphal along the Imphal-Dimapur road and the town is under the administrative jurisdiction of Lamsang sub-division. Besides Sekmai River and the Nongpok Ningthou and Koubru Hills, some villages like Kanglatombi, Maharabi and Tengdonyan are spreading as main villages of non-Scheduled Castes. Most of the important offices of administration are located at Imphal. Many people are dependent on the nearby hills to meet their basic needs. Shrubs and branches of trees found in these hills are still used as fuel for cooking. Vast paddy fields surrounded the town in the southern and northern parts.

A number of social researchers have analysed the changing pattern of village structures in many contexts. In India, including Manipur, decadal Census Operations study hundreds of selected villages across the States. They have adopted some criteria for selecting the villages in order to adequately represent geographical, occupational and ethnic diversity. Sekmai, a dominant SC *Loi* of Manipur was one of the fifteen selected villages of Manipur for a socio-economic survey conducted in 1961. In this survey, the non-Scheduled Caste households were excluded. This monograph found that these SC populations are too backward in many aspects. There is some literature available on the *Loi* locales of Manipur but there is dearth of scholarly studies on the subject from a sociological point of view.

According to T.C. Hodson (1908: 9), "Sengmai (now Sekmai), a village on the Manipur-Kohima cart road about 1.6 km from Imphal, is said to have moved from the south." Census 1961[8] shows that out of 15 villages in Manipur, Sekmai was selected to study the socio-economic life of the SC population in mid-December 1960 and later the report was published by the government. This report claims to be the first of its kind in Manipur. It says that there is no written record as far as the origin or history of the village is concerned. But Mr. Kh. Nilamani (74 years) said that in ancient times when there were constant wars and battles, most of the inhabitants from Nongpok Sekmai (now in Thoubal district) came and settled in the present village which was considered to be a safe place (cited from Census of India, 1961). Many inhabitants are believed to be the descendants of those ancient settlers. This survey highlighted that the immigrants did not bring any changes on the status of the villagers and therefore, the age-old traditional life remains intact which is marked by the absence of caste hierarchy or any caste-based statuses. The *Loi* of this village are treated as Scheduled Caste while inhabitants of Nongpok-Sekmai are yet to be included in this category despite having the same ancestors and place of origin. Here, one question emerged as to why and how Sekmai has been included in the list of SC and Shikhong-Sekmai excluded.

Phoubakchao: A Non-Scheduled Caste Loi Locale

In historical records, Phoubakchao village is found in the Manipuri court chronicles written by royal pundits from time to time regarding the establishment of *Loi* villages in the state. As per historical records, Phoubakchao was declared as *Loi-lam* during the reign of king Kongyanba (1324-1335 AD) along with other three other villages, namely, Heiyel, Hangul and Waikhong (Indira, 2003).

Phoubakchao is a small village in the south-west corner of Loktak Lake. *Pucca* and *kutcha* houses surrounded by fishing farms make this village different from other *Loi* villages but are somehow similar to Thanga village. There is only one *kutcha* road connecting other villages. There is a lineal form of settlement in the village with only one row of households. Community-wise, this row is divided into two; namely, Muslim and Meitei *Leikai*. Again, it is broadly sub-divided into *Awang*, *Makha*, etc., taking direction as the referral point. The settlement area of the two major communities, i.e., Meitei and Muslims, in Phoubakchao village are separated by small inhabited paddy fields and fishing farms. There are a few isolated Meitei households in the village. There is no government office except the Phoubakchao High School, but this too remains almost dysfunctional. Villagers informed and lamented on the pathetic condition of the school, the only educational centre for youths in the village.

Phoubakchao village falls under the jurisdiction of Wangoi sub-division and is located 49.1 kilometres south from Imphal. According to the 2011 Census there are 670 households. Most of the area is covered with fishing farms while in Sekmai it has paddy-fields. There are a few hamlets in the village but such small settlements have almost disappeared in the selected *Loi* locale. There are no hills except for a small-elevated tract. The population is 3,588, with females slightly more than males (Census, 2011). The village has a literacy rate of 61.28 (Census, 2011) percent which is lower than Sekmai (82.96 percent). The majority of the inhabitants are farmers, traders, daily-wage earners or mobile labourers, rickshaw drivers and *Maibas* or *Maibis* (priests and priestesses). Most of the houses are made of bamboo, straw and mud.

Though there is no exact meaning of the word 'Phoubakchao', inhabitants of this *Loi* village narrated that they had migrated from different places like Imphal, Kakching, Moirang, Thoubal, etc. There is no written record about the origin of this village but some statistical data is available. For many years the villagers have been complaining to the *Pradhan* about the pathetic condition of the village. Despite numerous complaints and demands, there is slow progress in the overall development of Phoubakchao village. At the same time, the *Pradhan* argued that shortage of developmental funds was the main reason for the village's underdevelopment.

Loi Locales: Similarities and Differences

Rural and urban areas across *Loi* locales were visited and it was found that, under certain conditions, rural inhabitants in the *tehsils* and the pattern of rural settlement were divided in terms of political ambition. By considering the Census definition of town as urban and village as rural, the actual physical structure in Manipur is different from it. More or less, most of the *Loi* locales seem to be rural in terms of their physical structure, geographical set-up, settlement pattern and social structure. However, the *Loi* are in a transitional stage from rural life to the urban way of living in the sense that their trades, standard of living, transport systems, etc., are well connected with adjacent towns, especially after the introduction of private transport services. Private transport vehicles have been passing through the villages in selected *Loi* locales for the last few years.

The percentages of Scheduled Caste and Scheduled Tribe population in Imphal West district is 2.99 and 47.49, respectively. Of the total population of Sekmai, 52.54 percent belong to SC. There are no SC or ST individuals in Phoubakchao. *Loi* locales in Imphal-West present a mixed picture of both rural and urban characteristics. Sekmai, located near the national highway is developing fast while Phoubakchao remains underdeveloped. The location of the field areas is between 30 to 60 kilometres from Imphal City, the State capital.

Lois participate in many activities. Their traditional assigned occupations are no more ascribed. In present times, there is the possibility of changing their occupation. On the other hand, some *Loi* villages are still continuing their traditional occupation like fishing, pottery, basket making, salt manufacturing, distilling traditional liquor, etc. In fact, all the districts in Manipur have a rich composition of multi-ethnic groups. In other words, no single ethnic group or caste/community inhabits a village or town. It is also true for both the selected *Loi* locales under the present study. Both the selected *Loi* locales are dominated by *Lois* who are Meitei-Hindus. There is no caste conflict while claiming social status in the caste hierarchy of Manipur. The study found that Meitei *Lois* and Meitei Muslims are inhabitants of Phoubakchao village since time immemorial. But it is also a fact that no inter-community marriage has ever taken place in these *Loi* locales. Among the *Loi* villages, Phoubakchao of Imphal-west district has the lowest literacy rate which is also far lower than the state and national average. Since there is no college, the youth of both Meitei and Muslims went to the nearby town to acquire degrees. Compared to Sekmai, the literacy rate of Phoubakchao village needs to be improved. Modern amenities like communication, electricity, drinking water, education facilities, postal services, hospital, etc. can be taken into account. Since private vehicles (like autos, buses, mini-buses, jeeps, etc.) ran throughout the village/town, there is no problem of movement. There is no hospital in Sekmai, except dispensaries/primary health centre (PHC). Whether they function or not, they can claim to have these facilities but the same are not available in Phoubakchao. Consequently, serious patients have to go to the city for treatment. Language is one of the most important elements to identify the origin of a person. *Meiti-lon* is the dominant standardized official language of the State; all the Meiteis speak *Meiti-lon* with different accents. *Meiti-lon* or the Manipuri language is the lingua franca among Manipuris. Despite the standardized *Meiti-lon*, the accent of respective *Loi* villages varies. All *Lois* except Muslims[9] have different common-place language which is the unique feature of being a *Loi*. But, many *Lois* maintain regular communication with others and they could switch their accent to standardized *Meitei-lon*. In another study, Devi (2002) found a similarity between 'Meiteis' and '*Lois*' in the matter of religious worship and she asserted that language and the present trend in the behaviour of both these groups call for further studies. But, there is a tonal difference between the *Lois* and the Meiteis in the Imphal areas. She traced the impact of Hinduism on Meitei society in general and the *Lois* in particular. According to her, the *Lois* became the lower caste Meitei community due to the impact of Hinduism. But Indira (2012) observed that the religious belief of *Lois* possesses elements of naturism, animism, ancestral worship and Hinduism. It is a fact that *Maiba* (priest) and *Maibi* (priestess) are busy throughout the year conducting various rituals and people still considered them as the 'traditional priest and priestess' who play a significant role in any ceremony.

Conclusion

In brief, we can say that the *Loi* inhabitants of *Loi* locales have suffered from constitutional injustice by the delay their inclusion in the list of SC or by denying their identity as Scheduled Castes. Such constitutional injustice to some sections of the *Lois* is despite the fact that all the *Loi* locales shared a similar historicity and experiences. Though *Lois* are treated as Scheduled Caste and Non-Scheduled Caste, the age-old stigma is applicable to all of them but it is gradually fading away in the daily interaction of the people with other non-*Loi* communities within or outside the village. Most of the *Loi* locales are at the junction of hills and valleys or at the borders of district administrations and this has a negative underpinning to their overall development. By analyzing the profiles of the *Loi* locales; it re-affirms Srivastava's (2005) contention that 'Indian villages are never self-sufficient'. No *Loi* village remains autonomous though *Lois* are located near the foothills of the state. It means all the selected *Loi* locales were well connected to the state/national highway, district and other roads. However, it does matter whether the connecting roads are *pucca* or *kutcha*. Thus, village studies can be an important unit in shaping rural sociology in Manipur.

To conclude, it is important that the government should make a state-level survey immediately and list all the deserving *Lois* who could have been included in the Scheduled Caste list in the early 1970s by taking into account their historicity, socio-economic condition, educational status, political participation, etc., so that the aim of social justice under the Constitution of India truly delivers justice to all those left out or excluded *Lois* from the SC list. Moreover, the survey should take note of all the technical errors found in the various criteria adopted by the Kakasaheb Kalekar Commission in January 1953 and the Presidential Notification in defining the *Lois* of Manipur. Instead, there is an urgent need to formulate more rational and inclusive criteria towards identification and inclusion of deserving *Lois* in the list of Scheduled Castes.

Note: This paper is one of the revised and updated outcomes from the author's Ph.D. entitled "Reservation and Empowerment: A Comparative Study of Scheduled Caste and Non-Scheduled Caste *Lois* of Manipur" (An unpublished Ph.D. thesis, Department of Sociology, Panjab University: Chandigarh. 2016).

NOTES

1. Among the Meitei, a dominant community, *Lois* have been stigmatized historically as one of the weaker sections of society. Literally, the word 'Lois', applied to inhabitants of a number of villages spread over distant places from Imphal who have for long been in subjection (Devi, 2016: 5).

2. Devi, M. Lilee. 2015a. *Juxtaposing Social Inclusion and Exclusion of Lois in Manipur.* IRJHRSS, 2(6): 136.
3. Loi villages and towns have been collectively conceptualized as 'Loi locales' in this study.
4. OSEC Human Dimension Seminar (2008) on 'Constitutional Justice,' held at Warsaw. Available at http://www.osec.org/conferences/hds_2008.html (assessed on 3 December 2017.)
5. European Commission for Democracy through Law (2010) 'Individual assess to Constitutional Justice,', available at http://www.venice.coe.int/WebForms/documents/default.aspx?pdffile= CDL-AD(2010)039rev-e (accessed on 1 Sept 2017).
6. RoL vs State of Manipur. 1995. [In the High Court of Assam, Civil Rule 800 of 1994, Civil Rule 839 of 1992, Civil Rule 317 of 1995, Civil Rule 141 of 1995, Misc Case 521 of 1995, Civil Rule 901 of 1993, Writ Appeal 10 of 1995] available at http://www.lawyerservices.in/Representative-of-Lois-Versus-State-of-Manipur-1995-11-17 (accessed on 10 Aug 2017).
7. Shri Heikham Surchandra Singh & others vs The Representative Of 'Lois' (9 October, 1996) available athttps://indiankanoon.org/doc/1021766/?type=print (accessed on 2/1/ 2016).
8. Census of India, 1961. *Village Survey Monograph: Sekmai.* Volume XXII, Part VI (12). Census Publications, Manipur.
9. The Manipuri Muslims (known as Meitei *Pangals*) are not original settlers but came to Manipur in different periods. Kings allowed them to marry Manipuri women and accommodated them in Meitei society by enlisting them in many new lineages. It brought a reciprocal exchange of cultural information between the Meiteis and Meitei Pangals. Manipuri Muslims also adopted *Meiti-lon* as their mother tongue and they are the only community after the Meiteis who spoke *Meiti-lon* [Singh, O. Ranjit. 2007. 'Influence of Meitei culture on the Muslims in Manipur', *Journal of North-East India Council for Social Science Research,* 31 (2): 64-65].

REFERENCES

Agnes, Flavia. 2011. 'The concubine and notion of constitutional justice', *Economic and Political Weekly,* Vol. 46, No. 24, pp. 31-33.

Borah, Saroj. 2015. 'Social Justice and Indian Constitution', *International Journal of Law and Legal Jurisprudence Studies.* Vol. 2, No. 1, pp. 1-5. Available at http://ijlljs.in/social-justice-and-indian-constitution/ (accessed on 3/10/2017).

Baxi, Upendra. 2010. 'Caste Census and Constitutional Justice', *Economic and Political Weekly,* Vol. 45, No. 37, pp. 25-29.

Census of India, 1961. *Village Survey Monograph: Sekmai.* Vol. XXII, Part VI (12), Census Publications: Manipur.

Chandrachud, Abinav. 2010. 'The insulation of India's Constitutional Judiciary', *Economic and Political Weekly,* Vol. 45, No. 13, pp. 38-42.

Christropher, L. Eisgruba. 1997. 'The living hand of the past: History and Constitutional Justice', *Fordham Law Review,* Vol. 65, No. 4, available at http://ir.lawnet.fordham.edu/flr/vol65/issue4/21 (accessed on 30/10/2017).

Devi, L. Bino. 2002. *The Lois of Manipur-Andro, Khurkhul, Phayeng and Sekmai.* New Delhi: Mittal Publications.

Devi, M. Lilee. 2013. 'Conceptualising Social Exclusion and Lois: A Case of Loi Population', in Singh, L. T. and Singh T. B. (eds.), '*Social Exclusion and Inclusive Development.*'. New Delhi: *Sunmarg,* pp. 143-164.

_______ 2015a. 'Juxtaposing Social Inclusion and Exclusion of Lois in Manipur', *IRJHRSS*, Vol. 2, No. 6, pp. 136.

_______ 2015b. '*Hinduism and Caste System in Manipur: Socio-political Repercussion for Loi Communities*', IJERMT, Vols. 1 and 2, No. 1, pp. 68-72.

Desai, A. R. 1994. *Rural Sociology in India,* New Delhi: Popular Prakashan.

European Commission for Democracy through Law (2010) 'Individual assess to Constitutional Justice,', available at http://www.venice.coe.int/WebForms/documents/default.aspx?pdffile=CDL-AD(2010)039rev-e, accessed on 1 Sept 2017.

Government of India. 2011. *Primary Census Abstract, Census of India, 2011.* New Delhi: Census Publications of the Office of the Registrar General.

Holland, Geoff. 2010. 'Standing as a Barrier to Constitutional Justice: Can we create a new public law paradigm', *Bond Law Review*, Vol. 22, No. 3.

Hodson, T. C. 1908. *The Meiteis—A study of the tribes of the Brahmaputra Valley,* London: DNP.

Indira, Khangembam. 2003. *Social organisation and religion among the Lois of Manipur.* Unpublished Ph. D. Thesis, School of Social System, JNU, Delhi.

_______ 2012. 'Religious belief system in contemporary Manipur: Role of Maibas and Maibis in Lois society', in Sudhir, H. (ed.). *Social history of Manipur.* New Delhi: *Sunmarg* Publishers and Distributors.

Misra, S. Narayan. 2013. 'Constitutional Democracy, Judiciary and Social Justice in India', *Odisha Review.* pp. 16-20.

OSEC Human Dimension Seminar on 'Constitutional Justice,', 2008, held at Warsaw. Available at http://www.osec.org/conferences/hds_2008.html (assessed on 3/12/ 2017).

Singh, O. Ranjit. 2007. 'Influence of Meitei culture on the Muslims in Manipur,' *Journal of North-East India Council for Social Science Research,* Vol. 31, No. 2, pp. 64-65.

Srivastava, Vinay Kumar. 2005. 'Indian village', *The Eastern Anthropologist,* Vol. 58, pp. 3-4.

13

INTERROGATING CASTE: LOCATING THE SCHEDULED CASTES IN A MULTI-CASTE ASSAMESE VILLAGE

Sarmistha Das

ABSTRACT

The aim of the paper is to understand the meaning of caste in the mundane and everyday life experiences of people. While the tentacles of social discrimination seem to wane away from Indian society, its challenges continue to persist. Thus, the paper aims to raise certain elementary questions like: what is caste? How do people in their everyday practices negotiate caste?

The paper also focuses on an important site of social interaction in the village, i.e., 'the satra', and aims at understanding the meanings that people give and derive from it. How the polity, economy and social rhythm of the satra vis-à-vis the village gives meaning to the idea of being who they are in the village.

Key Words: caste, Satra, multicast, kaibarta, detribalization, neo-vaishnavism

Introduction

Notwithstanding the cardinal features of caste like hierarchy and binaries of purity and impurity as indicated in the accounts of Ghurye (1932) and Dumont (1966), the paper probes the working definitions of caste, its everyday practices as to how people identify themselves with it as a group? To what extent do the people believe in the institution and has there been any change in its functioning?

Like most villages across Assam, the village under study too is multi-caste with a hierarchical social organization. This is reflected in the residential organization of the village. In terms of the notions of purity and pollution, the Brahmins occupied the innermost corners in the village which is surrounded by the *kalita* and *koch*. Hunter (1998, 184) mentions *Kalita*; next, if not equal to the *kayastha* in rank. *koch*; also, descendants of an ancient dominant aboriginal race, who have given up their crude habits and customs and embraced Hinduism (ibid) followed by the *kaibartas* (traditional fishermen) and *hari* (traditional sweepers). Thus, the village grew surrounding the *satra* with the 'pure' castes succeeding the *satra* (neo-*vaishnavite* monastery). The villagers use the term *hira* as a synonym of *hari* in the village. While the organization of the village seems normal at one point, at another the villagers distinguish themselves from neighbouring villages. The presence of *satra* clearly demarcates the village from its neighbouring areas. Hence, the village is also popularly known as a *satra* village.

Understanding the Village

To understand the village, one must look at it vis-à-vis the *satra*. The *satra* for long continued to be the nerve centre of the village. Popular lore in the village reifies the position of the *satra* as a patron giving shelter to the villagers. A popular lore on the origin of the *satra* indicates two processes of *detribalization* and *sanskritization* in the village as concurrent to the origin of the *satra*. The tribal king (chieftain) in the process of giving away his traditional practices adopted the new religious practices of neo-*vaishnavism* for which he donated the entire land including its common spaces in the village to the *satra*. Thus, all land along with its common resources was now under the control of *satra* (Deka, 2008). In one sense, it can be argued that the everyday religious, social and economic life of the villagers revolved around the *satra* as most of the decisions were now taken by the *satra*.

Thus, membership to the *satra* became coveted as it meant an access to agricultural land in the village. Therefore, taking refuge in the *satra* and becoming a neophyte became the unstated rule in the village. By its nature, the *satra* was accommodative; all the villagers irrespective of their caste took *saran* (religious refuge) and became adherents. The *satradhikar* (abbot) did not reside in the village; in his absence the decisions of the *satra* were taken up by members of the *satra parichalana samity* (*satra* management committee). Membership to this body was solicited yet restricted. The members of this body included the 'influential villagers' (which was restricted to caste). It was only by the virtue of their social position (in the caste hierarchy) that they could become members of this group, thus, making group membership exclusive. Major decisions like who would till the land and for how long were taken by this body. While villagers had access to land, irrespective of their caste, yet the *Brahmins,* by their influence (as most members of the committee were *brahmins*), controlled major decisions. Thus, caste became a benchmark to identify an individual's position in the production process. If the *brahmins* were on top of the social ladder, the scheduled castes, i.e., the *kaibartas* and *haris* were at the end and engaged as sharecroppers in the production process. Thus, in terms of participating in the production process, there were clear demarcations. On top were the *brahmins* and other castes like *kalitas* and *kochs* from the village and at the bottom were the *kaibartas* and *haris*.

The processes of individual engagements in the production process were manifold. The groups engaged in the decision-making process of the committee would participate in the major/minor activities of the village including deciding on agricultural activities. The groups who were not a part would engage in the production process without being a party to any decision making and would simply follow orders. Besides agriculture, at times they also help the *satra* in other activities like cleaning the *satra* wetland and its premises. Overtly, the village had two agrarian categories of landowners (the *satra* and the representatives of the SPS) and the sharecroppers (the rest of the villagers).

Not only economic, but the social and religious facets were also were taken care of by the *satra*. For instance, the social life of the villagers revolved around the festival of Holi (*Doul jatra)* celebrated in the Assamese month of *Fagun* (February-March); this is an annual festival. Traditionally, it was connected to the social rhythm and life of the people. While the festival is still celebrated in the village, it has lost its mass appeal. A two-day festival begins with the *jatra* (journey) when *Jadav Rai* (the idol of Krishna, inside the *satra)* goes for a stroll (*gaon phura*) across the village. The *jatra* begins on *Doul purnima*[1] with *Jadav Rai* moving through the village and out of the sacred space inside the *satra*. The two-day festival ends with the celebration of Holi, when the *Jadav Rai* re-enters the temple after a ritual bath. This is followed by songs and dances with a huge congregation of men, women and children participating. Traditionally, such congregations included people across caste groups. The *jatra* would cover the length and breadth of the village. But today such congregations have become reclusive and restrictive. The notion of shame and self-respect amongst the marginalized has pushed them out of these congregations. Therefore, the festival, which at one point, used to unite the villagers, has today lost its traditional charm. One can today hear voices of dissent which refutes the rationality of the festival. Instead, the movement has become restricted. The *jatra* is being confined to a specific area and would not include the *kaibarta* and *hira* settlements, thus ending its universal appeal. They (*kaibarta* and *hira*) lament their inability to participate in the festival at different levels because of the notions of purity and pollution. The process that was considered open and unrestricted has today become reclusive and closed.

While the reservations on inter-dining and practice of untouchability were not obvious, the villagers' narrative suggest its presence. One clear manifestation of this was the withdrawal of people from the 'dictates' of the *satra*. On grounds of such discriminatory practices the scheduled castes, specially the *kaibartas,* vividly recall an instance when one of the *satradhikars* came to collect the annual tithe (*gurukar*) from the villagers. It was then that the upper castes members did not let the *kaibartas* offer their tribute to the *satradhikar*.

Mr. G (an influential *kaibarta* in the village) narrates:

> During one of his visits to collect the annual tithe, the *satradhikar* had camped on the outskirts of the village for a couple of days. This was one of those occasions when everybody in the village wishes to appease him. Thus, irrespective of their caste, all the villagers would offer him their tributes. The tributes included mostly edibles, besides agricultural

> produce. Once a *kaibarta* man was not permitted to offer his tribute. This enraged many of the villagers. This was the beginning. Soon the protest spread horizontally across villages and many from the neighbouring villages too raised their voices in protest and participated in it. This was followed by a huge congregation of men from many villages in the neighbouring areas. These protests resulted in the withering away of the traditional power of the *satra* and the emergence of alternative places of worship in the form of *naamghars*.

People in the village have their own understanding of caste. For them, caste is beyond an endogamous cycle. There are many instances of inter-caste unions; however, there are no accounts of inter-religious alliances. For the villagers, their membership of a caste group is directly related to their access of agricultural land (*khatopathar)* under *satra*. Thus, for them, caste is more than social and is a part of the economic order. But over the years, such an understanding of caste has changed and the new avatars of caste have helped germinate the seeds of '*brahminical* patriarchy' within all the castes. Thus, over the years, restrictions on women and their mobility have increased manifold among the *kaibartas*.

Interestingly, most accounts had least reference to women in agriculture. While women were present significantly in the agrarian production process at different capacities, especially during harvesting and planting, their participation, over the years, had declined in tandem with the changes in the nature of agriculture.

M, a *kaibarta* woman in her early fifties, narrates similar accounts of honour and shame which have forced young women out of the traditional sources of supplementary income:

> Fishing was always considered as one of the much-anticipated activity of the day amongst women in the village. Apart from adding to the income, it also gave us a break from the tedious household chores. We went out for fishing in groups and mostly we used *jakoi, khaloi* (traditional fishing equipment). Walking up to the wet-lands, fishing there and coming back gave us some space which was strictly ours. We could talk about our mothers-in law, husbands and other issues on which we otherwise could not raise an opinion.

While M continues fishing, she misses the company of other women, who no longer go out with her. She adds that the young generation is not interested in any such activity. None of her daughters (who are now married) were interested in fishing; neither were her daughters-in-law.

She claims that they enjoy 'wasting' their time on the phone; they do not understand the importance of skill or the kind of satisfaction that one gets from community fishing. She was also displeased with the withering away of such traditional bonds which revolved around community fishing and women. She rues the fact that women from the neighbouring *Lalung Gaon* still continue such community fishing and it has been productive, both economically and socially. But the new consciousness amongst the women and men from the *kaibartas* impels them to abandon most of their traditional practices.

Changing Discourses

In the post-independence period, the agrarian relationships and livelihood practices in the village have undergone significant transformation on account of the role played mainly by two factors. They are: interventions by the state and lower-caste assertions. The State interventions have had both positive and negative impacts on the agrarian economy of the village.

The most significant state intervention came in the form of land reform. These reforms were followed by land redistribution amongst the landless peasant families. This has had a positive impact upon the villagers. It not only provided land to them but also led to the breaking up of the traditional authority of the *satra* which dominated their social and economic life owing to its control over all the land in the village.

However, the second form of state intervention came in the form of blocking the river *Kolong* at its mouth at *Hatimura*. The river was the lifeline for the village. It was blocked to prevent the inflow of water to the downstream areas of Nagaon city, the district headquarters. This was allegedly done by the government under pressure from the urban elites in Nagaon city with scant regard for the agrarian economy of the floodplains of the river resulting in a devastating effect on the socio-economic life of the villagers. The river today is but a pale shadow of its original self.

The land reform initiative of the state was emboldened by lower-caste assertions first witnessed in the early 1970s in the village. Such initiatives have had a significant role to play in the agrarian economy. The assertions of the lower caste in the village received the support of the *Ek Saran Bhagawati Samaj*, a splinter neo-vaishnavite group of the lower castes which came into being in 1973 and which had a strong following in Nagaon district. The association with the *Bhagawati Samaj* paved the way for the segregation of the lower-caste villagers from the control of the *satra*. The movement had spread as horizontal solidarity (Srinivas, 1995). The lower castes have set up their own *naamghars* and have stopped celebrating most of the festivals (e.g., Holi) and rituals patronized by the *satra* which they traditionally celebrated with much fanfare. Thus, there is a break in the traditional relationship of the villagers with the *satra* at the social and cultural level.

It has been already mentioned that traditionally the satra owned all the land in the village. The households of the officials of the *satra* which belong to the *brahmin* and *kalita* castes, enjoyed usufructuary rights over *satra* land provided to them by the *satra*. Such land included agricultural land, *bari* land and *basti* land. When the Land Ceiling Act 1973 came into force, the *satra* had to surrender land above the ceiling. However, the land under the possession of the above-mentioned households of the castes was not brought under the Act. Such land was treated as family land and not as *satra* land although the latter was the case. It is, however, not that they owned a considerable amount of land. Most of the households owned from 10 to 15 *bighas*.

It is to be noted that the *satra* had a total of 651 *bighas* in the village before the implementation of the Land Ceiling Act. The ceiling surplus land of the *satra*, however, was distributed among the other categories of villagers. Though this provided many marginal and landless peasants, especially *kaibartas*, with some *bighas* of land, this was much less than what the upper castes secured after redistribution. A *kaibarta* villager stated that they could get 12 *bighas* of land as their uncle was close to the revenue officials. However, leaving out the land under the possession of the *brahmins* and *kalitas*, the *satra* and the wetland areas (which were declared as commons), hardly 250 *bighas* of land was left for redistribution among more than 200 other families.

It can be inferred from this that the share of land that individual lower-caste families got after its redistribution was quite small and did not significantly change the economic status of many of them. This is testified by the fact that today incidences of landlessness among the *kaibarta* villagers are quite high and there are as many as 40 landless families among them. However, despite such segregation, it is to be noted that the *satra* remains the largest land holder with 50 *bighas* of agricultural land. The *satra* also continues to give employment to the landless lower-caste families in the village who are directly engaged as sharecroppers.

While most of the villagers have access to some amounts of land, the data on fragmentation indicates its skewed distribution among different castes. The data on fragmentation indicates: The village is numerically dominated by the SCs and they also have the maximum landholdings. However, the land fragmentation data indicates a different picture. From 1973 to 2013 there was an increase of 200 per cent. Compared to the SCs the Others and OBCs (numerically less) have less land fragmentation with 50 Per cent. Hence, despite having access to land, the SCs in the village continue to be marginal landholders as there have been many cases of excessive land fragmentation.

Here one needs to note that although the Others and OBCs have undergone land fragmentation, they continue their agricultural practices together. Among the SCs, a split in agricultural land means a division of agricultural activities as well. As a result, agricultural activities become unproductive. Adding to this unproductive agricultural cycle, the disappearance of the erstwhile commons has further multiplied the crisis of livelihood choices for them. Such instances act as precursors hastening the process of migration out of the village.

Though the village is dominated by the lower castes, the upper castes continue their socio-economic dominance. While in the post-independence period, the lower castes have been able to assert themselves through various social mobilization efforts and government policies, only a few could benefit in terms of tangible benefits. While fragmentation of land in general affected the entire village, it was adverse in terms of the scheduled castes. Since the members of the *brahmin* and *kalita* castes have found permanent employment outside the village because of their education, there is less pressure on their land stemming the process of land fragmentation. The lower castes, however, because of lack of education, have hardly found any sustainable permanent employment outside the villages. As a result, there is increasing pressure on their agricultural land leading to its fragmentation and landlessness. This has compelled the poor lower-caste villagers to look for unskilled and semiskilled livelihood opportunities in distant places. There is also a minor trend in the village where one can see some lower-caste villagers shifting to non-agricultural activities. However, owing to various reasons, such examples are few and far between.

It is to be mentioned that today only in the *satra* land is sharecropping exclusively practised. The other landowners in the village practise both sharecropping and a new system of contractual arrangement *(chukti)* with those who lease land. This new practice is much more favourable to landholders than the landless peasants. In *chukti,* irrespective of the produce, a peasant has to give a fixed amount to the landowner. This system puts a lot of pressure on a peasant because even if there is a crop failure, he must give the landowner the amount of crop or its monetary equivalent fixed by the contract. This took away whatever human considerations that existed in the erstwhile sharecropping *(adhi)* system where a sharecropping peasant had to give half of whatever was produced.

Therefore, the lower caste landless and the marginal peasants still prefer to work in *khatopathar.* The *satra,* in its turn, being the largest landowner of the village, is in a position to provide more livelihood opportunities to these poor peasants than the other landowners including the lower caste landowners. This economic power of the *satra,* besides its social position, has been the source of its continued influence in the village.

Various new government pro-poor schemes came to the fore. These schemes not only provided food items (especially rice) at a much subsidized rate; they also provided housing and various employment opportunities in the schemes under the Mahatma Gandhi National Rural Employment Guarantee Act (MGNREGA) mainly in building roads in the area. While these schemes took care of the basic necessities of the poor villagers, they had a discouraging effect on the interest of the villagers in agriculture which was already becoming difficult owing to the lack of irrigation and labour. Thus, the villagers gradually began withdrawing from agriculture and many youths did not have any productive activity. Around this time, news of migrants from nearby villages sending remittances from their places of work outside the state became a talking point in the area and it caught the imagination of the village youths. This situation prepared the ground for their migration to other states of India. Many have mortgaged their land to generate funds for their migration. Similar cases of non-farm employment are also found amongst the rural migrants from different parts of the country. For instance, Parthasarathy et al (1998) argues that the rural unemployed go out searching for jobs and are willing to do whatever comes their way. Studies also show that there is a co-relation between agricultural land holding and rural migration.

The issue of farmers' migration, however, has been a much debated one. A section of scholars argues that this migration is an outcome of the process of change that has occurred in the traditional agrarian sector (scholars like Arjan De Haan, 2002). The latter is breaking up under the onslaught of new forces of production and paving the way for a new production relation in the country side. These scholars uphold migration as a welcome and necessary process of change. Another section of scholars, however, is critical of this process of rural migration. They argue that this process has been hastened not by the availability of some better and sustainable opportunities outside agriculture, but because of an extremely sluggish agricultural sector devoid of necessary government support including irrigation, subsidized power, minimum support price, etc., turning agriculture into an unproductive sector.

However, this enthusiasm regarding migration gradually declined not only in the village but also in the larger area. While some youths have indeed contributed to the economic well-being of their families in the village as well as in the neighbouring villages, there are many more cases of failure and fiasco. The migrants could not find jobs that matched their expectations; in a number of cases, their families had to sell their land for failure to return the money they had borrowed for the migration. The absence of young male members from the family also created many problems for their families as well as in the village. There have been cases of injuries and broken health due to illness. Thus, the bad experiences outside, indebtedness, loss of land, etc., have created a situation of hopelessness among the returnees. However, in the absence of any government scheme either to support agriculture or to facilitate the employment of youths in non-farm sectors, it might create a condition of lumpenisation of these youths which is already showing some early indication.

It is worthwhile to note that unlike some pockets in India where agricultural modernization along with the green revolution were introduced to upgrade agricultural productivity, Assam did not witness any such push. Therefore, the class of rich farmers on the one hand and the class of pauperized peasantry on the other, born out of the green revolution as discussed by Jodhka (2004) are not found in the state. However, the agrarian structure of Assam is characterized by class differentiation and pauperization which is to be understood in its own special context as the present study indicates.

However, various other issues like lack of government initiatives and lack of proper implementation of various pro-poor schemes have been some of the major issues that continue to overshadow the rural agrarian economy of the state.

Conclusion

To conclude, we can argue that the two processes of land redistribution and scheduled caste assertions in the village have undoubtedly emboldened the scheduled castes to some extent but its overall impact on them remained uncertain. Hence, while the scheduled castes in the village today have their own religious space (*naamghar*) away from the clutches of the *satra* indicating the affirmative side, instances of land fragmentation and unemployment indicate a gloomy picture of their economic status.

Disappearance of family farms rampant among the *kaibartas* also append to their economic challenges.

At this juncture, therefore, it becomes essential to take cognizance of the status of scheduled castes in the village. While state initiatives on improving the conditions of the scheduled castes are on, there still lies a grey area (with issues like corruption, nepotism and social networking topping the chart). There is also a growing consciousness among the scheduled caste youth to break away from the traditional practices of livelihood and engage in new forms which in the long run looks promising to them. For instance, the young boys shy away from engaging themselves in fishing which, if carried out in an organized way, maybe in the form of a cooperative, can help them generate a lot more revenue. The growing consciousness also has an adverse effect on the women. Men who have become conscious of their identity have begun exercising a much more constraints on their women, especially on their movement. Women who were traditionally engaged as help (apart from acting as *ruwoni* and *daoni* during the harvest season) in the upper caste houses are no longer engaged so. Also, the scheduled caste men prevent their women from going and working in MGNREGA work, as the sexuality of women is always guarded to protect the purity of the caste (Dube, 2000). Moreover, the move away from the village in search of new job avenues has increased the number of female-headed (scheduled caste) households in the village from none to 6. For instance, these female-headed households today must undertake economic and social-cultural custody of the members left behind without moving beyond the contemporary boundaries of caste 'Biradari' (Padi, 2012). On the one hand, from after studying the village, we can say that caste as a system has diminished and there is change but its features in terms of pollution and purity continue to linger and have taken new forms following the contemporary changes that have reshaped caste.

REFERENCES

de Haan, A. 2002. 'Migration and Livelihoods in Historical Perspective: A Case Study of Bihar, India', *Journal of Developmental Studies*, Vol. 38, No. 5.

Dube, Leela. Nov, 2000. 'Doing Kinship and Gender,' *Economic and Political Weekly*, Vol. 35, No. 46.

Deka, Rameshwar. 2008. *Dakhinpat Kachari Satrar Samu Etibriti in Smriti-Grantha Kolong-Haria*. Nanda Singh, ed. Guwahati: Dristi.

Ghurye, G. S. 1932. *Caste and Race in India*, Bombay: Popular Prakashan.

Louis, Dumont. 1970. *Homo Hierarchicus: The Caste System and its Implications*, University of Chicago Press.

Jodhka, S. S. 2004. 'Agrarian Structures and their Transformations' in *Oxford Handbook of Indian Sociology*. Veena Das, ed. New Delhi: Oxford UP, 7th edition.

Padi Ranjana. 2012. *Those who did not Die*, Sage.

Parthasarathy, G., et al. 1998. 'Determinants of Rural Non-Agricultural Employment: The Indian Case.' *Indian Journal of Agrarian Economics*, Vol. 53.

Srinivas, M. N. 1955. 'Caste can they exist in India tomorrow,' *Economic and Political Weekly*, Vol. 7, No. 42.

14

SOCIAL JUSTICE: FUSION OF POLARITIES, A PEEP INTO THE APPROACH TO THE SCs OF TRIPURA

Paul Pudussery

ABSTRACT

Social justice may be considered as the exercise of altering, disrupting and subverting arrangements that promote marginalization and exclusionary processes. It is an active engagement of reclaiming, appropriating, nurturing and engendering the inherent rights of equity, equality and fairness in social, economic, educational and personal dimensions. Social justice is a social reconstruction by a process of deconstruction with certain determined impetus to have inclusive society by fusing certain polarities that exist in any given society. This conscientious effort has to be a positive discrimination so as to set a stage for the fusion of polarities of various types. This paper is a study of how the state of Tripura has engendered this fusion. Tripura has declared thirty four communities as Scheduled Castes. In 1982, a Department of Welfare of Scheduled Castes was established for overall growth and development of the Scheduled Caste community. The total population of Scheduled Castes is 6,54,918 and the literacy percentage is 89.45. The number of SC-dominated villages is 168 (40 per cent above the SC population) and 236 (20-40 per cent SC population). The Government of Tripura has developed special packages for SCs from 2013-14 to 2017-18 for their socio-economic development. Development works taken up are in the area of education, health, housing, drinking water, link roads, power, irrigation and income-generating schemes. This study will appraise the construction of a society by positive discrimination.

Key Words: social justice, Tripura, scheduled castes, educational, social enhancement, financial stability

Introduction

Tripura is a state in North-East India. It shares borders with Bangladesh, Mizoram and Assam. It is surrounded by Bangladesh on its north, south and west. The length of its international border is 856 km (84 per cent of its total border). The state is connected with the rest of India by NH 44 that runs through Assam, Meghalaya, North Bengal, Kolkata and other parts of India. Although the state is small with a population of only over three million, Tripura is the second-most populous state in the North-Eastern region. The social composition of the population of Tripura is diverse. Around one-third of the population belongs to the Scheduled Tribes. According to the 2011 Census, the state's population is 36.74 lakh with a density of 350 persons per sq. km. The population pattern and demography have always been fluctuating. In 1901, Tripura's population was 1.73 lakh, with tribals making up nearly 52.89 per cent of the whole. By 1941, the total population rose to 5.13 lakh with a barely 50.09 per cent tribal majority. But by 1981, the tribal population dipped to 28.44 per cent of the total population of 2.05 million because of several socio-political developments. According to the 2011 Census the Scheduled Tribe population is 31.8 per cent of the total population

Classification of SC/ST (and also OBCs) as backward classes of citizens is a reasonable classification permitted by Article 14 of the Constitution of India. However Article 16(4) is exhaustive on the subject of reservation in favour of 'backward' classes of citizens, as explained in the judgment of Supreme Court in Writ Petition No.930 of 1990 (*Indira Sawhney vs UOI*). The Census 2011 data shows that the SC population of the State was 6,54,918 (17.8 per cent). The total SC males was 3,34,370 and SC females was 3,20,548. The demography of Scheduled Castes in the state is not confined to any particular location or 'paras' or 'bastis'; it is scattered in all regions.

The SC literacy rate has increased to 89.45 per cent in 2011 from the earlier level of 74.68 per cent in 2001. During the intra-census period of 2001-2011, an increase of 14.77 per cent is noticed for SC literacy. The scheduled caste-population of the state comprises 34 communities recognized by the state as well as the Government of India. A separate department was set up known as 'Department for Welfare of Scheduled Castes' in 1982 bifurcating the Department for Welfare of Scheduled Tribes (STs) & Scheduled Castes (SCs). The following list indicates the number of Scheduled Castes and their population as per the 2011 Census.

Sl. No.	*Name of SC community*	*Total population (as per 2011 Census)*	*Literacy Age (7-above)*	*% of literacy*
1	Bagdi	510	331	78.44
2	Bhuimali	272	198	83.90
3	Bhunar	178	131	86.75
4	Chamar,Muchi	13579	9898	83.20
5	Dandashi	5	5	100.00
6	Dhenuar	65	54	94.74
7	Dhoba	56513	45893	90.88
8	Dum	41	31	81.58
9	Ghasi	204	160	90.91
10	Gour	6854	4808	82.71
11	Gur	86	61	83.56
12	JaliaKaibarta	106849	85577	90.29
13	Kahar	357	252	84.56
14	Kalindi	135	95	86.36
15	Kan	27	22	88.00
16	Kanda	2574	1775	82.91
17	Kanugh	49	34	82.93
18	Keot	302	209	84.62
19	Khadit	18	10	62.50
20	Kharia	1409	763	64.50
21	Koch	815	576	81.59
22	Koir	102	73	81.11
23	Kol	1079	755	80.32
24	Kora	117	76	75.25
25	Kotal	9	6	85.71
26	Mahisyadas	153034	125362	92.34
27	Mali	55009	43539	90.94
28	Methor	1851	1419	86.79
29	Musahar	327	257	87.41
30	Namasudra	215267	167666	88.18
31	Patni	7235	5688	88.94
32	Sabar	4429	2223	63.99
33	Dhuli,Sabdakar,Badyakar	9344	6792	85.75
34	Natta,Nat	1643	1264	86.63
35	Generic	14630	10873	84.76
	All Scheduled Castes	654918	516876	89.45

The following chart will illustrate the growth of the SC population in Tripura

Population scenario as per date of last 5 Census operations

Sl.No.	*Census year*	*Total population*	*SC population*	*Percentage (%) of SC population*
1	1971	15'56342	1,92,860	12.39
2	1981	20,53,053	3,10,384	15.11
3	1991	27,57,205	4,51,116	16.36
4	2001	31,99,203	5,55,724	17.37
5	2011	36,73,917	6,54,918	17.80

Educational Change

According to the Census report, the literacy rate among the scheduled castes is on the rise. The overall literacy rate of the state in 2001 was 73.20 per cent while the SC literacy rate in the corresponding period was 74.01 per cent, which is a very positive indication in respect of their development. The chart below reflects the position in this regard.

Category	*Position of 1991(%)*		*Position of 2001(%)*	
	Overall	*S.C.*	*Overall*	*S.C.*
Total	60.44	56.66	73.20	74.01
Male	60.20	67.25	81.00	80.09
Female	39.79	45.45	64.90	67.20

As per Census 2011 the literacy rate of scheduled castes has increased to 89.40 per cent from 74.01 per cent which is a grand success. This increase in literacy rate was possible because of the concerted effort by the government which is supported by leaders from the same community. In an interview with a five-time member of state legislature from the scheduled caste-dominated area, he reaffirmed that this increase in the education level was only due to the support of the government. He went on to elaborate that it is also due to the belief in equality held by the ruling party for the last many years. He believed that education is the key to social change both in terms of understating the nuances of life and financial stability. This financial stability brought about new marriage alliances with the other so-called superior castes. These marital alliances are bringing about changes in the strict following of caste. According to a Member of the State Legislature (MLA), the change in educational status has brought about a social transformation leading to fusion.

The following table of jobseekers is a clear sign of the higher level of education that is being imparted to the community. Many of them are leaving their traditionally assigned jobs for other possible employment. It is also an indication that the economy of the state is not adequate to employ so many. It also indicates lack of investment in industry which generates jobs. The reason for a lack of investment can be studied from various perceptives. This paper does not study that but may mention that geographical isolation is a factor that one has to reconcile with. The fact that the members of scheduled castes are looking for jobs different from theirs is another indication of fusion in society.

According to the Economic Review 2015-16, job seekers among different categories are:

UR	*ST*	*SC*	*OBC*	*EX. S*	*PH*	*TOTAL*
359116	161933	1125594	53797	1039	6037	693516

This paper explores the concept of social inclusion and how it is transmitted in actuality both at the macro-institutional level and at the meso-practice level which has had an impact on the life and society of scheduled castes in Tripura. The rapid socio-economic development of persons belonging to various scheduled caste-communities has always been a priority for the state government. Two special development packages comprising 17 and 15-points were launched in 2000-2001 and 2003-2004, respectively, for the welfare of the Scheduled Castes. Based on the successful implementation of these special packages and the feedback received, it is proposed to launch another special package for the welfare of scheduled caste-communities to be implemented over a period of five years from 2013-2014 to 2017-2018.

The commitment of the state government to the overall development of the scheduled castes and its focus is on the 293 SC-dominated villages across the state which is described as SCSP areas. Of these 179 villages have SC population in the range of 20 to 40 per cent and 119 have an SC population of 40 per cent and above. According to government sources 17 per cent of the plan fund is utilized annually in these areas for its development. The said fund is utilized for development of SCs in different sectors like agriculture, horticulture, animal resources, fisheries, health, education, drinking water, roads, electrification, irrigation, etc. The author visited the SC-dominated areas and some of these developments are visible. It is also possible for a traveller to see the transformation in these areas brought about by an inclusive policy. This socio-economic transformation has brought about a fusion of different castes in a healthy manner.

Infrastructure Development

The state government has taken many steps to bring about a change in the lives of SCs who are living in villages that are not dominated by them. The basic infrastructural facilities provided to them include all-weather roads, telecommunication, health care facility, electrical power supply, safe drinking water, sanitation, irrigation, etc. The government has allotted money to construct a multi-purpose hall with a seating capacity of 300-500 for the purpose of skill development, cultural and other democratic activities. These efforts have benefited not only the target group but the general population as well. These specific steps have contributed to building bridges between and among different castes and brings about the idea of a melting pot giving every individual a social standing despite the kind of caste stigma attached elsewhere in the country.

Land allotment

The government has allotted land to many homeless persons and land-less scheduled caste families in different areas of the state where land was available. Such allotment policy and financial assistance at the rate of Rs.75,000 per family to construct dwelling houses for persons in the BPL category has brought about a higher confidence level among them. It was evident in the interviews that this confidence level has enabled them to interact with other castes.

Housing for *Safai Karmacharis*

The government has provided for the *safai karmacharis* (cleaning staff) living in Agartala Municipal Council area and other *nagar panchayats* by giving them land and financial assistance to build houses. The government is also considering a housing complex for them.

Vocational Training and Financial Assistance

The government has imparted training for interested youth from SC families to produce leather goods, handicrafts, electronic and other items having good market viability. The trained youths were provided required assistance as well as soft loans from financial institutions to set up and run their enterprises. Assistance was provided to people engaged in pisciculture with soft loans and facilities to make new ponds. The farmers were provided with Kisan Credit Cards to avail credit for agricultural and allied activities. The people who were involved in traditional laundries were given new machines and other facilities. Traditional musicians were provided with equipment to form a band party. The women were provided seed money to start small businesses.

Educational scholarships were provided to many students to pursue their dreams. Pre-matric scholarships will be provided to all eligible SC students studying in classes VI to X. Post-matric scholarships will be provided to all SC students studying in Class XI and above in colleges/ university. Special coaching in core subjects like Science, Mathematics and English will be organized for SC students. All girl students belonging to SC families having an income of less than Rs.1.25 lakh per annum and studying in classes IX to XII were provided bicycles free to facilitate their movement to schools.

Social Enhancement

The government made provisions to promote culture and other literary activities by instituting awards such as the 'B.R. Ambedkar Socio Cultural Awards.' This award recognized individuals who worked for the welfare of the scheduled castes. A special award in memory of Adwaita Malla Barman has been instituted in the field of literature related to the scheduled castes.

Appointment to government jobs as per reservation was strictly adhered to. The issue of scheduled caste certificates was strictly scrutinized to ensure authenticity.

Conclusion

The schemes envisaged under the Protection of Civil Rights Act, 1955 and the SC/ST (Prevention of Atrocities) Act,1989 and the 33-point welfare schemes for scheduled castes in Tripura have brought about a tremendous transformation in this community. The non-existence of exclusive scheduled caste villages is a significant contributing factor in bringing about fusion. The economic and social agenda of the government provided a greater impetus and stability to these communities. The training and timely financial assistance lifted many families out of poverty. The commitment of the government and officials require special mention as the transformation in this community was possible only because of their concerted effort. A focus group consisting of seven post-graduate students shared the view that they never experienced any negative discrimination because of their caste. They felt bad that others could not enjoy the privileges they did because of their caste. A few were of the opinion that it may be time for Tripura to think about stopping the special privileges granted to people based on caste. The schemes may have to be based on economic status rather than on caste considerations.

Social Justice: Fusion of Polarities: A peep into the approach to the SCs of Tripura was an attempt to illustrate how real transformation can be brought about by the concerted effort of the government and people in power. The story of Tripura is an inspiration for those who wish and work for transformation. The data indicates that Tripura is in a right direction in engendering a society that is based on humanity rather than caste which is a social construct.

REFERENCES

Karmakar, K. G. 'Agriculture and Rural Development in North-Eastern India: The role of NABARD,' *ASCI journal of Management*, Vol. 37, No. 2, pp. 89-108.

Ahluwalia, Montek S. 2000. 'Economic Performance of States in Post-Reforms Period,' *Economic and Political Weekly*, Vol. 35, No. 19, pp. 1637-1648.

Bajpai, M. 2002. '"A Decade of Economic Reforms in India: The Unfinished Agenda,' Working Paper No. 89, Centre for International Development, Harvard University, http://www.ksg.harvard.edu/CID/cidwp/089.pdf.

Barbora, Sanjay. 2006. '"Rethinking India's Counter-insurgency Campaign in North-East,' *Economic and Political Weekly*, Vol. 41, No. 35, pp. 3805-3812.

Bareh, H. M. 2001. 'The Gathering Storm in Tripura.' *Encyclopedia of North-East India.* Vol. 8. Delhi: Mittal Publications.

Basu, P. K. 1996. 'The Communist Movement in Tripura: Its Evolution (1935-75).' *Encyclopaedia of India and her States.* Vol. 9. Ed. Verinder Grover and Ranjan Arora. New Delhi: Deep & Deep Publications.

Bhattacharya, B. B. & S. Sakthivel. 2004. 'Regional Growth and Disparity in India: A Comparison of Pre and Post-Reform Decades,' http://iegindia.org/worksakthi244.pdf.

Bhattacharya, H. 1996. 'The State and Social Changes in colonial Tripura.' *Encyclopaedia of India and her States.* Vol. 9. (ed) Verinder Grover and Ranjan Arora. New Delhi: Deep & Deep Publications.

Bhattacharya, S. 2005. 'The North-East Frontier. Discovery of North East India.' Vol. 1. (ed). S. K. Sharma and Usha Sharma. New Delhi: Mittal Publications.

Brass, P. 1991. *Ethnicity and Nationalism: Theory and Comparison*, New Delhi: Sage Publications.

Coghlan, D. 2016. 'Retrieving a philosophy of practical knowing for Action Research.' *International Journal of Action Research*, Vol. 12, No. 1, pp. 84-107. doi: 10.1688/IJAR-2016-01-Coghlan.

Ghosh, Madhusudan. 2006. 'Economic Growth and Human Development in Indian States,' *Economic and Political Weekly*, Vol. 41, No. 30, pp. 3321-3329.

GOI. 1997. '"Transforming the North East: Tackling Backlogs in Basic Minimum Services and Infrastructure Needs,' High Level Commission Report to the Prime Minister, Planning Commission, http://planningcommission.nic.in/reports/genrep/ne_exe.pdf.

Hawkes, Jon. 2001. *The Fourth Pillar of Sustainability: Culture's Essential Role in Public Planning.* Victoria: Cultural Development Network.

Humanshu. 2007. 'Recent Trends in Poverty and Inequality: Some Preliminary Results,' *Economic and Political Weekly*, Vol. 42, No. 6, pp. 497-508.

15

DR. B. R. AMBEDKAR AND SCHEDULED CASTES:

A BRIEF SCENARIO OF SCHEDULED CASTES IN TRIPURA

Surojit Sen Gupta

ABSTRACT

Ambedkar's concept of social justice stands for liberty, equality and fraternity of all human beings. He stood for a social system that is based on right relations between man and man in all spheres of life. As a rationalist and humanist, he did not approve of any type of hypocrisy, injustice and exploitation of man by man in the name of religion. He stood for a religion that is based on universal principles of morality and is applicable to all times, to all countries and to all races. It must be in accord with reason and must be based on the basic tenets of liberty, equality and fraternity. He considered the caste system as the greatest evil of Hindu religion. The varna system, according to him, is the root cause of all inequality and is also the parent of the caste system and untouchability. He addressed the problem of untouchability and came out with concrete proposals for its removal and the upliftment of the marginalized and the excluded. He believed that the root of untouchability lay in the caste system and caste in the hands of the orthodox has been a powerful weapon for persecuting the reformers. He felt that no socio-political reform movement could be successful without the annihilation of caste. He wanted justice for untouchables as well as the weaker sections of society by making provision in this regard in the Constitution itself. Ambedkar stood for a social system in which a man's status is based on his merit and achievements and where no one is noble or untouchable because of his or her birth. He advocated the policy of preferential treatment for the socially oppressed and economically exploited people of the country. Thus, against in this background, the present paper will be an attempt to understand sociologically Dr. B. R. Ambedkar's perspective of the Hindu social system and his notion of social justice.

Key Words: hypocrisy, injustice, exploitation, Ambedkar, Hinduism, social justice, Safai Karmacharis

Introduction

Bhimrao Ramji Ambedkar, affectionately known as Babasaheb, was born in a community that suffered oppression for centuries. The social oppression and disability attached to him on the ground that he was born to *Mahar* parents could not prevent him from realizing his dreams. His love for learning led him to obtain the highest academic degrees available to any person during those days. Dr. Ambedkar graduated from Bombay University in 1912. Thereafter, he went abroad to pursue higher studies. He was one of the most qualified persons of his time who had such high academic distinctions to his credit as M.A. and Ph.D. from Columbia University, and M.Sc. and D.Sc. degrees in Economics from the London School of Economics. He also studied Law at Grays Inn, London, and visited the famous University of Bonn.

Dr. Ambedkar ranked high among the intellectuals of his time. He was a versatile genius who wrote on such diverse subjects as Anthropology, Sociology, Economics, Philosophy, Religion, Law, History and Politics. His burning passion to fight against injustice made him a natural leader of the oppressed and downtrodden sections of Indian society who were persecuted for centuries. Ambedkar has created a unique place for himself in the history of India by sheer dint of his scholarly brilliance, untiring zeal and tenacious efforts for the uplift of the downtrodden. His social thought was thus dominated by his urge to lift the 'untouchable' community and break the shackles of casteism and Brahmanism. He is naturally, therefore, looked upon as a great emancipator of those who had been suppressed for centuries.

Dr. Ambedkar's social thinking was a result of his total dissatisfaction with the humiliating treatment meted out to members of his community by the so-called high-caste Hindus. His philosophy, therefore, had the objectives of the attainment of social amelioration, political enlightenment and spiritual awakening for his community. Due importance to the economic well-being of the masses was essential for this. To him, political thought embodied a social dynamism with equal rights for man and woman. His deep faith in the Fundamental Rights, the dignity of the individual, social and economic justice, the promotion of social progress and better standards of life with peace and security in all spheres of human life enriched his political philosophy. Dr. Ambedkar's role as a saviour of the weaker sections of society is no less than that of any reformer of the Hindu religion throughout the centuries. He doggedly fought against the two principal inhuman malpractices in Hindu society, that is, untouchability and casteism.

Untouchability which was religiously practised during Dr. Ambedkar's time was the most inhuman and cruel practice. Without annihilating casteism, Hindus cannot be a modern society—a civilized one—nor can there be democracy in the real sense of the term in which human rights are well protected. Dr. Ambedkar made a thorough study of the caste system which has been an intractable problem of Hindu society. Differing with Western scholars like Senart, Nesfield and Risley on the issue of the caste system, Dr. Ambedkar noted that in spite of the composite make-up of the Hindu population, there is a deep cultural unity and that classes have become castes through imitation and excommunication (1979). The Brahmins first started rigidity in the caste system by introducing the custom of endogamy (but not in the same gotra), enforced widowhood, sati minor-girl marriage, etc. Persons belonging to the other castes followed the rituals observed by Brahmins to get a respectable place in society and later on such customs and practices got codified in the *Manusmriti* and the other shastras through which the practice of untouchability was perpetuated in its worst form (Mishra, 1991). Dr. Ambedkar did not keep himself confined to academic research. He was a great fighter and an able organizer. He organized Harijans to fight the menace of untouchability to get a respectable place in society.

Hindu Social System—Dr. Ambedkar's Perspective

Dr. Ambedkar attempted an incisive analysis of the Hindu social organization which he found to be tradition-bound, conservative and insular. He criticized the Hindu social system and religious laws as being inhuman, unscientific and irrational (Rajasekhariah, 1991). They placed the 'untouchables' in a desperate and helpless position. As a result, they remained oppressed, unorganized and poor. It was the deplorable state of these helpless human beings that motivated Dr. Ambedkar to trace the historical origins and development of the cruel practice of untouchability, the caste system and the Shudras themselves. He identified the hypocrisy and conspiracy of upper-caste Hindu thinkers, who, by virtue of their advantageous position, created inhuman, illogical and irrational social and religious laws and inflicted untold human miseries on the 'untouchables' and on their social, economic and cultural lives. Thus, these people remained oppressed, suppressed and poor in the Hindu social hierarchy through the ages. Perhaps, it was such appalling conditions that prompted Dr. Ambedkar to write remarkable treatises such as (1) Annihilation of Caste; (2) Who Were the Shudras and How They Came to be the Fourth Varna in Indo-Aryan Society?; and (3) The Untouchables: Who Were They and Why They Became Untouchables?

Dr. Ambedkar's social philosophy may be said to have two aspects: the negative and the positive. In its negative aspects, he wanted to destroy the existing unjust social order by denouncing and rejecting the irrational division of society into four varnas or classes, viz., Brahmana, Kshatriya, Vaisya and Shudra based on the principle of 'division of labour' and heredity. Dr. Ambedkar refuted this theory of chaturvarna and argued that it not only divides the society artificially into water-tight compartments but also leads to 'division of labour.' It is opposed to the principles of natural law and the spirit of human development. He forcefully argued that the chaturvarna system was created deliberately to deprive the Shudras of their social, economic, educational and cultural rights.

In fact, Dr. Ambedkar refuted the chaturvarna theory and argued that there were only three varnas—the Traya Varna—in Aryan society. According to him, the Shudras were not a separate varna but were a part of the

Kshatriya varna. They emerged as the fourth varna from the conflict between the Kshatriya kings and Brahmins as they were denied the sacred thread by the latter. Owing to this denial, the Shudras were socially degraded and demoted to the rank of the fourth varna. In support of his argument, Dr. Ambedkar quoted *Purushasukta*, *Satapatha* and *Taitriya Brahmana*. He also cited Western scholars such as Max Mueller and Max Weber and pointed out that in all their works, reference is made only to three varnas in the early Aryan society.

Dr. Ambedkar also denounced the caste system which was a direct outcome of the chaturvarna theory. It was mainly responsible for the origin and development of the institution of caste in India. In course of time, the four varnas came to be divided into hundreds of castes with many more sub-castes, thus dividing, sub-dividing and fragmenting Indian society. The caste system divides society into separate units, each one markedly different from the other. This compartmentalization is maintained by instilling, among the members of a particular caste, feelings of prohibition, separation and fear. This division of society into castes and sub-castes has shaken the very roots of the Indian social structure and has caused tensions and caste wars.

There is a great controversy as well as confusion and distortion about the origin of the practice of untouchability. There is no unanimity among historians, sociologists and thinkers on the issue. The pertinent question is: When the 'untouchables' are not a part of the chaturvarna scheme, where do they belong? They are called avarnas, i.e., they have no varna; rather, they are outside the varna scheme. To understand the psychological, historical and sociological issues involved in the theory of the origin of untouchability, Dr. Ambedkar undertook an in-depth research and analysis which was mostly speculative in approach owing to paucity of historical documents and wrote his findings in his valuable work on 'untouchables' (Ambedkar, 1948). He held that the 'untouchables' are distinct from 'impure'. All orthodox Hindus committed the mistake of identifying the impure with the 'untouchables'. While the impure as a class came into existence at the time of the Dharma Sutras, 'untouchables' came into being much later. It is interesting to note his concluding observation here: "We can therefore say with some confidence that untouchability was born some time about 400 A.D. It is born out of the struggle for supremacy between Buddhism and Brahminism which completely moulded the history of India..." (Ambedkar, 1948).

Thus, Dr. Ambedkar rejected the Chandala theory to explain the origin of untouchability and showed that untouchability arose out of an accident in history much later, that is about 400 A.D. The so-called untouchables were originally Buddhists. With the decline of Buddhism, they were sucked into Hinduism and subjected to indignity and infamy (Rajasekhariah, 1991). Vested interests belonging to the upper-caste Hindus were certainly behind this move; they had to be protected at any cost even if it meant that a whole section of people were to be treated as less than humans. Having segregated one section of people as beyond redemption, they had perforce to find a religious ground to justify such segregation. Furthermore, Dr. Ambedkar held that 'impurity' and 'pollution' are terms associated neither with secular ideas nor with profane practices. They definitely belong to the realm of sacred or religious doctrine. Dr. Ambedkar successfully exposed this hypocrisy and the misrepresentation of the shastras by building up a more scientific explanation to the origin of untouchability by pointing out that it has no racial basis. It was on these grounds that he tried to convince those who objected to its abolition (Rajasekhariah, 1991). He said that untouchability could be completely eradicated once its opponents knew that it has no racial basis. Hence, the significance and value of his study and research on the origin of untouchability (Rajasekhariah, 1989).

Dr. Ambedkar was in fact struggling with the unholy nexus between religion, caste and untouchability. Since the caste system and untouchability are deep-rooted in the socio-economic, religious and cultural spheres of life, he came to the conclusion that unless and until the religious basis in the form of chaturvarna and caste is demolished, untouchability cannot be removed. He called for a total annihilation of the caste system and its allied practices. His major objective was to transform the very nature of Hindu society so that a free and independent India could proudly claim to be a democracy. He was striving to transform a social organization which was tradition-bound, conservative and insular, which had seldom yielded to pressures whether from within or outside, to restructure itself into a modern, progressive and open society (Rajasekhariah, 1991). He also had the insight to realize that the Hindu religion with its innumerable castes and sub-castes posed a serious problem in any effort towards unification of India politically, socially and economically. Therefore, Dr. Ambedkar totally denounced the caste system and its allied practices. But more than finding a mere diagnosis of this deep-rooted malady, he was in search of a cure that would make free India a healthy, cohesive and progressive political system, based on democracy, secularism and socialism.

Ambedkar's Notion of Social Justice

Justice is a very complex concept as it has a number of sources and dimensions. It has been examined by different people from different viewpoints within the limits of the time, place and circumstances they lived in. Social justice is one of the dimensions of the concept of justice that stands for organization of society based on the principles of equality, liberty and fraternity. Its greater emphasis is on the principle of equality, both social and economic and fraternity with a view to create such human social conditions that ensure free and fair development of all human beings. As such, the concept of social justice sometimes requires unequal or preferential treatment for certain sections of the population that have been deprived of certain values for ages to bring them on an equal footing with other sections of the population.

Ambedkar's concept of social justice stands for the liberty, equality and fraternity of all human beings. He stood for a social system that is based on right relations between man and man in all spheres of his life. As a rationalist and humanist, he did not approve of any type of hypocrisy, injustice and exploitation of man by man in the name of religion. He stood for a religion based on universal principles of morality and is applicable to all times, to all countries and to all races. It must be in accord with reason and must be based on the basic tenets of liberty, equality and fraternity. He considered the caste system as the greatest evil of Hindu religion. The varna system, according to him, is the root cause of all inequality and is also the parent of the caste system and untouchability.

Ambedkar stood for a social system in which man's status is based on his merit and achievements and where no one is noble or untouchable because of their birth. He advocated the policy of preferential treatment for the socially oppressed and economically exploited people of the country. The Constitution of India, which was drafted under his chairmanship, contains a number of provisions that enjoins the state to secure to all its citizens, justice, social, economic and political, along with liberty, equality and fraternity. It also contains a number of provisions that guarantee preferential treatment to the downtrodden in various sectors (Raghavendra, 2016). Article 17 of the Indian Constitution declares untouchability as abolished. Ambedkar, in his speech before the Constituent Assembly for the passage of the Constitution, said, "I have completed my work; I wish there should be a sunrise even tomorrow. The new Bharat has got political freedom, but it is yet to raise the sun of social and economic liberty."

The positive aspect to Dr. Ambedkar's social philosophy was his concern for justice to the 'untouchables' in particular, and to all the people of India in general. He was fully aware of the fact that it is difficult to get justice from people so deeply engrossed in a religion which, according to them, had given its seal of approval to the practice of the caste system. Dr. Ambedkar's main concern was the secularization and democratization of Indian society and polity as a prerequisite for dispensing justice to one and all. He always maintained that there cannot be an economic and political revolution in India unless the caste system was totally abolished. He made it clear that only a secular India in which the death-knell of casteism is sounded would be fit for a socialistic pattern based on equality and justice (Ambedkar, 1936). The measures suggested by Ambedkar for uprooting the practice of untouchability can be divided into social, political and constitutional categories which followed the establishment of an egalitarian and just society. These social measures included: abolition of the caste system, encouraging inter-caste marriages and inter-dining, creating social awareness among the people about the irrationality of the caste system and the practice of untouchability, organizing the people to fight against these evils and abolition of the scheduled caste ghettos under the New Settlement Movement Act, 1942 and assimilating the 'untouchables' with upper-caste Hindus. The political measures included creating opportunities for the Depressed Classes for effective participation in the political process and granting them a fair share in the political power of the country through reservation of seats, separate electorate and protective discrimination (Rajasekhariah, 1991).

Dr. Ambedkar had hoped that these and many other political and constitutional safeguards would help the people to liberate themselves from the clutches of caste politics and pave the way for the emancipation of the Depressed Classes. But his efforts did not yield the desired results. It is rather unfortunate that the traditional and insular nature of Hindu society did not accept the politico-legal and constitutional measures envisaged by Dr. Ambedkar. Hence it was more in despair than as a political ruse or expedient that this great leader was compelled to search for a faith which would promise a destiny—political, social and religious—to the untouchables to enable them to realize their fulfilment as persons and human beings. Dr. Ambedkar naturally began to feel the clawing hand of frustration. His zeal, unflagging as ever, could not but search for a spiritual answer to the problem. Finally, he found the answer in Buddhism. So he, along with his countless followers, embraced Buddhism to derive solace and justice.

Dr. Ambedkar's social philosophy emerged from his intense social urge and relentless struggle for the emancipation of the servile classes of India—the Shudras and the untouchables. He revolted against the tradition-bound and insular Hindu society which oppressed and suppressed the downtrodden and the underprivileged. He developed a particular kind of socio-ethical philosophy that was characteristically his own. He steadfastly stood for human dignity and freedom, socio-economic justice, material prosperity and spiritual discipline.

Dr. Ambedkar's thoughts on social justice were progressive. He did not believe in violence; he considered the Press to be a powerful tool for social change for justice and freedom. He published *Mook Nayak*, *Janata* and *Samata* magazines, but they remained largely unsold, perhaps because of the progressive and unconventional thoughts expressed therein. If there are prohibitions on the social evil of untouchability in the Constitution, then this credit goes to Ambedkar to a great extent. Ambedkar's greatest achievement was that he made the downtrodden feel their separate powerful existence; the credit goes to him that he brought all the downtrodden, untouchable castes under one name, Scheduled Castes. If Ambedkar had not pursued special reservation facilities for scheduled castes in the field of education and government services of the central and state governments, their condition would have remained as before—laden with sorrow and suffering. He enshrined the principles of reservation for improvement of the scheduled castes to enable them to progress educationally, economically and socially by providing extra support to them in the form of reservation and concessions to uplift them to the level of the advanced classes. It is clearly seen at present that many legal provisions have been made to give social justice to all classes. In this way, many schemes and programmes have been begun for the all-round development of the country and a measure of development has been achieved through it.

Dr. Ambedkar was a crusader of social equality justice. He never made any compromise with injustice, never cared for prestige and self-aggrandizement. He was an uncompromising rebel against social injustice and inequality. He worked relentlessly for the regeneration of humanity, for the well-being of mankind and for the transformation of man and society. He was a great social liberal. His vision was to produce a new social order based on the principles of justice, equality and fraternity. Thus, the idea of justice, equality, liberty and fraternity was the crux of his activities (Mallik, 2011). Dr. Ambedkar wanted economic and social equalities before political equality; he tried his best to ensure that the downtrodden got a proper place in society. Hence, he gave more importance to social justice than political justice; on equal opportunity with individual liberty was laid much emphasis to root out the differences created by the caste system of the country.

Scheduled Castes—Situation in Tripura

The demography of scheduled castes in Tripura is not confined to *paras* or *bastis* or localities. According to the Census 2011, the population of scheduled castes in Tripura accounted for 6,54,918 persons which is 17.8 per cent to the total population (Census, 2011). The scheduled caste population by and large live inter-mingled with other communities in the same village or neighbourhood. The social distance between scheduled castes and other communities is negligible. In Tripura, 34 scheduled caste communities are recognized and they are: (1) Bagdi, (2) Bhuimali, (3) Bhunar, (4) Chamar/Muchi/Chamar-Rohidas/Chamar-Ravidas, (5) Dandasi, (6) Dhenuar, (7) Dhoba/Dhobi, (8) Dum, (9) Ghasi, (10) Gour, (11) Gur, (12) Jalia Kaibarta/Jhalo-Malo, (13) Kahar, (14) Kaliadi, (15) Kan, (16) Kanda, (17) Kanugh, (18) Keot, (19) Khadit, (20) Kharia, (21) Koch, (22) Koir, (23) Kol, (24) Kora, (25) Kotal, (26) Mahisyadas, (27) Mali, (28) Mehtor, (29) Musahar, (30) Namasudra, (31) Patni, (32) Sabar, (33) Dhuli/Sabdakar/Badyakar and (34) Natta/Nat (Government of Tripura, 2016). The interrelationship of scheduled castes with other communities in Tripura generally appears to be harmonious, not only in the economic field, but also in a social context. The scheduled caste groups are almost equally important as a community and apparently there is nothing to indicate sectorisation or polarization of scheduled caste communities in matters relating to business dealings, politics, education, religious functions, social get-togethers, etc. Any such apprehension is further thwarted by the fact that social interaction between different communities with regard especially to marriage is very common. As a matter of fact, at a superficial level, there is no distinction among the scheduled castes in Tripura.

Developmental Activities for the Welfare of Scheduled Castes in Tripura

Rapid socio-economic development of persons belonging to various scheduled caste communities has always been a priority for the state government since the establishment of the Department of Welfare for Scheduled Castes in 1982. Since then, the state government has taken different initiatives for the development of scheduled castes in both the rural and urban areas. In this regard, it is worth mentioning here that the two special development packages comprising 17-points and 15-points that were launched in 2000-2001 and 2003–2004, respectively, for the welfare of scheduled castes has brought far-reaching changes in the state. Based on the successful implementation of these special packages and the feedback received, another special package for the welfare of the scheduled caste communities was implemented over a period of five years from 2013-2014 to 2017-2018. Details of this package for the development of the scheduled castes in various segments in the state include:

Infrastructural Development

Necessary action is taken for providing basic infrastructural facilities for communication like weather, road, telecommunication, health care facility, electrical power supply, safe drinking water and sanitation, irrigation, etc., in the uncovered scheduled caste populated areas on a priority basis. Efforts are also underway in the state to construct a multi-purpose hall with seating capacity of 300-500 in scheduled caste-dominated areas for the purpose of skill development, cultural and other democratic activities.

Economic Development

Landless scheduled caste families belonging to the BPL category are allotted available *khas* land as per guidelines. The remaining homeless as well as landless scheduled caste families under the BPL category are provided financial assistance at the rate of Rs. 75,000 per family to construct dwelling houses. *Safai karmacharis* living in Agartala Municipal Council area as well as in other *nagar panchayats* are provided available land and financial assistance for construction of dwelling houses to the extent possible. In view of the non-availability and high cost of land in urban areas, the construction of a housing complex is also considered for them.

To exploit available and new opportunities, assistance for upgrading skill is provided through training to interested youths from scheduled caste families. Production of leather goods, handicrafts, electronic and other items having a good market is given special attention while imparting vocational training. Trained youth are provided necessary assistance as well as soft loans from financial institutions to set up and run their enterprises.

New water bodies are created and existing ones renovated and developed for improving production of fish and income of scheduled caste families living on pisciculture. These water bodies are provided to cooperative and self-help groups (SHGs) formed with scheduled caste families. Further, scheduled caste families having suitable land are also assisted for creation of water bodies. For pisciculture, soft loans are also provided to fishermen belonging to the scheduled castes.

Interested scheduled caste families are assisted through subsidies and soft loans to set up modern laundries, giving particular attention to upgradation of traditional laundries being run by scheduled caste washermen.

Financial assistance is also provided to traditional scheduled caste professional musicians like band party, *dhaki*, etc., to pursue their activities on a commercial scale.

Necessary action is taken to form SHGs with women belonging to scheduled caste families and extending necessary assistance and soft loans to them to run micro-enterprises as per market requirements.

Market sheds are constructed in market areas in scheduled caste dominated areas, both in urban and rural areas, and interested youth and SHGs with members from scheduled caste families are provided assistance and soft loans to set up their business.

Educational Development

Special coaching facility is provided to eligible candidates belonging to scheduled caste families to enable them to come compete successfully in various competitive examinations of all-India and state services such as IAS/IPS/IFS/TCS/TPS/TFS, etc. Educational loans are also provided to scheduled caste students to pursue higher studies. Pre-matric scholarships are provided to all eligible scheduled caste students studying in classes VI to X. Post-matric scholarship is provided to all eligible scheduled caste students studying in classes XI and above in colleges and university. There are also 32 hostels with good facilities run by the government for scheduled caste students. Special coaching in core subjects like Science, Mathematics and English is organized for them. Special emphasis is given for training of youth belonging to the scheduled caste in computer application (both software and hardware) and trained youth are extended necessary assistance.

Social Development

Special efforts are made and necessary assistance extended for promotion of culture and other literary activities for the scheduled castes in the state. Awards are given in recognition of talent for outstanding achievements. The B.R. Ambedkar Socio-Cultural awards are given for significant work relating to the welfare of scheduled castes every year. A special award is launched in memory of Adwaita Malla Barman in the field of literary activities relating to the welfare of the scheduled castes. Provision of reservation for scheduled castes in appointment and promotion in government services and admission in various educational institutions is strictly enforced and eligible persons are assisted for availing benefit of reservation as admissible under the law. The procedure for issuing certificates to persons belonging to notified scheduled caste communities is strictly followed and carefully scrutinized to ensure that they are issued only to eligible persons.

Conclusion

To conclude, resting on Ambedkar's thoughts, the Indian Constitution guarantees equal rights to all based on social justice and human dignity. It is observed, however, that Ambedkar's ideas of social justice could not be realized in a proper manner over the years. As such, his concept of justice will have to be propagated by institutions through civil society. Ambedkar was concerned about the overall development of the vulnerable sections of Indian society and he chose to demolish existing caste discrimination by enacting the Constitution. Therefore, Ambedkar's ideas of social justice remain relevant in contemporary Indian society in promoting constitutional and legal methods to uphold the rights and dignity of vulnerable sections.

Dr. Ambedkar wanted the scheduled castes to follow some principles in life so that they attain a respectable status by their own efforts as a community. He recommended 'Pancha-Sutras' for them: (1) Self-Improvement: Making one's own efforts for one's improvement without expecting much from others; (2) Self-Progress: Making self-efforts for achieving progress in life; (3) Self-Dependence: Learning to lessen one's dependence on others and attaining finally self-reliance; (4) Self-Respect: Maintaining self-dignity and never sacrificing it for any reason; and (5) Self-Confidence: Developing confidence in oneself, in one's capacities and in one's efforts, and in this regard the scheduled castes in Tripura are no exception. At the same time, the participation of the scheduled caste community in the process of modern politics, education, economic and other processes has undergone a significant change in their lifestyles in Tripura. Caste has been made freed from its traditional local and vertical matrix. The coming into existence of new opportunities, education, economic, political participation and welfare programmes brought about an increase in horizontal solidarity. Internal differences of a caste are undermined now and different sections of a caste are coming closer and getting united. Urbanization has also increased spatial mobility among the scheduled castes in Tripura. The Westernized style of life and modern ideology has played an important part among the scheduled castes. Thus, the spread of equalitarian ideology, governmental welfare programmes and social mobilization reveal that a fundamental change has taken place among the scheduled castes in Tripura.

REFERENCES

Agarwal, Sudarshan. 1991. Dr. B. R. Ambedkar—*The Man and His Message*, New Delhi: Prentice Hall of India.

Alva, Joachim. 1943. *Men and Supermen of Hindustan*, Bombay: Thacker & Co. Ltd.

Ambedkar, B. R. 1936. *Annihilation of Caste*, Bombay New Book Co.

Ambedkar, B. R. 1946. *Who Were the Shudras*? Bombay, Thacker & Co. Ltd..

Ambedkar, B. R. 1948. *The Untouchables: Who were They and Why They Became Untouchables*? New Delhi: Amrit Book Co.

Ambedkar, B. R. 1979. *Dr. Babasaheb Ambedkar: Writing and Speeches*, Vol. 1, Education Department, Mumbai: Government of Maharashtra.

Guru, Gopal. 2002. 'Ambedkar's Idea of Social Justice', In: Ghanshyam Shah (ed.), *Dalits and the State*, New Delhi: Concept Publishing Company.

Iyer, Krishna, V. R. 1990. *Dr. Ambedkar and the Dalit Future*, Delhi: B. R. Publishing Corporation.

Jatava, D. R. 1997. *Social Philosophy of B. R. Ambedkar*, New Delhi: Rawat Publications.

Kuber, W. N. 2001. *Builders of Modern India—B. R. Ambedkar*, Publications Division, Ministry of Information and Broadcasting, Government of India, New Delhi.

Lal, Shyam. 1998. 'Ambedkar and Social Justice,' In: Shyamlal and K. S. Sazena (eds.), *Ambedkar and National Building*, Jaipur: Rawat Publications.

Larbeer, Mohan, P. 2003. *Ambedkar on Religion: A Liberative Perspective*, Delhi: ISPCK.

Mackenzine, J. S. 1918. *Outline of Social Philosophy*.

Mallik, C. 2011. 'Justice and Equality in Dr. B. R. Ambedkar's Vision of India,' Doctoral Dissertation, Kolkata: Jadavpur University.

Notification. 2016. List of Scheduled Castes in Tripura, Department of Welfare for Scheduled Castes, Agartala: Government of Tripura.

Raghavendra, R. H. 2016. *Dr. Ambedkar's Idea on Social Justice in Indian Society, Contemporary Voice of Dalit*, New Delhi: Sage Publications.

Rajasekhariah, A. M. 1989. *B. R. Ambedkar: The Quest for Social Justice*, New Delhi: Uppal.

Sharma, Sanjay, P. 2003. *Dr. Ambedkar a Crusader of Social Justice*, Jaipur: RBSA Publishers,

Sing, Surendra. 1997. 'Dr. B. R. Ambedkar's Contribution to Social Justice,' In: Mohammad Shabbir (ed.), *B. R. Ambedkar Study in Law and Society*, Jaipur: Rawat Publications.

Special Package for Development of Scheduled Castes in Tripura, 2017 -2018, Department of Welfare for Scheduled Castes, Agartala: Government of Tripura.

Yadav, Shushma. 2006. 'Social Justice: Ambedkar's Vision,' Dr. Ambedkar Studies Centre Lecture Series No. 2, Dr. Ambedkar Studies Centre, Jammu: Department of Sociology.

16

SOCIAL JUSTICE AND THE SCHEDULED CASTES: A SIKKIM NARRATIVE

Debasish Chowdhury

ABSTRACT

Ensuring social justice across the board in a vast country like India with its hierarchically stratified society and highly disparate economic distribution has always been and continues to be a formidable challenge. Delivery of social justice may be understood as the task of ensuring that the collective essentials of a society, its wealth, opportunities, authorities and privileges are fairly shared without prejudices by each of its constituent elements. And dispensing social justice would, therefore, only act as an enabling future. The arguments and counter-arguments involving this policy of extending discriminatory privileges to select social groups notwithstanding, legislative approval to the continuance of this policy till date remains a compulsion in Indian politics that none of its elected governments irrespective of its ideological inclinations had so far dared to ignore either at state or at central level.

This paper is an attempt to draw insights from the state of Sikkim where the scheduled caste population constitutes a very low number compared to other parts of the north-eastern states of India. It is a boon for the state that affirmative action initiated for the historically underprivileged by the Government of Sikkim has always been in the right direction. Education has been the most viable source which has contributed largely to the development of the SCs in the state. And it is for this reason that Sikkim has been able to meet the demands towards ensuring social justice for the deprived. Though now it may seem like a utopia to strive for an individual's rights and fight for justice, in course of time this utopia shall drive the progress of the society with an undiminished zeal.

Key Words: social justice, hierarchically stratified society, industrialisation, sustainable, utopia, hypogamous

Introduction

Ensuring social justice across the board in a vast country like India with its hierarchically stratified society and highly disparate economic distribution has always been and continues to be a formidable challenge. Given that a large majority of her people are backward on the count of almost all accepted parameters of social metrics such as economy, education, access to health services and even to political authority and given further that millions of them live in countless denominations with each of them having its own social, linguistic, cultural and even religious background and placed in socio-economic settings of extremely diverse kinds, from difficult-to-cultivate mountain ranges and barren plain lands to fertile and highly cultivable plain lands to hilly terrains, ensuring social justice to each such group under a common policy umbrella indeed is fraught with challenges that are far more complicated than one may like to envisage.

Broadly speaking, delivery of social justice may be understood as the task of ensuring that the collective essentials of a society, its wealth, opportunities, authorities and privileges are fairly shared without prejudice by each of its constituent elements. Since, such a state of being in any society is hardly feasible without its operating social institutions getting duly empowered; it is essential that adequately empowering its social institutions is a prime concern in the task of delivering social justice. By turn, it suggests that all relevant entitlement such as education, healthcare, social security, labour rights, etc., be made inclusive and accessible to all concerns. Institutions put in charge of dispensing these entitlements fairly to each of its individual elements irrespective of caste, creed or community considerations to facilitate their performing, acting and living a life of one's own choice based on individual merit and attainments must also get duly empowered and energised. Dispensing social justice, seen in this context, therefore, would only act as an enabling feature.

Such a state of affairs is hardly achievable but for a well-oiled institutional mechanism that must have in place the authority to implement and monitor a broader system of public services. This, in turn, necessitates having in place appropriate taxation policies duly equipped with market regulatory, progressive features but for which fair distribution of wealth, equal opportunity, equality of outcome, etc., in short, all that a just society must ideally have makes no real sense. The concept of social justice, it would be evident then, must serve a specific goal that despite its dynamic content must appear a tangible one seeking to at least reduce, if not abolish completely, the inequalities that holds the progress of society in general.

The Legacy

Post-independence, when the framers of the Indian Constitution embarked upon the task of giving the newly-liberated nation its first Constitution, they did take note of this pressing social necessity to remove inequalities that thrived in this land for millennia together and accommodated in the Constitution such enabling features as they deemed prudent to help remove disparities to serve the cause of ensuring social justice to its citizens across the board. Accordingly, the concept of differentially facilitating its people across the spectrum depending on their current social standing was mooted and favoured. Consequentially, the colonial era 'depressed class' was redefined in the Constitution by segregating it into two distinct categories, namely, the Scheduled Castes and the Scheduled Tribes and, by granting them formal recognition and granting legitimacy to accord them a favoured treatment though special privileges for a limited time period, the Constitution of India sought to address the issue of social justice.

By envisaging that such favoured treatment to the select groups identified to have been in the depressed category and proposing that such favoured treatment to the people of this category be extended for a period of 10 years to begin with, the Constitution (Scheduled Castes) Order, 1950 listing 1,108 castes across 29 states were released in its First Schedule. The Constitution (Scheduled Tribes) Order, 1950 further lists 744 tribes across 22 states in its First Schedule[1] granting each of these social groups special privileges striving to restore equality and reduce depravity. These lists, however, were not exhaustive and subsequent amendments were made to add more such castes and tribal groups in these two lists while Article 46 that says, "the State shall promote, with special care, the education and economic interests of the weaker sections of the people, and, in particular of the Scheduled Castes and Scheduled Tribes, and shall protect them from social injustice and all forms of social exploitation" was provided for in the Constitution to serve the interest of these groups. Interestingly, seven decades down the line none of the groups listed in the First Schedule or added into it subsequently has ever been dropped from it to take it out of the coverage of these Constitutional provisions hinting, rather sadly, that the exercise somehow did not deliver its desired objectives stated at its commencement.

Views and Counterviews on Positive Discrimination

Extending discriminatory privileges to traditionally deprived and disabled communities with the objective of reducing social inequality as provided for in the Constitution, however, from the very start, has been a highly contentious issue. In the pre-independence era, extending of such privileges to select social groups was seen as a tool of the then colonial rulers to divide and rule the people while post-independence, it has often been seen as a wrongly legitimized benefit to only a select set of people on the basis of their birth that has been perpetuated at the cost of 'merit'. As for the discriminatory privileges provided for in the Constitution, the people of India have often taken an obdurate stance on both sides of the divide with a readiness even to die either supporting or opposing the cause. The self-immolation of Rajiv in Delhi opposing implementation of the Mandal Commission Report or, in recent times, the *Patidar* movement in Gujarat led by Hardik Patel demanding inclusion of his community within the ambit of the reservation cover vividly describes the searing tension entwined so deeply in the social fabric of this vast country surrounding this issue of discriminatory privileges more commonly known as the 'Reservation Policy'.

Defenders of the policy of positive discrimination argue that society is obliged and needs to adequately compensate for the deprivation it had thrust upon its own people for a millennium on the excuse of caste, creed and community. Those opposing the policy argue that such policies seriously compromise merit and that such policies do not uphold the fundamental principle of natural justice by imposing penalty on individuals who had played no direct role in the perceived miscarriage of justice. The arguments and counter-arguments involving this policy of extending discriminatory privileges to select social groups notwithstanding, legislative approval to the continuance of this policy till date remains a compulsion in Indian politics that none of its elected governments, irrespective of its ideological inclinations, had so far dared to ignore either at the state or at the Central level.

Table 1

	Language	*People*	*% of Total*
1.	Nepali	338,606	62.61
2.	Bhutia	41,825	7.73
3.	Hindi	36,072	6.67
4.	Lepcha	35,728	6.61
5.	Limbu	34,292	6.34
6.	Sherpa	13,922	2.57
7.	Tamang	10,089	1.87
8.	Rai	8,856	1.64
9.	Bengali	6,320	1.17
10.	Urdu	2,930	0.54
11.	Tibetan	1,977	0.37
12.	Punjabi	1,364	0.25
13.	Malayalam	1,021	0.19

Source: K. S. Singh: People of India, Sikkim: Vol. XXXIX, 1993, ASI, Calcutta, p. 412

Sikkim: A Basic Profile

Sikkim, despite its late inclusion in the Indian Republic in 1975 as its 22nd state and the special protection it receives under Article 371 on a host of administrative and policy-related matters, too does provide for such discriminatory privileges for the socially disadvantaged groups residing in it. To appreciate the status of social justice in this tiny state, it is pertinent to look at its basic profiles.

A tiny hill state of breath-taking natural beauty situated in the Himalayan range, Sikkim is only about 7096 sq. km in size. The size of its geographical territory makes it the second smallest state of India. With approximately 6.53 lakh plus population at present (projected figure taking the 2011 Census as base), it, however, qualifies as the least populous Indian state at present. With its only airport yet waiting a formal commissioning, this landlocked state is connected to the rest of India only by road. Being placed in a high rainfall zone, landslides are routine features that frequently, even if for short duration, disrupt road links connecting it to the rest of the country through the Bengal corridor. National Highway 10 (NH 10), its prime and most-used road link to the rest of the nation serves the state as its lifeline.

Its small size and low population strength notwithstanding, by being home to a number of distinctly identifiable language, culture, custom and ethnic groups, Sikkim, like the rest of India does have a highly variegated pluralist culture of its own kind in which Nepali is the lingua franca and the Nepali ethnic group constitutes the largest segment of its population. In fact, as of now, it is the only state in India having a Nepali ethnic majority population. Besides the Nepalis, it is home to a host of other language groups such as the Lepchas, the Bhutias, the Limboos, the Newari, the Kulung, the Gurung, the Manggar, the Sherpa, the Tamang and the Sunwar besides Hindi and Bengali in a limited way. It may be interesting to know that 'Sikkim' literally means 'new home' in the Limboo language. Table 1 at pre-page shows the linguistic distribution of population in Sikkim as per the Census 2001 (Linguistic details of the Census 2011 could not be availed) clearly reflecting on the fact that the Nepali-speaking people are the dominant majority (Table 1) in this state.

With its population density approaching about 90 per sq. km., Sikkim, however, is more thickly populated than Arunachal Pradesh which, incidentally, has the largest land area amongst all the north-eastern Indian states. The decadal population growth in the state has been computed to be at about 12.0 per cent and is trending downward over the years. With its female population count registering a rise from 875 in 2001 to 890 per thousand males in 2011, the female-to-male ratio also seems to be displaying reasonably encouraging trends. Inclusive of the population of Gangtok, which is the capital city of the state, the proportion of urban population in Sikkim stands at about 24.5 per cent of its total population. It may however deserve a mention here that it is the urban population, over the last decade or so, that has actually grown at an alarming rate of 150 per cent resulting in a noticeable fall in its rural population strength and hinting at large-scale migration of people from rural to urban/ semi-urban centres.

In the absence of large-scale industrialisation typical of India's north-eastern states, the mainstay of the state's economy is anchored in agriculture and tourism and hospitality-related services inclusive of the transport sector. A glance at the total area under cultivation of principal crops reveals that both crop yield as also the area under cultivation has been receding over the past few years, a nominal though steady decline (Table 2).

Apparently, this seems to be a direct consequence of the changing dynamics of the economy at the national level as also the contribution of migration of labour from the agricultural sector to urban-centric economic sectors luring them to look for quick cash return-giving engagements. As regards education, Sikkim has done fairly well and is placed well amongst the northeast Indian states. With its average literacy rate currently standing at 81.42, Sikkim has registered a rise by about 15 per cent as per the 2001 Census figures. This, by any standard, is highly encouraging particularly for the reason that this enhancement in the literacy rate also registers a significant growth in the rate of average women literacy as well.

Table 2

Year	*Principal Crop*	*Area under Cultivation ('000 ha)*	*Production ('000 tonnes)*
2009-10	Food grains (cereals)	65	104
	Food grains (pulses)	13	13
	Oilseeds	10	9
	Total	88	126
2010-11	Food grains (cereals)	63	99
	Food grains (pulses)	13	12
	Oilseeds	10	8
	Total	83	119
2011-12	Food grains (cereals)	63	97
	Food grains (pulses)	07	6
	Oilseeds	09	8
	Total	79	111
2012-13	Food grains (cereals)	60	100
	Food grains (pulses)	06	6
	Oilseeds	08	7
	Total	74	113

Sources: Recompiled with data taken from Directorate of Economics and Statistics, Ministry of Agriculture (Statistical Yearbook, India 2015)

Sikkim, as of now, is the only state that has made education up to the level of graduation free for its indigenous citizens as also for all those settlers in Sikkim who come under the purview of the Sikkim Subjects Regulation 1961 as amended vide relevant notification issued on January, 1962 and also to those residing here and are covered by GoI order dated August 07, 1990. Currently servicing the higher educational academic aspirations of about 15,000 students enrolled at various levels in its institutions of higher education alone, such an endeavour for a state of the size of Sikkim with its limited revenue earning is indeed a commendable effort.

The Scheduled Castes in Sikkim

Three years after Sikkim became part of the Indian Republic in May 1975, Presidential assent to The Constitution (Sikkim) Scheduled Castes Order, 1978 was obtained according to which all Nepali-speaking Hindus, Sikhs and Buddhists belonging to the *Damai*, *Kami*, *Lohar*, *Majhi* and *Sarki* groups and resident in the state of Sikkim were included in the scheduled caste category. Table 3 shows that the scheduled caste population in Sikkim is less than half the estimated national average of 15 per cent of the total population. The Sikkim Legislative Assembly, as of now, has a capacity of thirty-two (32) seats of which twelve (12) are reserved for scheduled tribes of BL origin and two (2) for Scheduled Castes. There has been a consistent demand from the 'Limboo-Tamang' community resident here for their inclusion in the ST reserved category though a solution to this is yet awaited. On December 18, 2014, the '*Majhi*' community was dropped from the list of recognized scheduled castes in Sikkim and this perhaps may be the only instance when a community could be migrated out of the purview of the scheduled list and consequently out of the purview of the advantages of the discriminatory privileges earlier accorded to them without the fuss that is normally anticipated in such action.

This goes favourably to substantiate the state government claim that the affirmative action initiated by it towards facilitating development and furthering social justice for the historically under-privileged has been and continues to be in the right direction.

Table 3

Name of State/District	*Area*	*Population*			*Scheduled Caste Population*			*% of SC*
		P	*M*	*F*	*P*	*M*	*F*	
Sikkim	Total	610,577	323,070	287,507	28,275	14,454	13,821	4.6
	Rural	456,999	242,797	214,202	20,335	10,496	9,839	4.4
	Urban	153,578	80,273	73,305	7,940	3,958	3,982	5.2
North District	Total	43,709	24,730	18,979	982	536	446	2.2
	Rural	39,065	22,274	16,791	804	441	363	2.1
	Urban	4,644	2,456	2,188	178	95	83	3.8
West District	Total	136,435	70,238	66,197	5,935	3,117	2,818	4.4
	Rural	131,187	67,528	63,659	5,663	2,978	2,685	4.3
	Urban	5,248	2,710	2,538	272	139	133	5.2
South District	Total	146,850	76,670	70,180	6,053	3,058	2,995	4.1
	Rural	125,651	65,848	59,803	5,042	2,569	2,473	4.0
	Urban	21,199	10,822	10,377	1,011	489	522	4.8
East District	Total	283,583	151,435	132,151	15,305	7,743	7,562	5.4
	Rural	161,096	87,147	73,949	8,826	4,508	4,318	5.5
	Urban	122,487	64,285	58,202	6,479	3,235	3,244	5.3

Source: Census of India 2011, RGI as picked from Basic Statistics of NE States, a NEC document.2

Enabling Features in Practice

It is well known that traditionally the scheduled castes were cowed down by a host of infirmities, the prominent of which may be identified as social, economic, religious and educational. In Sikkim, the social disadvantages of being a scheduled caste is and has never generally been as intense as is the case elsewhere in the country. Inter-caste and inter-group marriages here, by and large, are not seen as taboo and though exact statistics are difficult to obtain, hypogamous marriages in which the bridegroom comes from a scheduled caste community while the bride belongs to a higher caste community including even Brahmins are not too uncommon. It may however not be fair to undermine the fact that though such inter-caste and inter-group marriages often are a tacit hint at the economic and educational standing of the family of the bridegroom which, in many instances is at least, if not better, of a comparable standard with that of the bride's family. In fact, the state government here sees such inter-caste marriages as an effective tool to promote social parity and takes proactive measures to encourage them, particularly if one of the spouses in such a marriage is from the scheduled caste community. Accordingly, as a supportive gesture, the state government has implemented a scheme that provides a cash reward of 20,000 to any newly-married couple provided that one of the spouses in such a marriage is a scheduled caste. The spread of education has always been viewed as a key tool for promoting social justice. Facilitating delivery of education with ensured emphasis on access, equity and inclusivity for the disadvantaged, as such, needs to be taken up with a sense of priority and Sikkim, on the educational front, despite its many limitations in terms of physical, infrastructural and manpower resources, has done a fairly commendable job.

Table 4

District /State	*Total SC Population*	*Literates*			*% of Literacy*
		M	*F*	*T*	
North District	982	349	246	595	60.59
South District	6053	2228	1881	4109	67.88
West District	5935	2086	1634	3720	62.68
East District	15305	5828	4946	10774	70.40
Sikkim	28275	10491	8707	19198	67.90

Source: Primary Census Abstract 2011 Data: RGI

The literacy rate figures (Table 4) as it stands now for the scheduled castes, is a critical social indicator of social progress; for instance, it vindicates that efforts to reach out to the disadvantaged have delivered reasonably well.

The proportion of scheduled castes to the total population in Sikkim (4.6%) is less than even one-third of the estimated national average of 15 per cent (refer Table 3). A 7 per cent quota has been earmarked for the scheduled castes to enable them pursue education in various educational institutions within and outside the State and this is indicative of the priorities accorded to their development. An exclusive scheme for scheduled castes under the Chief Minister's merit has also been launched in 2016 that, after conducting a State-wide selection process, fully sponsors the education of scheduled caste children at schools of national repute both within and outside the state.

At least, three scheduled caste children, a local researcher confirmed, could manage to qualify in the selection process in the current year and are now studying outside the state at full government expense. Sikkim has also provided for full free education up to the graduation level at all its state-run institutions of higher education. Under this scheme, the institutions run and managed by it do not charge any fee from the students who are eligible to be beneficiaries. Even other fees payable to the affiliating university are borne from the public exchequer making education virtually freely available to all eligible aspirants.

On the economic front, Sikkim does not have a spectacular success story to tell but even as early as in 2006-07 its aggregate household income distribution, if compared to other neighbouring states of the North-east, was reasonably fair. Distributing its households into three categories, namely, rich, middle and poor wherein households having annual income exceeding Rs 3 lakh were placed in the rich bracket, those having annual income between Rs 0.75-3 lakh were placed in the middle category and those with an annual income below 0.75 lakh were put in the poor bracket, it is clear that the people of Sikkim do not lag behind most of their neighbouring states. With 8.27 per cent of its households falling in the rich category, 69.45 per cent in the middle and only 22.29 per cent in the poor bracket, Sikkim was even then reasonably placed if compared to its neighbouring states as far as distribution of its household economy was concerned. Interestingly, even this distribution of household economy does not, at least in the middle and poor categories, indicate any discernible caste-centric bias. However, pursuant to its stated objective of servicing the cause of social justice, the scheduled castes in Sikkim continue to enjoy the benefit of 7 per cent job reservation on all directly employable state government-run offices and also public sector undertakings operating within its jurisdiction. In the 32-member state legislative assembly too, two seats are reserved for the scheduled castes to provide them with a space even in the policy-making exercises.

Further, to support the scheduled castes, scheduled tribes and the other backward classes, the Sikkim Scheduled Castes, Scheduled Tribes and Other Backward Classes Development Corporation has been established to support and finance income-generating ventures of the intended target group. The corporation supports and funds projects planned by the target group towards uplift and furtherance of their economic standing in agriculture and allied; artisan and traditional occupation, technical trades, hotel, guest house, lodge, restaurant and other small-scale business projects including the transport sector. It would, however, be fair to acknowledge that while funding under various loan schemes is a routine feature of the corporation, details in respect of the recovery status of the loans extended by it is a rather grey area and demands a little more serious attention to ensure that the scheme does not die out due to unreasonable fund drainage through the bad debt route.

Sikkim, by and large, counts amongst the most peaceful of all the north-eastern states. Reports of caste-linked atrocities, as such, are few. However, to ensure speedy disposal of cases of atrocities on scheduled castes and scheduled tribes, all session courts in Sikkim have been designated as special courts with adequate empowerment to try and speedily dispose off such cases. A state vigilance and monitoring committee has also been constituted in pursuance of the relevant provisions of the Prevention of Atrocities against Scheduled Castes and Scheduled Tribes (PoA). Under its authority, this committee routinely reviews and monitors various relief and rehabilitation-related works relating to SCs and STs living here. Training of police personnel on a regular basis to sensitise them on matters pertaining to SCs and STs is routinely carried out.

Closing Comments

Going by the above narrative, it may be easy to say that Sikkim has been true to its responsibilities towards the need to ensure social justice for the deprived and that, in general, it has carried out its responsibilities in a sensible fashion. Yet, it remains for one to appreciate that given the tiny population of less than thirty thousand that it needed to cater for and, further, despite the many central as well as state-sponsored schemes that it had put into operation for decades now, its inability to succeed to even achieve hundred percent literacy for the scheduled castes places the picture in a rather different perspective.

To consider that having a reservation policy in place in itself is a guarantee of having ensured social justice is a myth. The injustice meted out over centuries is perhaps hard, if not impossible, to be removed only through reservation. Besides, the perspectives that such policies often cost the larger society heavily in the long run by making serious compromises on quality also needs to be aptly dealt with to ensure that it does not lead to hardened animosity between those benefitting from such privileges and those who subscribe to the view that the legitimacy accorded to reservation is devoid of any sound rationale.

Some argue that extending reservation has only succeeded in creating a creamy layer from among the backwards by enabling few of them to avail its benefits multiple times while denying a larger segment of such backwards any access to the discriminatory privileges guaranteed to them. Creating adequate infrastructure and allowing every one equal opportunity are measures, according to them, fundamental towards delivering real social justice in an apt and sustainable manner.

Ensuring social justice tacitly suggests that our striving to create a win-win scenario for all its constituent elements must continue to go on unabated. As of now, it may seem like utopia but then utopias drive the progress of a society or a civilisation. Today's utopia can turn out to be the reality of tomorrow provided there remains a persistent will to pursue it with undiminished zeal.

REFERENCES

Basic Statistics. 2015. A NEC document.
Bhandari, L. et al 2007. The North East and Sikkim.
Constitution of India.
Drall, N. January 2013. Facilitating Social Change: A Government of Sikkim Publication.
Primary Census Abstract, 2011.
Sikkim Government Gazette Extraordinary, July 05, 2014, No. 263, No. 279.

17

IMPACT OF SOCIAL JUSTICE IN NORTH-EAST INDIA:

A STUDY FROM THE STATES OF ASSAM, MANIPUR AND TRIPURA

C. J. Thomas and Padmakshi Kakoti

ABSTRACT

Indian society is a cluster of many castes, ethnic groups and identities. Caste-based divisions continue to dominate under the banner of segregation, exploitation and sometimes violence. The discourses on discrimination and explicit inequality have become vital themes of the country in recent times. These are deep-rooted and embedded in the socio-economic and religious lives of a particular section in society thus thoroughly augmenting the practice of deprivation and discrimination. Through centuries, large numbers of people have been subjugated and experienced social discrimination due to caste hierarchies and as such efforts have been made to redress their issues and bring about possible changes. In recent times, the policy of PD has gained grounds in many developed and developing countries of the world. And India is no exception to this. To bring equity, the deprived and the economically feeble class of individuals in society are ensured of a special right referred to as reservation being a part of PD policies. The policy of reservation as a way of protecting their rights, adapted by the state to bring about a social transformation of the scheduled castes only, is also known as 'protective discrimination'.

The geographical spread of the study is limited to the states of Assam, Manipur and Tripura. The study attempts to examine primarily the education status and its level of achievement among the scheduled caste communities in these three numerically strong SC populated states of North-East India. It also tries to ascertain the quality of higher education in these states vis-a-vis employment status. This paper is an effort to be acquainted with the measures undertaken by the Government of India for SCs, namely, the reservation policy and its impact on the socio-economic and political condition of the people of these selected states of the North-East.

Key Words: scheduled caste, Employment, Education, Political representation, Positive Discrimination, Reservation

Introduction

The concept of 'positive discrimination' and 'social justice' go hand in hand. As implied for the backward and marginalized sections in society, these concepts have attained a new momentum in India because of the massive disparity in the socio-economic status of the people. The ideals of a welfare state are cardinal to the protection and promotion of the socio-economic status of an individual. India, like other developing countries of the world, has adopted the policy of PD in order to uplift the socially and economically weaker sections of the population. After independence, this policy came to be more spelled out as the castes came to play a benign role and changed the perception of equality. The caste system became intrinsic to Indian society and so PD, through the reservation-quota system, steeped in questions of equality, social justice and merit. Dating back to the history of PD, it originated in the United States of America with the notion of affirmative action and, as a consequence, it has taken place in many developed and developing countries worldwide. Literally, termed as 'positive action' in the United States, the concept of affirmative action is based on equality since discrimination by its name only denotes a negative aspect. The Americans initiated affirmative action programmes in favour of the Blacks in various spheres of society since 1964.

The geographical spread of this study is limited to the states of Assam, Manipur and Tripura and it attempts to examine primarily the education status and its level of achievement among scheduled caste communities in these three numerically strong SC populated states of North-East India. It also tries to ascertain the quality of higher education in these states vis-â-vis employment status. This is an effort to be acquainted with the measures undertaken by the Government of India for the SCs, namely, the reservation policy and its impact on the socio-economic and political conditions of the people of these selected states.

Education is one vital element by way of which society socializes all its members and, in the long run, is a way of progress. In a democratic country like India, access to education is open and for all. In spite of many constitutional measures and guaranteed rights especially for the underprivileged, as mentioned in the Constitution of India, there is an acute disparity noticed even today. The reservation or the quota system came as a respite but the socio-economic condition of the marginalized has created a huge gap which is yet to be filled up. The SCs are the worst affected in comparison to STs and other backward categories. Literacy rates among them are region-specific. Rural-urban disparity is another matter of concern coming to terms with educational attainments. Education opens up avenues for employment. When the rate of illiteracy is higher, automatically providing job security becomes meagre. This is common to the SCs in India in general. They are still comparatively less educated and more backward.

In any developing county, education acts as a metaphor and has often been described as being analogous to power. A healthy and efficient education system can only usher in social mobility. And it is expected that with economic transformation along with various developmental schemes and reservation facilities, marginalized groups will match the privileged sections of society. The process of building high quality human resource becomes at stake if the impoverished do not get their share of benefits, and in the long run could not meet the demands of the socio-economically discriminated.

As regards the collection of empirical data, primary data is collected through extended door-to-door interviews using questionnaires and schedules. Questionnaires have been prepared keeping in view three important modules: a) for family/households; b) academic institutions; and c) non-government organizations. The structured interview schedules consisted of questions to measure the socio-economic status of the SCs, their empowerment in education and in political areas, the role of academic institutions in achieving the goals and targets set for the SCs and the accountability of the NGOs working for their welfare.

The material collected for the study was mainly done through both primary and secondary sources. The primary data was collected from respondents in the field and various techniques were employed to extract information like interview schedules, interviewing resource persons and stakeholders, discussion and participant observation. Secondary sources were obtained from books, selected articles, journals and published works, newspapers and magazines, reports prepared by government agencies, universities, research institutions, NGOs, data available online and collected from various government portals and official records from all the three states to support the present study.

In this study, tables, as an important method of communicating and displaying the analyzed data, have been prepared in terms of percentage to identify the differences in all the States. The study also attributes to the SPSS (Statistical Package for the Social Sciences).

Table 1: Sample size of the present study

Sl. No.	*States in North-East India*	*No. of Samples*
1	Assam	3542
2	Manipur	833
3	Tripura	1405
	Total	5780

The above table, therefore, mentions only the family/household samples that were possibly collected from all the three reference states. There was a total of 5,780 samples from each of the States out of which data of 3,542 households from Assam, 833 from Manipur and 1,405 from Tripura have been studied.

The SCs have been conceived as one of the more oppressed and backward groups in Indian society. They suffer from the stigma of discrimination and untouchability. However, through the enactment of various laws and constitutional measures, the SCs have been given a platform to raise their economic standards in the present Indian society. There has been a slight positive shift noticeable in their living standards even though large stratums of the economically weak community still remain a cause of concern. The question of awareness and harnessing the benefits availed to them has become a prime subject of study today. To understand certain notions of the PD policies deployed for the benefit of the SCs, the present study will try to overview the impact of the reservation schemes in changing the general condition of the SCs in these particular States.

The present paper is expected to give meaningful insights towards modifying the operational content on the system of education in these States of the North-East. Students from the SC communities in the region are still far below the national average of educational upliftment and, therefore, programmes implemented for their benefit have so far not been able to meet their needs. And, most importantly, since Indian school education is, by nature, elite class oriented and prepares an individual for prestigious white-collar jobs, it becomes more imperative to draw the distinction. And, hence the true character of the demands for the job market does not suffix the requirements of the marginalized communities. Thus, through the present findings, it will be easier to understand the present state of education and educational problems, the needs of the SC communities and consider the viable changes done through PD policies in the pattern and content of education. It is highly worthwhile to understand the phenomenon of initiating PD programmes in the country and especially to the SCs in particular in a proper perspective and devise some measures to further improve their condition.

The Indian Constitution, going by its lawful and protective rules, adopted justice and equality as its prime principles to organize the socio-political system of the nation. In fact, the measures to ensure equal protection of the laws involves the element of protection as well as that of compensation or reparation to offset the systematic and cumulative deprivations suffered by lower castes in the past (Singh, 1991). The framers of the Constitution felt that the inequalities that have arisen out of the caste system would penetrate deeper into the lives of individuals and it should be stopped with some discretionary measures. It was for this reason that the concept of equality came into vogue and was given a place in the Constitution under Articles 14, 15 and 16 and an express mandate for affirmative action. This was to bring in the scheduled castes and scheduled tribe population under the banner of a protective discrimination policy so that they are given preferential treatment in the socio-cultural and political life of the country. In due course of time, these provisions meant for particular group/groups of individuals came to be recognized as the 'reservation system' and came to be equated with the AA programme in the United States. The efforts made by social reformers like Mahatma Gandhi, B.R. Ambedkar and Vinoba Bhave in tackling the problems of caste-based discrimination are appreciable and befitting. The constitutional measures and legal and governmental policies and procedures adopted by them are the biggest contributions towards the backward community for a certain level of social change and development. These changes and mobility should act as channels to raise the present status of the SCs in the traditional system of the caste hierarchy.

The policy of PD in India is caste-based. It relies mainly on reservation through quotas. Caste is a determinant factor in Hindu society and has been predominant since ages. It determines an individual's status and dignity. There were many big thinkers and reformers in the country who have perpetuated and also condemned the caste system. The social reformers received a good response from society in the 19th and early 20th centuries but there was an ardent need to procure legal provisions for the SCs for their equal rights and privileges and integrate themselves in the main order. It was only after Gandhiji's 1932 fast in opposition to the Communal Award's provision of separate electorates for untouchables that Congress leaders were willing to countenance the positive use of law for providing various facilities to them (Galanter, 1986). Amongst them Dr. B.R. Ambedkar, who had a different approach towards the SCs, strived for an egalitarian order. According to him, the lowest strata of people in society are the scheduled castes and they should be recognized, get proper education and strive for their rights so that they are not dependant on sympathy but live a life of dignity. Though Ambedkar did not coin the term 'dalit' for the untouchables, his philosophy behind the fight for their rights has emerged into widespread popularity in India today. Ambedkar focused on two aspects of social exclusion. One was the exclusionary nature of the caste system (underpinned by untouchability), which denied resources and opportunities to members of the lower castes and the second was a set of policy measures to ameliorate the effects of exclusion (Thorat and Kumar, 2008). Ambedkar emphasized the fact that all people should have respect for each other, protect their inherited rights and stand for solidarity. He, in his deliberations on social democracy in the Constituent Assembly, mentioned that "it means a way of life which recognizes liberty, equality and fraternity which are not treated as separate items in a trinity. They form a union of trinity in the sense that to divorce one from the other is to defeat the very purpose of democracy. Nor can liberty and equality be divorced from fraternity." As the chairman of the Drafting Committee of the Constitution, he prodigiously incorporated the AA programmes for the SCs in education, employment and electoral politics. On the basis of this, the Constitution included a number of provisions which dealt with compensatory preference for the backwards like Articles 15(4) and 16(4). Articles 46, 335, 338, 340, 341, 342, 366 (24) and 366(25) were cited as important and relevant. Pt. Jawaharlal Nehru, the first prime minister of the country, put forward his views to eradicate untouchability for the benefit of the dalits. He remarked that "the communal problem as it was called was one of adjusting the claims of the minorities and giving them sufficient protection from majority action. Minorities in India...are not racial or national minorities as in Europe; they are religious minorities...Religion transcends the racial differences, which fade into one another and are often hard to distinguish".

The issue of graded inequality is a characteristic feature imminent in the Indian caste-based society. This is more pronounced as we go deeper into the caste-based hierarchical system which still persists in the country. This has led to the inducement of certain measures common to all subjugated groups to rectify and overcome the problems of inequalities. But in spite of all efforts and strategies applied to control the disparities, the exclusion of the low caste untouchables persists. The affirmative action programme or the policy of positive discrimination in India can be viewed solely as an anti-discriminatory measure, primarily focused on the stigmatic caste system. The quota or reservation policy in India, which is the core of AA, is essentially a policy of preferential treatment for certain disadvantaged groups (Deshpande, 2013). But, in spite of the implementation of such programmes in India, the condition of the scheduled castes is still under the scanner and by and large it has remained the same. The reasons for the ground reality behind such ineffectiveness are many and have raised questions like what is the impact of such policies in terms of employment, education and political empowerment, whether the benefits accrue equally to the SC population living in rural and urban sectors, or, with globalization taking root in the national economy and the market being the main driving force instead of the state, is the policy of PD losing its relevance?

The current position in India with regard to the caste system and reservation policies is complex and diverse in the context of affirmative action and the achievement of equality in the workplace as well as in the educational attainment of an individual. India needs a more fluid system of positive discrimination policy which cannot only provide support to the disadvantaged without completely undermining the merit of the individual but can also reinforce the social divides that are existent within the community. These programmes have grown over the past two decades. In addition to the quotas in education and employment, the government has also launched a variety of programmes to lower the cost of education for SCs. These include a number of schemes such as provision for pre and post-scholarship/fellowships, introduction of mid-day meals, free stationery, uniforms, books, etc. One scheme, funded by the central government, provides four years of remedial tutoring to select secondary school students to prepare them to gain entrance into colleges and universities (Desai and Kulkarni, 2008). Such remedial coaching increases the college preparedness of students reserved quotas encourage parents to educate their children thus immensely reducing dropout rates at the secondary level. In terms of government employment too, education can substantially increase the earning potential of SC communities. With minimum primary level education they can opt for lower level government jobs instead of doing a manual job in the private sector. Hence a number of reasons contribute to a potentially positive effect.

Though initially the process of emergence of SC communities in the country began as a transformative reform movement, it ultimately led to a reformative social movement removing all inequalities and addressing the issues and problems that lay underneath the caste system. This became a widespread movement and the North-East, once termed as a cluster of scenic beauty and serenity came in its grip. The status of SCs in this region has always been a chequered one since they have undergone series of deprivation and seclusion from the mainstream. And this is why PD policies became more pronounced in this part of the country than in the rest of India. The SC groups inhabiting the states of Assam, Manipur and Tripura in particular, have long been undertaking a struggle for their upliftment. The worst affected are in the rural areas living a life of discomfort and drudgery. Besides an ample physical resource base and with the advancement of modern science and technology, the status of scheduled castes in this part of the region and their historical background are the most influencing factors in the case of occupational patterns. In order to make the study a comprehensive one, we have drawn up a framework of the scheduled caste population inhabiting the three important states of the North-East, namely, Assam with the highest concentration, Tripura the second highest and Manipur with a subtle concentration. This chapter is an attempt to understand the state profiles in general and the different resident SC communities in particular.

Assam is considered to be one of the leading states with a vast majority of scheduled caste population, the highest amongst all the North-Eastern states. Caste plays a slightly significant role in the socio-economic condition of the people of Assam as the state has the history of the least rigidity of the caste system, unlike other parts of the country. Altogether, there are sixteen different sub-castes amongst the SCs in Assam, each with a distinct identity and culture. The *kaibartas* are the largest concentrated group engaged in fishing. The essential exclusion of the SCs in Assam lies within the periphery of village settlements where a majority of the population comprises either landless labourers or marginal agricultural farmers. Among the Hindu population in Assam, the largest concentration of the backward communities, as enumerated in the Constitution, belongs to the scheduled castes. The present population according to Census 2011 is 31,205,576 (approx.) of which the total scheduled caste population is 1,825,949 (approx.). This SC population roughly constitutes only 7 per cent of the total in the State, which is a considerable strength.

The caste structure in both the Brahmaputra and Barak valleys is however different from the rest of India. The population here is constituted of various ethnic groups with diverse social attributes. It is relatively simple since there are not many occupational-based caste distinctions. The districts surveyed in the course of the present study deliver an interesting ethnographic insight into SC communities. There are a multitude of caste groups living together in the same village, each having their history of migration with a multiple set of occupational behaviours. Most SCs are by and large non-agricultural professional people who specialize in occupations like fishing, goldsmithy, carpentry, cloth-washing, pottery-making, sweeping, leather-tanning, etc. The rest are either agricultural farmers or landless agricultural labourers. However, the study confirms that the fishing community forms the majority with six caste names, namely, *namasudra, kaibarta, jhalo, patni, jalkeot* and *hira,* and these are among the sixteen scheduled caste groups of Assam recognised by the Constitution of India Order 1950(a) Part II, Assam. Of the different castes, a good number from varied communities are engaged in different professions. The professional castes in the state can be named *hira*, *brittial bania*, *namasudra*, *kaibartta*, *sutradhar,* etc.

A land of great diversity, Manipur is a combination of people from different tribes, castes, culture and religion. The original inhabitants of the land are *Meiteis*, *Nagas*, *Kukis* and *Meitei Pangals*. The *Meiteis* dominate the valleys of Manipur. The central valley of the state which covers only 10 per cent of the total inhabited land comprises of the *Meiteis* in majority, along with Manipuri Muslims and the scheduled tribe population. The remaining 90 per cent is occupied by the hill tribes belonging to different ethnic groups. The SCs in Manipur came into existence only after the Scheduled Castes and Scheduled Tribes List (Modification) Order, 1956. Under this order, the number of recognized scheduled castes communities that are scattered in the region is seven: *dhobi/dhupi*, *lois*, *muchi/ravidas*, *namasudra*, *patni*, *sutradhar* and *yaithibi*. Among these seven, the *lois* and the *yaithibis* are the original settlers in the land whereas the rest are recent immigrants from different parts of the country who came in search of a better livelihood at different times. The *lois* form the majority and comprise an important section of the population of Manipur. This group belongs to one of the earliest indigenous settlers known as *chakpa* and if we look into the history of the scheduled caste population of Manipur, it refers to the transformation of the *chakpas* into SCs.

Tripura is the second most populous State in the North-East with a diverse composite culture. The scheduled caste population in the State is only 17.82 per cent of the total population and it is as a marginalized section of the State that it has been unable to keep pace with the rest of the population. There are seven prominent scheduled caste communities scattered in the region which include the *namasudras, mahisyadas, jalia kaibarta, dhoba, mali, chamar* and *patni*. The *namasudras* alone account for more than a third of the total SC population in the State. The SC groups in Tripura are basically migrants from other parts of the country. The population of SC migrant workers is increasing both in the rural and urban areas, as the indigenous inhabitants of Tripura continue mostly to aspire for white-collared jobs which get them higher earnings. The social distance between the SCs and other communities in Tripura is maximum. The basic statistics of 2015 show that the total SC population in the State is 6,54,918 of which males are 3,34,370 and females 3,20,548 (approx.).

Occupation plays an important role in determining the socio-economic condition of the people in a locality or community. The occupational status of the population reflects their relative dependence on the various economic activities carried out by them, which would also cite the traditional occupation of the respective communities. The status and nature of the family business determines the present occupational status of the population in the surveyed States. Table 2 indicates that though a larger section of the population has changed or shifted from traditional occupations, yet a good number still depend on agriculture to meet their daily expenses. Information has been collected from the respondents about the nature of their self employment and their present occupation. Many have shifted from fishing and pottery to other lucrative petty businesses. This has brought many changes in their lifestyle too, since they have abstained themselves from following traditional occupations like fishing, pottery, goldsmith, etc. A sizeable number of the respondents also work as vegetable vendors and drivers. Youngsters think that farming and fishing are jobs with low social prestige and this is why we find that there is a phenomenal change in the occupational structure that pulls them out of traditional occupations to newer more income-oriented occupations.

Table 2: Status of self-employment

Sl. No.	*State*	*Yes*	*%*	*No*	*%*	*Total*
1	Assam	1299	36.67	2243	63.33	3542
2	Manipur	460	55.22	373	44.78	833
3	Tripura	547	38.93	858	61.07	1405
	Total	2306	39.90	3474	60.10	5780

There are many SC families that have been carrying on their traditional business and have established themselves over the years. There is also a tendency amongst them to pass on their business to their next generation which is why there is no inclination towards government jobs or careers. Traditionally, the *lois, dhobi, namasudra,* etc., are engaged in fishing, washing and agriculture, respectively. The representation of both males and females in such occupations is equals that of other communities. Although a majority of the populace as seen in the table are engaged in their parental occupations and are self-employed, a segment of the respondents are agricultural farmers and do not get a regular income. But in all the three States, there is a fairly good representation of families engaged to varied occupations.

The occupational status of the population is reflected on the relative dependence on their traditional occupational mode. With time, the SC population in these three states has to a great extent undergone change. The youth have tried for alternative occupations such as petty businesses, cottage and private industry, etc., instead of following their traditional occupations. And those respondents who could receive formal education have looked for better job opportunities within or outside the state. This has also resulted in a decline in the number of persons carrying out traditional occupations. With the spread of education, there is a vertical movement in the occupational behaviour of the respondents in the referenced States. This is a kind of qualitative change in the economic well-being of the SCs as a significant number of the population has moved upward vertically along the occupational structure. Therefore, it is seen that though small in number, a many individuals have left their traditional jobs and are engaged in others. One reason for the lower classes changing their occupation is the tendency to acquire upward mobility and restrict the inequalities in their economic conditions. This implies a slight variation in their social position and condition.

Literacy is another important index of educational development and is assumed to be the first step of empowerment. There was a time when it was not possible to educate people from these communities as they were surviving under acute hardship to earn a livelihood. But now, with the initiatives from the government as well as implementation of different schemes and programmes for their sole benefit, the situation has comparatively improved to a great extent. Statistically, there seems to be a higher degree of variation in educational attainment and literacy rates across the three states of the region.

The education policies initiated by the government has emphasized on factors based on priorities like opening of primary schools, introducing *Anganwadi* centres and adult education centres in areas predominantly inhabited by SCs. The national programme of *Sarva Shiksha Abhiyan* (SSA) has been implemented in most of the school curriculum with a special focus on education for the marginalized and initiated in SC-dominated areas. Besides, various other development programmes covering agriculture, irrigation, co-operatives, health, etc., have been undertaken and designed for the welfare of SCs living in remote villages of the states. But the end results are not satisfactory.

During the course of the field study, it was found that most of the respondents of the older generation, i.e., in the age group of 60 or above, did not complete the primary level of education or are total illiterates, although they have been enthusiastic in providing good education to the younger generation. An attempt has been made to give data regarding the composition of institutions and students in the surveyed SC-inhabited areas emphasizing on the present education condition as shown in Table 3.

Table 3: Institution Type

Sl. No.	*Institution Type*	*Assam*	*%*	*Manipur*	*%*	*Tripura*	*%*	*Total*	*%*
1	Elementary school	221	92.47	-	-	10	17.24	231	66.38
2	Secondary school	10	4.18	23	45.10	42	72.41	75	21.55
3	College/University	6	2.51	22	43.14	4	6.90	32	9.20
4	Technical Institute	-	-	-	-	-	-	-	-
5	Professional degree institution	2	0.84	6	11.76	2	3.45	10	2.87
6	Open Universities/ Distance Education	-	-	-	-	-	-	-	-
7	Others	-	-	-	-	-	-	-	-
	Total	239		51		58		348	

The statistics clearly state that the number of higher educational institutes is low in Assam and Tripura, while academic institutes for higher learning exist in Manipur. The picture of the type of educational institutions located in various rural and urban zones is dismal. It has been observed that there has been under-investment in primary education while secondary and tertiary education has been given the most importance. But the need of the hour is to educate the child at the primary stage since, in India, primary schools are most often termed as 'poor man's school.' In Manipur, both government-aided and privately-run educational institutions co-exist, while in Assam and Tripura government institutions are many but in a poor deplorable condition. It is observed that every family sends their wards to government schools in the village, but the level and quality of teaching is so poor that it does not improve the standard of knowledge of the children. In such conditions, they are not able to be at par with their urban counterparts and the dropout rate also becomes seemingly high. Though the intake of students from SC categories is more from rural areas, the number of dropouts is almost equivalent. The causes of poor literacy in the States as mentioned above have compelled students to lose interest in further studies. And the ones who complete their secondary education do not continue their further and mostly opt for grade IV jobs. This situation is more pronounced in Assam and Tripura. Though efforts has been made by the Central and the State government to educate the people through different policies and programmes, the literacy pattern is still discouraging among the SCs in the Brahmaputra and Barak valleys of Assam. However, in many cases, to remove the existing disparities among the SCs and to develop an interest in education free books, uniforms, Teaching and Learning Methods (TLMs), etc., have been provided. This is clear from the survey done at Manipur. It also explored that in both the situations, guardians are willing to provide higher education to their children despite their social status and economic condition. While many are aware about the scholarship schemes and funds they are unable to allow their children to continue their studies because of financial problems.

Therefore, education seems to be a component in their social mobility. The SCs generally become the subject of mismanaged policies of the government followed by lack of information. A notable part of the population from the three States (from field data) are still alien to the concept of PD and do not even know the terms 'reservation' and 'scheduled castes'. The position of the SC population in all the states has remained static to a considerable extent but there is a definite sign of upward mobility in education and occupation, though the number is very low.

India, being one of the supporters of these programmes, has failed miserably. Except for the policy of PD as also implied for social justice, India has not been able to do much in the field of educational development. One-third of the population still lives below the poverty line and those in the rural areas are living in abject poverty and hunger. Statistics reveal that the government has failed to fulfil all the requirements for the development of marginalized groups. Given such circumstances, a holistic approach is quintessential for bringing these communities and groups who have for long been deprived of their rights to the forefront. Expansion of educational infrastructure is one important sector. In recent times, enrolment in the primary, secondary and higher institutions is increasing constantly and accordingly, to accommodate the increased number of students the government has to initiate more plans to develop educational infrastructure. The Right to Education Act of 2009 has made provisions for establishing schools at an approachable distance. But there has been a structural change in education after inclusion of private partnership. This has led to private investment in school education as well as in tertiary education. There should be more contributions by government educational institutions than private agencies.

North-East India, amidst its plurality and diversity, is endowed with scores of opportunities and resources. However, it has failed miserably to prosper since there are a multitude of problems ranging from insurgency, lack of motorable roads, unemployment, etc. In such an under-developed situation, educational development remains a far cry. Education is recognized as a great motivating factor and an agency of social change. While it is a fact that the North-Eastern states are known for their unique ethnic identity and culture and are less vulnerable to the rigid Indian caste system as compared with the rest of the nation, yet it has been deemed necessary to understand the cause of poverty, poor literacy rate and backwardness of the SC community in this region. How far has the PD policy been able to remove the disparities and create a positive impact on communities scattered in different parts of the selected states (study area) is a matter of concern. A deeper understanding is necessary to confront the truth of the matter. The SC population scattered in all the three States of the North-East are not equally distributed. There exists a huge gap between the SCs and the upper caste population in all of the States. In order to comprehend the present nuances and state of affairs as regards the implementation of PD policies, various SC communities have been studied to gauge the parameters of their level of educational attainment, income of the family, their standard of living, economic parameters like job opportunities, allocation of funds and welfare schemes. Economic exploitation and economic disadvantages continue to sustain the degraded social condition of the SC population. Hence the problems cited above are similar to the educational scenario in each of these states in the North-East.

The geographical location of the region is a remarkably glaring problem in the North-East today. The location of a school is often the deciding factor on whether to send children to school and till when would the child be able to continue studies. As for children from higher castes in the NE, the condition is more grim in SC-populated zones where a majority of the children are either forced into labour or do not attend school at all. The States mostly affected are Assam and Tripura where, according to the survey, the number of drop-outs is large. SC groups in Manipur have a slightly different status as their socio-economic condition is not as low as that in other parts of India. Under the rubric of poor implementation of educational policies of positive discrimination, especially at the school level in these States, there is a very crucial dimension of unequal representation. But despite many shortcomings, several schemes have been implemented for the betterment of the communities in the region. This has helped in facilitating social mobility and status change among the SCs. However, the coverage of many programmes in favour of them seems to be inadequate and there is no proper monitoring system by way of which they could be accentuated in the right track.

From the observations made in the three largely SC-dominated States of the North-East, three key issues have been keenly undertaken, namely, the massive privatization of educational institutions, lack of funds and development of the syllabi. In recent years, the region has witnessed a massive privatization of education. The general condition is such that upper castes and well-to-do families are sending their wards to private schools and low-income families to government schools thereby compounding the whole socializing process. Thus, the problem of social hierarchy has resurfaced again. In order to facilitate the concept of equality and education that is open to all, the government should take initiatives to control the mushrooming growth of private schools and higher educational institutions. Government-funded institutions must be strengthened and provided all basic amenities and financial support. In this respect the North-Eastern states have always faced an acute shortage of funds in education. A shift in the policy approach needs to be resorted to by the government to check the trend for privatization. Reform measures should be in line with democratic ideals and work for the upliftment of the marginalized sections. Thus, in the present study, the entire rural population can be considered marginalized when compared to the urban and semi-urban localities, where PD policies have not touched the lives of the SCs to a great extent.

It has been noted that formal institutions of education are conditioned more for the urban class and culturally-advantaged groups. A glaring disparity is seen between urbanized SCs and rural SC dwellers, where education has taken a back seat in most of the places of the region. Education, seen as an indicator of urbanism and modernity, has been able to touch the lives of the SCs but not to the extent where they could remove the growing disparities and inequalities. Therefore, it is most daunting among these populations that they either abstain from getting educated or indulge in their ancestral occupations to secure a better future.

The table shows the overall percentage of desire of families passing on their occupations to their children.

Table 4: Desire to let children succeed in one's own occupation

Sl. No.	*State*	*Yes*	*%*	*No*	*%*	*Total*
1	Assam	566	15.98	2976	84.02	3542
2	Manipur	165	19.81	668	80.19	833
3	Tripura	185	13.17	1220	86.83	1405
	Total	916	15.85	4864	84.15	5780

The convincing factor is that in all the three States, family traditions are no longer passed on. A relatively better condition has been noticed. This is one reason of the positive impact of the PD policy where children from even the poorest families are sent to school rather than made to follow their parents' profession. With regard to employment too, there is a significant variation between the numbers of respondents working in the three States. Manipur has evidenced the highest percentage of respondents working either in the private or public sector, while Assam and Tripura show a low percentage.

As discussed, the PD policies have in one way or the other benefitted the marginalized to a considerable extent. Unlike as in other parts of the country, the marginalized communities in Assam, Manipur and Tripura are characterized by one or more factors like caste, gender, age, place of residence, ethnicity and religion. The present paper tried to investigate the impact of reservation policies on educational attainment and government employment based on the primary data from the survey in the three States.

Among a the sizeable number of SC-populated districts in the states, education of girls from the communities, high incidence of dropouts, low student-enrolment, absenteeism of teachers, habitation without a single schooling facility, schools without teachers, single-teacher schools, schools without buildings, etc., are some of the hurdles prevailing in the State today. While comparing the three States it is noticed that in Manipur, preferential treatment is accorded to the oppressed sections in of admissions to educational institutions and appointments in government service. And this has improved their social status and economic condition to a considerable extent thereby raising them to the level of the advanced sections and integrating them with the upper caste mainstream in Manipuri society. Since poverty is a glaring reason from the socio-economic point of view, parents feel it inconvenient to send their children to school. Another important factor that acts as a hindrance to educational attainment is the viable sources from which required information could be acquired to avail governmental benefits and utilize the schemes/facilities meant exclusively for reserved SC categories. The following table highlights the percentage of respondents adhering to the basic sources about the schemes provided by the government for them. Comparing all the three States, it is understood that since a majority of the people are in the rural areas, the required information is outsourced by the gram *panchayats* or the village councils and who are educationally sound and aware get the information from various sources of mass media.

As stated earlier, reservation contains three main areas; legislative seats, education and public employment. There is no such precise definition on the criteria for eligibility to the caste or tribe status and it has hence opened the door for arbitrariness. The question of caste subject to positive discrimination has been and still is the subject of debate and has been subject to change over time. The positive discrimination policies in India in terms of the reservation system or quotas have long been in Indian history since the days of colonial rule. The Indian government's approach towards marginalized social groups has been primarily shaped by the

Constitutional provisions. Since educational attainment is directly linked with employment generation, persons with higher qualifications are more likely to secure government jobs than others.

An important phenomenon regarding employment is that without proper higher education or with no minimum educational qualifications, SC individuals cannot get better jobs. Most people in villages are poor daily-wage earners, and only one member out of ten families has been able to secure a permanent government job. Educational backwardness is one reason responsible for their low participation in jobs. Relating to the employment status of the SCs in present times, Table 5 highlights the number of family members working in government services, status of availing quotas of the reservation policy for jobs, percentage of SCs getting in institutions and number of employed SCs getting all benefits from the government in time.

Table 5: Criteria for application of reservation policies in institutions

Sl. No.	*Nature*	*Assam*	*%*	*Manipur*	*%*	*Tripura*	*%*	*Total*	*%*
1	Economic condition of the individual	21	8.79	6	11.76	12	20.69	39	11.21
2	Social stratum	10	4.18	34	66.67	37	63.79	81	23.28
3	Merit of the individual	13	5.44	11	21.57	9	15.52	33	9.48
4	Political backing								
5	Others	195	81.59					195	56.03
	Total	239		51		58		348	

It is true that the reservation system has benefitted SCs to a considerable extent giving them scope for development. But it does not always ensure a fair privilege for really poor families. During the course of the survey, respondents from the three States have deliberated on the problem. Getting reservation for the backward communities is a good sign, but the benefits have always been availed more by the privileged section within the SCs. This definitely has a bad effect on the education system and the quality of education has deteriorated to a considerable extent. Thus, comparing all the important parameters associated in the form of socio-economic justice in the fields of education and employment, it has been observed that the position of the SCs in these States indicate a positive change. The affirmative action programmes and the ones related largely to imparting social justice with regard to education are only applicable in the matter of procuring higher educational degrees. One can enjoy the benefits of reservation only when one attains the minimum eligibility criteria for admission in higher institutions. It is noticed that a majority of the SC population has not been able to reach up to that level. So is the case with employment facilities. Employment by way of reservation can only be accessed when one possesses the required qualifications for the job. The policy per se has not been able to provide the ladder for development on many grounds and, as such, the policy has started benefitting only the creamy layer amongst the SCs leaving the poor behind. The policy needs to be reworked so that it becomes more inclusive for a large section of marginalized groups.

But in politics, the scenario in these States is the opposite. Through the reservation system, political leaders from backward communities have gained the maximum benefit, right from contesting in the elections to creating a vote bank for themselves. Again, reservation is working as vote banks for political leaders of this region. The *panchayats* also play an important role in creating a political atmosphere in SC-villages. In the field of politics, Tripura ranks the highest in voting in India, since a majority of the population is involved in politics. But the scenario of political awareness is minimal in Assam and Tripura. According to the study, the SCs in Tripura are actively connected to politics to improve the poor state of the economy. But, most of the responding families opposed government policies and the distributing system. The study highlights the fact that the ones who are into politics are highly influential for their own benefit. They are the least interested in the prosperity of their community. There are instances when they are hesitant to reveal their identity as members from SC communities. Politics has brought about stagnation in the overall development of the SCs in the three states. The PD policy can have either a positive or negative effect on poverty and this is attributed to the fact that political reservation among the SCs has reduced poverty to a considerable extent. In most of the cases, the party members generally do not work for the benefit of the SCs nor do they make them aware of their rights and privileges.

Conclusion

The debates that are juxtaposed before the policy of positive discrimination have foreseen many challenges so far and in India this policy is still under surveillance. So far as the policies and programmes are concerned, it finally accrues to violence. The hierarchical stratifications are so deep-rooted in our country that it is impossible to curb them all in one go. Despite the fact that they have always been there in our society for centuries, positive discrimination has been able to bridge the gap to a considerable extent. This is possible only when the standard of the disadvantaged groups are raised to a level where they could compete and be at par with the upper class. The scheduled caste population should no longer believe in the notion that they are socially stigmatized and hence are backward. However, the making of compensatory discrimination as a means to eradicate the discrimination system in the country and the fight to seek social justice has not been developed much; it only acts as a boost for the oppressed classes.

This paper tried to analyze the achievements through the adoption of the PD policy in the selected States of the North-East where a sizeable number of the population is under the threat of caste discrimination. The demography of the place is one big reason behind the policy implementation. Despite educational opportunities by way of the reservation system for SCs, they are still lagging behind. There are still many who remain uneducated. The level of literacy has been unsatisfactory particularly in Assam and Tripura. Moreover, the traditional occupational structure of these communities is a barrier that inhibits them from attaining higher education. The educational aspirations of school students (mostly in the remote interiors) are lower than college students. But a majority were not at all willing to take up traditional or parental occupations. The respondents, mostly from Manipur, were overwhelmingly in favour of obtaining government jobs which can be cited as a consonance to the reservation policy.

Despite many policies and programmes adopted for the SCs, there has been continuous deprivation and elimination from the mainstream or the upper classes in society. The situation is grimmer in the three North-Eastern States that form the basis of this paper. This has posed many questions. Reservation or quotas against achieving the expected educational attainment for the marginalized cannot be the only answer to curb the disparities that have created waves in India since long. The population of SCs in the respective North-Eastern States have also been fighting to assert their rights and privileges to keep pace with the mainstream. Along with the rest of the country, in these States too, the need of the hour is to make these affirmative action programmes more effective instead of confining them to reservations alone. Opportunities for education and employment are not evenly distributed. Widening socio-economic differences are particularly evident at the upper levels of education. It has often been noticed that the politically and economically more affluent class optimize the benefits of the opportunities. As a result of such advantages, they are able to obtain higher positions in employment. The study, thereby, emphatically focuses on some important areas which still needs attention both by the Central and State governments in terms of its educational provisions.

Due to lack of adequate infrastructure like power, transport and communication, skilled labour force, shortage of capital and low credit facilities, these states show a wide disparity. The SCs in the urban areas are comparatively more developed than the rural ones. Industrialization, in the modern era, has been taking place at a very slow pace in these states; as such; there is an absence of large and medium scale industries that can provide scope for employment. However, the States have given emphasis to the development of small scale and cottage industries such as sericulture, handloom, handicrafts, and various self-employment schemes like *Pradhan Mantri Rojgar Yojana* (PMRY), especially for the educated SC youth. Such policies have not yielded the expected result so far. The States even after implementing the PD policies are not in a position to give gainful employment to a large section of educated SC youth. That is why the states, even after experiencing the rapid expansion of education, have seen an alarming increase of educated youth. Among the SCs, this phenomenon is widespread and can be identified by inferior jobs, poor social status and low income. This has finally raised problems such as loss in production and deterioration of skill and morale of the unemployed population and finally an increase in criminal and other anti-social activities, thus, accelerating damage to society as a whole. The policy makers, therefore, should take it as a responsibility to re-devise certain policies which alleviate the problems of unemployment and provide lasting solutions to it.

The three surveyed states populated by SCs in a majority indicates that over the last few decades, these states witnessed the emergence of a sizeable number of middle and lower middle class SC population both at the local and state level, which has created much potential to revolt. PD policies have been functioning in two ways; one genuinely orienting this class of people and the other not being able to address the economically backward, especially in the villages. This indicates that among the various SC sub-groups, the new policies have not yet been able to create mobility and improvement in their status. These policies have been able to touch the lives of a smaller section from the community, but the majority, who are rural dwellers and under the shadow of extreme poverty and illiteracy, have been deprived still. This can be effective when policies related to job reservations in the private as well as public sectors are opened. And this would be possible when there is ample opportunity and access to quality-based education at the school and higher educational institution levels, not necessarily meant for the elite classes. The shattering effects of caste segregation in education vis-a-vis the employment sector in these states have remained submissive and in a helpless position.

Therefore, special efforts and interventions need to be taken from time to time to oversee that positive discrimination programmes do not turn out to have a negative impact based on prejudices, stereotypes and protection of the assigned privileges. Most of all, there are issues which also need the conscious efforts and engagement of the SC groups themselves, both at the State and Central level. International as well as national mechanisms of solidarity can also help in this regard to further fuel the cause. In the light of the above discussion on effective strategies and on the basis of the survey report and policy prescription, it is understood that every person should receive a fair chance to apply for government jobs as well as admission to academic institutions. Aspirants must be judged by merit and their abilities to perform and true potential should be recognized. In a developing country like India where human resource is an important factor, more skilled and educated people need to be nurtured. Thus, social inclusion as an important aspect of demography and should cater to provide harmony with equal opportunities for the marginalized.

REFERENCES

Chitnis, S. 1974. 'Education of the scheduled castes and scheduled tribes in Maharashtra,' in Shah, A. B. (Ed.), *The Social Context of Education*, New Delhi: Allied Publishers Pvt. Ltd.

Das, Bhakta. 1986. *A Glimpse of the Scheduled Castes and their Socio-economic Development in Assam*, New Delhi; Omsons Publications.

Das, N. K. (Ed.), 2013. *Exclusion, Discrimination and Stratification: Tribes in Contemporary India*, Jaipur: Rawat Publications.

Desai, Sonalde and Veena Kulkarni. 2008. 'Changing Educational Inequalities in India in the context of Affirmative Action,' in *Demography*, May, Vol. 45, No. 2.

Deshpande, Ashwini. 2013. *Affirmative Action in India*, New Delhi: Oxford University Press.

Dube, S. C. 1968. *Caste Dominance and Functionalism, Contribution to Indian Sociology*, Lucknow: New Series Publications.

Fredman, Sandra. 2012. 'Comparative study of anti-discrimination and equality laws of the US, Canada, South Africa and India,' in *European Community Programme for Employment and Social Solidarity—PROGRESS*, Luxembourg : European Commission.

Heredia, Rudolf C. 2012. *Taking Sides: Reservation Quotas and Minority Rights in India*, New Delhi: Penguin Books.

Namala, Annie. 2009. "Lessons learned from policies to address caste based exclusion in India", in www.un.org/esa/socdev/egms/docs/2009/Ghana/Namala.pdf.

Singh, M.P. 1991. *Reservation Crisis in India*, in V. C.Mishra (Ed.), New Delhi: Universal Book Traders.

Singh, Shyama Nand. 1991. *Reservation: Problems and Prospects*, New Delhi: Uppal Publishing House.

Singh, Soran. 1987. *Scheduled Castes of India: Dimensions of Social Change*, Delhi: Gian Publishing House.

Singh, Tejveer. 2016. 'Towards Social Justice: A Critical Analysis of Reservation Policies in India,' in *The Administrator*, Journal of Lal Bahadur Shastri National Academy of Administration, July, Vol. 57, No. 2.

Sowell, T. 2004. *Affirmative Action Around the World: An Empirical Study*, New Haven: Yale University Press.

Srinivas, M. N. 1966. *Social Change in Modern India*, Bombay: Allied Publishers.

Thomas, C. J., R. Gopala Krishnan and Ranjan Singh (Eds.), 2001. *Constraints in Development of Manipur*, New Delhi: Regency Publications.

Thomas, E. W. 2006. 'Is Positive Discrimination a Good Way to Aid Disadvantaged Ethnic Communities?, in *EPW*, Vol. 41.

Thorat, Sukhadeo and Chittaranjan Senapati. 2007. *Reservation in Employment, Education and Legislature—Status and Emerging Issues*, Indian Institute of Dalit Studies, Working Paper Series, IIDS, Vol. 2, No. 5.

Thorat, Sukhadeo and Narender Kumar. 2008. *In Search of Inclusive Policy: Addressing Graded Inequality*, New Delhi: Rawat Publications.

Yagati, Chinna Rao. 2003. *Dalit Studies: A Bibliographical Handbook*, New Delhi: Kanishka Publications.

Zweigenhaft, Richard L. and G. William Domhoff. 1998. *Diversity in the Power Elite: Have Women and Minorities Reached the Top?*, New Haven: Yale University Press.

INDEX